MILTON STUDIES

XXI ❧ *Edited by*

James D. Simmonds

UNIVERSITY OF PITTSBURGH PRESS

MILTON STUDIES

is published annually by the University of Pittsburgh Press as a forum for Milton scholarship and criticism. Articles submitted for publication may be biographical; they may interpret some aspect of Milton's writings; or they may define literary, intellectual, or historical contexts — by studying the work of his contemporaries, the traditions which affected his thought and art, contemporary political and religious movements, his influence on other writers, or the history of critical response to his work.

Manuscripts should be upwards of 3,000 words in length and should conform to the *MLA Style Sheet*. Manuscripts and editorial correspondence should be addressed to James D. Simmonds, Department of English, University of Pittsburgh, Pittsburgh, Pa. 15260.

Milton Studies does not review books.

Within the United States, *Milton Studies* may be ordered from the University of Pittsburgh Press, Pittsburgh, Pa. 15260.

Overseas orders should be addressed to Feffer and Simons, Inc., 100 Park Avenue, New York, N.Y. 10017, U.S.A.

Library of Congress Catalog Card Number 69-12335

ISBN 0-8229-3524-4

US ISSN 0076-8820

Published by the University of Pittsburgh Press, Pittsburgh, Pa. 15260

CONTENTS

MILTON STUDIES
XXI

SHUFFLING UP SUCH A GOD:
THE RHETORICAL AGON OF MILTON'S
ANTIPRELATICAL TRACTS

Lana Cable

READERS OF Milton's antiprelatical tracts commonly distinguish between his time-bound "low" polemical style and the "high" or "poetic" style of the occasional disgressions in which he anticipates an England whose millennial hopes have been realized. Such passages are taken to demonstrate Milton's identification of England's destiny with his own artistic promise: only the prospect of the millennium inspirits his prose with a consonance that resembles poetry. This discrimination between Milton's high and low prose style is also used to help explain away his sometimes scurrilous language: we are reminded that Milton himself excuses his muckraking as merely a resort to the common arsenal of pamphlet warriors, whereas his noble poetic flights announce his cordial departure from the requisite vulgarity. According to Joan Webber, "The language reaches such a height of intensity . . . because Milton now excludes the low abusive epithets that have been his previous weaponry."[1] But such distinctions do not sufficiently account for the unevenness that so clearly separates the antiprelatical tracts from, say, the artistically coherent *Areopagitica*. For the most disturbing conflict in the antiprelatical tracts is not between "high" and "low" styles, but rather between Milton's rational argumentative purpose and the vivid language with which he tries to illuminate it. In *Areopagitica*, Milton's imagery and his argument coalesce to form a unified moral, intellectual, and esthetic vision. In his antiprelatical tracts, on the other hand, the less experienced polemicist creates images that richly express his animus, but that, at the same time, strangely detach themselves from the historical and rational level of argument and even exercise over it a peculiar rhetorical tyranny. For example, consider the memorable and scandalizing scenario from *Of Reformation*, in which the "seething pot" of spiritual devotion in the bishops cools to a "skinny congealment of ease and sloth" that finally "gives a Vomit to GOD himselfe."[2] No matter that, as Thomas Kranidas justly reminds us, Milton merely writes these words in the vanguard of a polemical tradition derived ultimately from the Book of Revelation.[3] For,

3

even if we actually relish Milton's scurrility (and I would argue that we do), we are distracted by it from his main argument. Neither does it much help our reading to follow J. Milton French and attribute Milton's gross images to satiric convention: rhetorically, even his nonscurrilous "poetic" images disrupt the flow of his argument.[4] Indeed, few readers can recall anything of the antiprelatical tracts *except* Milton's startling images; regardless of whether their origins are "high" or "low," the images come to vivid life seemingly independent of their argumentative context, which labors grimly, often obscurely, and endlessly behind them.

This divergence between Milton's ostensible rational argument and the affective rhetoric of his imagery has been variously interpreted. K. G. Hamilton sees the rhetorical ascendancy of Milton's figurative language as a failure of dialectic, "a complex but static expression of the strength of his own conviction, rather than either a reasoned statement or an imaginative apprehension of the basis of that conviction."[5] Stanley Fish, on the other hand, turns Hamilton's charge of rhetorical stasis into a virtue. He finds that intentionally failed dialectic is just one of Milton's demonstrations of the insufficiency of rational processes as against regenerate intuition: "The prose and its forms are continually removing themselves from the reader's path of vision and leaving him face to face with Reality."[6] But a more jaundiced view of Milton's "Reality" is conveyed by Keith Stavely: "A writer whose goal is to see in the prejudices of his audience the human expression of divine wrath has no need for logical procedure or even for elegant rhetorical planning. He need only convince his audience, by the devices of diction, imagery, and syntax . . . that their hostilities do indeed partake of the grandeur of God's wrath."[7] Stavely's antipathy toward Milton's imagery of wrath stems from his belief that the imagery serves only to work up a rhetorical frenzy — "to approximate a tone of saintly zeal" — that needlessly supersedes Milton's "relatively sober and restrained" critique of "a sociological phenomenon, the behavior patterns of upwardly-mobile clerics."[8] Although Milton's interest in such clerics isn't even remotely sociological, Stavely makes a valid point. We may find ways of justifying Milton's affective language as such, but that does little to explain his discontinuous rhetorical handling of it. And as to satire theories, Milton may consciously employ satiric techniques, but he is not writing satire, not does he finally share the aims of the satirist. For instance, he does not, despite certain ringing denunciations, strike the Juvenalian stance of the solitary prophet lashing at the sins of the world. Neither does he jestingly lampoon his antagonists "all for the grim amusement of his circle."[9] However disillusioned with men and their causes Milton may become, his writings never show him seeking solace in the urbane discourse of the worldly resigned. The sophisticated pose of the Augustan satirist is far too secular, too morally and spiritually detached, to suit Milton.

Nevertheless, Milton does strike a characteristic pose, one that can be singularly offensive. As Stavely puts it:

Milton pretends that Armageddon has come. . . . We have . . . not political discourse or persuasion, not even political polemic, but a kind of millennial melodrama. . . . Returning again and again to denunciations of the fleshly corruptions wrought by popery and prelacy, Milton attempts to inflate these received Protestant attitudes and feelings into expressions of divine wrath. . . . Milton seek[s] no less than to make himself the voice of a nation of inspired prophets.[10]

Thus Milton's rhetorical effectiveness in the antiprelatical tracts depends largely on a readership that is predisposed to agree with him.[11] In this respect, Stanley Fish's characterization of *The Reason of Church-Government* applies to all the antiprelatical tracts: "Milton stands alone, or with those of his audience who, like him, are 'eye-brightened' and the prose continues to pressure the reader to enroll himself in that number. . . . it does not provoke the self of the reader to change, merely to acknowledge his position in the polarities it continually uncovers."[12] But if, like Keith Stavely, the reader rejects Milton's polarities, or sees them as elements of only one moral structure out of many humanly imaginable, then Milton's rhetorical discontinuities will continue to be disturbing, and the "arrogant humility" of Milton's stance will simply encourage what one critic laments as the reader's refusal to look and understand.[13]

If there is any getting around such a critical impasse, it will necessarily depend on an effort to comprehend Milton's rhetorical discontinuities without yielding to his terms—terms whose appeal is suggested as much by the resentment of Milton's detractors as by the enthusiasm of those who support him. We need, therefore, to consider the nature of this appeal, as well as to examine how the discontinuity between moral image and rational argument comes about.

Briefly stated, the antiprelatical tracts show Milton shifting back and forth between two rhetorics—that of the temporal world of men and events, the world of polemical activity and "clubbing quotations"; and that of the realm of moral Truth, a realm manifested through the free use of imagery. The language of the temporal world is factual, historical, rationally apprehensible, and affectively neutral. It is with this language, and within this world, that Milton claims to construct his argument. Here, accounts of English political events, reformation history, or the church fathers convey a plethora of busy activities—persons engaged in quarrels and coronations and councils, in suits and dispensations and missions. But Milton's temporal world comes to us largely unshaped by the kind of interpretive intelligence that would give it depth and significance: its details are abundant, but unmemorable. The language of Milton's moral realm, on the other hand, produces images that are unforgettable. These images develop from his assumptions of a higher reality, one that is eternal, suprarational, functionally (though not finally) dualistic, theocentric. In such a realm, meaning comes not from rational and empirical interpretation, not from historical analysis, but from relationship to God.

Critics who object to Milton's affective language understandably resent the rhetorical pressure of this moral realm, the pressure to see to it that they are "implicitly included" among "the elect people of God."[14] But, of course, moral meaning is not the same thing as rhetorical effectiveness—a point less clear perhaps to Milton than to his readers, and one to which we will be returning from many angles. Contrary to the claims made by Milton's moral realm, it is not, in fact, relationship to God that gives these images their rhetorical authority. It is not their theocentricity but their sensuousness that powers Milton's moral images. They are so pungent, so memorable in contrast to the rational argument that they gain rhetorical ascendancy over it without actually engaging in it. Their effect is to obscure and, ultimately, to overwhelm the argument rather than enhance it.

How this extreme discontinuity between moral image and rational argument occurs will shortly be demonstrated. But why it occurs is a question worth bringing up immediately because the answers to it are so much more elusive. Toward the end of a personal digression in *The Reason of Church-Government*, in which Milton vigorously defends his right to challenge the bishops, he makes it a point to remind his reader of the great distaste he finds in doing that very thing. Yet once more he is "put from beholding the bright countenance of truth in the quiet and still air of delightfull studies to come into the dim reflexion of hollow antiquities sold by the seeming bulk, and there be fain to club quotations" (pp. 821–22). This statement strikes at the heart of the rhetorical ambivalence of the antiprelatical tracts: exactly what does Milton mean when he speaks of Truth? His allusions to Truth in the antiprelatical tracts are girded with a demure reticence very like the Lady's in *A Mask Presented at Ludlow Castle*, when she primly declines to reveal "the sage / And serious doctrine of Virginity." Yet if Milton's polemical world, like Comus, is not fit to hear itself convinced, neither is his ideal poetic readership: "those especially of soft and delicious temper" would presumably come unstrung at the sinews to hear it, for they "will not so much as look upon Truth herselfe, unlesse they see her elegantly drest" (pp. 817–18). Complicating the issue, Milton himself seems at this point to share the fastidiousness of the latter party: whatever Truth may be, it clearly is something other than the sort of mundane business he is now compelled to engage in. But at the same time, he is so compelled precisely because of his convictions about what is or is not "true." Thus, in a personal as well as artistic sense, temporal realm (rational argument) and moral realm (imagery, affective language) remain ambiguously at odds, and Milton writes as if to say that any verbal activity — including polemics — can be either factual or true, but not both at once. Because Milton can neither separate nor reconcile these two realms and the modes of apprehension they imply, the antiprelatical tracts record a rhetorical agon from which no one — not fact, not Truth, not even Milton — emerges as victor.

For example, watch what happens to the temporal claims of rational discourse in this typical passage from *Of Reformation.* Milton is arguing that the worldly precedence of bishops is not supported by evidence from church fathers. He establishes his rational mode of argument through scrupulous marshaling of historical testimony:

Now for Episcopall dignity, what it was, see out of *Ignatius,* who in his Epistle to those of *Trallis* confesseth *that the Presbyters, are his fellow Counsellers, and fellow benchers.* And *Cyprian* in many places, as in the 6. 41. 52. Epist. speaking of *Presbyters,* calls them his *Compresbyters,* as if he deem'd himselfe no other, whenas by the same place it appeares he was a Bishop, he calls them Brethren. (P. 546)

For a few sentences, Milton sustains the historical level of argument, although he varies it by interpolating the objection of a supposed disputant and immediately answering it: "But that will be thought his meeknesse: yea, but the *Presbyters* and Deacons writing to him think they doe him honour enough when they phrase him no higher then Brother *Cyprian,* and deare *Cyprian* in the 26. Epist." (p. 546) With the next sentence, Milton still maintains the historical level of argument, but his apparent commitment to that level becomes impaired:

For their Authority 'tis evident not to have bin single, but depending on the counsel of the *Presbyters,* as from *Ignatius* was erewhile alledg'd; and the same *Cyprian* acknowledges as much in the 6 Epist. and addes therto that he had determin'd from his entrance into the Office of Bishop to doe nothing without the consent of his people, and so in the 31. Epist, for it were tedious to course through all his writings which are so full of the like assertions. (Pp. 546–47)

The proof from Ignatius "erewhile alledg'd" is Milton's own of just two sentences past, but by casting the allusion into an impersonal passive construction ("as . . . was . . . alledg'd"), he begins to distance himself from the act of citing scholarly evidence. In the phrases that follow, detachment wanes into sheer boredom, as his treatment of patristic testimony disintegrates. What had earlier seemed worthy of minute examination ("Cyprian . . . speaking of *Presbyters*, calls them his *Compresbyters*, as if he deemed himself no other") now is reduced to a kind of shorthand or ditto: "and so in the 31. Epist, for it were tedious to course through all his writings."

A case could be made here for a strategical Milton who deliberately subverts the trappings of historical evidence, ultimately to lay that "hors load of citations and fathers" at the prelatical doorstep. But that is not what's going on. Milton's well-known apologetic can be taken quite seriously: "I should not chuse this manner of writing wherin knowing my self inferior to my self, led by the genial power of nature to another task, I have the use, as I may account it, but of my left hand" (p. 808). The ennui is not a pose: Milton has committed himself to a task and a form of argument which he finds necessary but exceedingly disagreeable, and what we witness in a passage like this is the rumblings of a disgruntled sensibility. It is not the technical aspects of prose so much as its attendant presumptions of rational detachment that unnaturally restrict Milton to the use of his left hand. In this instance he permits the requisite historical citations for the case against episcopal dignity finally to wither in scholarly dust. But at the same moment a sign of vigor appears, with the first image in many sentences — an image of Rome, "the womb and center of Apostacy":

It were tedious to course through all his writings which are so full of the like assertions, insomuch that ev'n in the womb and center of Apostacy *Rome* it selfe, there yet remains a glimps of this truth, for the Pope himselfe, as a learned English writer notes well, performeth all Ecclesiasticall jurisdiction as in Consistory amongst his Cardinals, which were originally but the Parish Priests of *Rome*. (P. 547)

The words "womb and center of Apostacy" momentarily enliven a dry passage. But more importantly, they invoke a radically different level of discourse in which the terms for validating an argument are completely changed. Into a field of scholarly allusions and citations that can be infinitely extended (perhaps without altering the case), Milton suddenly intrudes a moral judgment that is totally independent of such evidence. After all, Rome's identity as apostate can neither be proven nor disproven, only acknowledged or denied. Striking as it is, however, this moral pronouncement is only of secondary importance as a rhetorical gesture. Rome's apostasy is useful here to Milton only as it accentuates "a glimps of this truth"—the equable consistory of cardinals that recalls the early church "Parish Priests of *Rome*." The immediate rhetorical import of the image of Rome stems not from Rome's presumed apostasy but from Rome's being presented as an image. The intrusion of an image signals Milton's shift away from the rational and historical level of discourse, on which he ostensibly bases his argument against the bishops, while it launches the nonrational, morally resonant, theocentric and eternal level of discourse. And as we will see, this level of discourse—despite its obvious aspiration toward the ideal and the abstract—is absolutely dependent on language that is sensuous and concrete. It is, of course, the prerogative of imagery to be sensuous. But my point is that in the antiprelatical tracts, Milton's moral perceptions and his moral intensity reside entirely in his sensory, affective language, and this language has almost no rational connection with the historical entities he discusses—be they fallible princes, time-serving prelates, superstitious monks, or corrupt institutions. This will become clearer as we go along, but for the present it is valuable to watch Milton's affective language take over the passage at hand.

Had Milton called Rome only "the center of Apostacy," his characterization of it would still have remained within the bounds of rational discourse. That is, one could conceivably agree or disagree with him as an exponent of partisan opinion. But by adding the metaphor "womb," Milton makes of Rome not a temporal location ("center") but a primal nurturer, and of her apostasy not a subject for partisan debate but an entity with a potent life of its own, a life quite distinct from the temporal life of historical men and places. As a polemical tactic, this is effective: imagery tends to preclude or outface rational argument. But that is just the beginning. Once introduced, the organic metaphor pervades the sentences that follow. Images of the body emerge and weave among other images in a scenario that burgeons with the copiousness implied by its origin in the word "womb." Significantly, the connection between the developing images and their original is pictorial only, not polemical. The words "womb of Apostacy" can logically have only negative connotations for Milton, whereas "the mysticall body" in the ensuing passage is clearly positive. But the natural affinities between image and image ("womb" and "body") are strong enough effectually to supersede the nonvisual indictment, "Apostacy." Because subsequent images tend to adhere to the image established, the "womb" eventually becomes less defined by the term "Apostacy" than it is enhanced by "a glimps of this

truth." For, in Milton's moral realm, truth is not what you call something, it is what you see. This subtle contest between intellectual definition and direct sensory representation ends with the latter in command.
From here to the end of the passage, the veridical claims of historical
evidence and reasoned debate are totally abandoned, while the affective
language of teeming imagery fills the polemical arena:[15]

Thus then did the Spirit of unity and meeknesse inspire, and animate every joynt,
and sinew of the mysticall body, but now the gravest, and worthiest Minister,
a true Bishop of his fold shall be revil'd, and ruffl'd by an insulting, and only-
Canon-wise Prelate, as if he were some slight paltry companion: and the people
of *God* redeem'd, and wash'd with *Christs* blood, and dignify'd with so many
glorious titles of Saints, and sons in the Gospel, are now no better reputed then
impure ethnicks, and lay dogs; stones & Pillars, and Crucifixes have now the
honour, and the almes due to *Christs* living members; the Table of Communion
now become a Table of separation stands like an exalted platforme upon the brow
of the quire, fortifi'd with bulwark, and barricado, to keep off the profane touch
of the Laicks, whilst the obscene, and surfeted Priest scruples not to paw, and
mammock the sacramentall bread, as familiarly as his Tavern Bisket. (Pp. 547–48)

One notices immediately the way Milton's images seem to multiply
themselves by doubling up at practically every point of syntax.[16] Nouns
pair with other nouns — "unity and meekness," "joint, and sinew," "Saints,
and sons," "impure ethnicks, and lay dogs," "stones & Pillars, and Crucifixes," "the honour, and the almes," "Table of Communion . . . Table
of separation," "bulwark, and barricado." Verbs and verbals move in
tandem — "inspire, and animate," "revil'd, and ruffl'd," "redeem'd, and
wash'd," "paw, and mammock." Adjectives team up too — "gravest, and
worthiest," "insulting, and only-Canon-wise," "slight paltry," "obscene,
and surfeted." All this doubling creates a veritable explosion of tangible
particulars, rapidly crowding the visual field.

But sheer force of numbers is just one of the ways Milton's affective
language overwhelms the rational argument. In addition to this, the organic metaphor for the church — generated by the glimpse of truth in the
womb of apostasy — now develops as "the Spirit of unity and meekness"
that can "inspire, and animate every joynt, and sinew of the mysticall
body." The image of the body transfigures the church from a historical
institution subject to the accidents of time, place, and human foibles to
an integral living being founded in eternity and imbued with truth.[17]
Similarly, the body metaphor transforms "the people of *God*," whose redemption by "*Christs* blood" makes them into "*Christs* living members."

The organic metaphor even alters the dimensionality of time. The
syntactic structure, "Thus then . . . but now," initiates a series of com-

parisons between past and present, but both are released from their ordinary chronological meanings by the imaginary with which each is characterized. "Then" calls up not the historical past with its patristic annotators and witnesses, but a seemingly timeless era that thrived before the spirit of the gospel had been formulated into a text: "Thus then did the Spirit of unity and meeknesse inspire, and animate every joynt, and sinew of the mysticall body." Milton's suprarational juxtaposition of the evanescent ("Spirit of unity and meeknesse") with the explicitly concrete ("every joynt, and sinew") vividly reifies an otherwise intangible abstraction, "the mysticall body" of the primitive church. So reified, "the mysticall body" from the ideal past is kept fresh by successive confirming images — "redeem'd, and wash'd with *Christs* blood," "honour, and the almes due to *Christs* living members" — to operate as a touchstone against which images from a fallen present are tested.

The contrasting vision of the "now" is delineated by increasingly homely, even vulgar particulars: "but now the gravest, and worthiest Minister . . . shall be revil'd, and ruffl'd . . . some slight paltry companion . . . impure ethnicks, and lay dogs; stones & Pillars, and Crucifixes . . . bulwark, and barricado . . . profane touch of the Laicks . . . obscene, and surfeted Priest . . . paw, and mammock . . . as familiarly as his Tavern Bisket." As ideal past alternates with fallen present, a rhythm is established: "then did the Spirit . . . but now the gravest," "and the people of *God* redeem'd . . . are now no better reputed," "stones & Pillars, and Crucifixes have now the honour, and the almes." But as if to show how thoroughly the temporal "then" and "now" have been redefined as the moral "ideal" and "fallen," the alternating rhythms continue beyond all possible temporal connection without any loss of emphasis. In "Table of Communion now become a Table of separation," both terms of the comparison are chronologically in the present: "now" simply announces the immediate unmasking of hypocrisy, as the "exalted platforme" visually converts the "Table of Communion" into its moral opposite, "a Table of separation." Then to complete the sentence, there is a climactic imagerial denouement. In the final manifestation of the image, "mysticall body," the symbolic body of Christ undergoes a mock transubstantiation. As with the table of communion, the true meaning of "the sacramentall bread" is vitiated right before our eyes: the image of "the obscene, and surfeted Priest" pawing and mammocking the sacramental bread visually converts the eucharist into "his Tavern Bisket."

Up to this point, Milton's images have been liberally filling up the scene, and their culmination in the minutely secular graphic detail of the priest's tavern biscuit has an interesting effect. The energetic populousness of all the preceding guarantees that instead of narrowing the visual field, the single image of the tavern biscuit spontaneously infuses it with broad secularity. As the sacramental bread converts to a tavern biscuit, so the setting of the church becomes the world epitomized by the tavern. Moreover, as the church and the sacrament are secularized by the prelates, so are the people, whose conversion from their Christian identity we now see has been in continual progress. Originally portrayed as the true bishop's "fold," "the people of *God*" and "Saints, and sons in the Gospel," they have passed through their prelatical repute as "impure ethnicks, and lay dogs" to "Laicks" with a "profane touch." The perceptions and spirit of a secular world, therefore, shape the people's conclusions, as signaled by the words that begin the next sentence, "And thus":

And thus the people vilifi'd and rejected by them, give over the earnest study of vertue, and godlinesse as a thing of greater purity then they need, and the search of divine knowledge as a mystery too high for their capacity's, and only for Churchmen to meddle with, which is that the Prelates desire, that when they have brought us back to Popish blindnesse we might commit to their dispose the whole managing of our salvation, for they think it was never faire world with them since that time. (P. 548)

The people "thus . . . vilifi'd and rejected" are actually changed by the labels that have been attached to them. Their pastoral simplicity rescinded, they use cynical tavern wisdom to assess a world grown morally ambiguous, where "vertue, and godlinesse" and "divine knowledge" have all become as effete and manipulable as communion tables and sacramental bread, things "only for Churchmen to meddle with." The measured irony of "greater purity then they need" and "a mystery too high for their capacity's" is both Milton's and the people's, for irony permits a worldly comprehension that does not embrace. The people's rejection of and by the bishops registers in the prelates' final secularizing gesture, "that . . . we might commit to their dispose the whole managing of our salvation." The commercial language "commit to their dispose" and "managing" converts "our salvation" to a vendible commodity. Milton's use of commercial imagery for religion will later be richly expanded and subtly complicated in *Areopagitica*, but here the structures of moral accountability remain completely simple. Truth is what we see. Predictably, therefore, Milton's visually simplistic representation of prelatical evil allows for an equally simplistic portrayal of its cure:

But he that will mould a modern Bishop into a primitive, must yeeld him to be elected by the popular voyce, undiocest, unrevenu'd, unlorded, and leave him nothing but brotherly equality, matchles temperance, frequent fasting, incessant prayer, and preaching, continual watchings, and labours in his Ministery. (Pp. 548–49)

Milton's reversal of the prelates' secularizing conversions is a material stripping away: the modern bishop must be "undiocest, unrevenu'd, unlorded." In the place of substantial things and forms Milton leaves only intangibles: attributes of character — "brotherly equality, matchles temperance"; and disciplinary habits and duties — "frequent fasting, incessant prayer, and preaching, continual watchings, and labours in his Ministery."

With this reassertion of the simplicities of the primitive church, we conclude a representation of the Christian myth on which Milton's moral perspective is premised: an original pristine landscape, here the primitive church, becomes corrupted and falls, then is shown the way of salvation. In purely Christian moral terms the scenario, barring an apocalypse, is complete. But in terms of its affective language, the scenario's return to simplicity is a decided falling off. Milton's stripping away of appearances creates an affective vacuum. Therefore, the final resurgence of prelatical imagery operates as if filling a void — an effect peculiarly enhanced by Milton's sustained syntactic structure: "which what a rich bootie it would be, what a plump endowment to the many-benefice-gaping mouth of a Prelate, what a relish it would give to his canary-sucking, and swan-eating palat, let old Bishop *Mountain* judge for me" (p. 549). The sensory anticipation raised by withholding completion of the clause "which . . ." through the teasing hints of "what a rich . . . what a plump . . . what a relish" positively dishes up the antecedent "brotherly . . . Ministery" to be engorged by the lip-smacking sibilants and masticating hyphens of "the many-benefice-gaping mouth" and "canary-sucking, and swan-eating palat." By the time we reach the end of the clause "which . . ." the image of the gourmandizing prelate so precisely suits the pejorative nickname "old Bishop *Mountain*," that this authority whom Milton calls upon to "judge for me" is inescapably caught chomping the evidence.

We may now fairly ask the question raised at the start of this analysis: what has happened to the claims of historical investigation, of rational argument? And the answer, not entirely facetious, is of course that the bishop ate them. For proof we need only look at the next sentence: "How little therfore those ancient times make for moderne Bishops hath bin plainly discours'd." It has? What plain discourse? What can "therfore" possibly follow from? The gourmandizing scene we have just witnessed? What would it mean to try to draw logical inferences from that? A scenario like the foregoing wreaks havoc with the kind of deductive reasoning Milton invokes by his use of the word "therfore." With no more ceremony than the start of a new paragraph, Milton drops an entire level of discourse and resumes on a different plane.

The resulting discontinuity is unsettling in several ways. First, it is disorienting, because there seems to be no connection between what we read now and what has gone immediately before, despite the bald claim made by "therfore." Second, even if we sort out Milton's terms sufficiently to recognize that the "true Bishop" of the scenario might be related to "those ancient times," while the scenario's "canary-sucking" prelate apparently belongs to the "modern bishops," we are still foiled by what follows:

but let them make for them as much as they will, yet why we ought not stand to their arbitrement shall now appear by a threefold corruption which will be found upon them. 1. The best times were spreadingly infected. 2. The best men of those times fouly tainted. 3. The best writings of those men dangerously adulterated. (P. 549)

No help here: once we revert to the rational and historical level of discourse, the terms that had seemed so stable in Milton's imagerial world no longer apply. The vague pronoun references ("let *them* make for *them* as much as *they* will . . . *their* arbitrement . . . upon *them*") simply accentuate that fact: morally speaking, the "theys" and "thems" are all one, for in this newly reasserted historical world, even "ancient times" turn out to be unreliable and corrupt. Gone are the facile distinctions, the clearcut moral types, the giveaway activities and appearances of brotherly laborers versus self-indulgent tavern biscuit mammockers.

But perhaps most disturbing, in the long run, is an effect few readers of Milton's prose seem willing to admit, although I suspect many have felt it. It is the abrupt loss of reading pleasure. Milton's scenarios are always richly sensuous — the longer he goes, the more graphic he gets. And that's fun, sometimes comic, even captivating. But for that very reason, it is also peculiarly problematic. Milton's images lure us into an esthetic experience that purports to embody moral truth. The effectiveness of that experience depends on criteria such as visual coherence, richness and suggestiveness of detail, symbolic resonance. All these rhetorical weapons can legitimately be conscripted by the prose artist to serve in the "wars of truth," but here, instead of serving the polemical task, they effectually compete with it. As we are drawn into the scenario by its sensory appeal, we may suppose that we are being given an illustration of the argument we have been reading; but our return to that argument once the scenario is complete shows us how mistaken we were. Repeatedly with

Milton's antiprelatical imagery, we are swept up by the affective language, carried with it to a crescendo, and then unceremoniously dumped. No point of contention is illuminated by this maneuver, no comment on the historical citations is made. Instead of using affective language to convey the moral import of a rational argument, Milton actually draws us away from a rational argument which has no apparent moral dimension, only to involve us in a supposedly moral world which has no perceivable rational foundation. Once the affective pressure of Milton's moral world reaches its climax, there is nothing left for him to do but abandon it and pick up the rational, historical argument where he left off. So, at the conclusion of an exuberant imagerial passage, Milton simply stops; then he resumes his historical argument in precisely the same unruffled tone as had prevailed before his imagery got going: "How little therfore those ancient times make for moderne Bishops hath bin plainly discours'd." Milton gives no sign of recognizing the obvious non sequitur.

What we get out of all this depends on our critical predisposition. With the satiric assumptions of French, or the historical ones of Kranidas, we we may remain detached enough to enjoy the images for their own sake as artistic and intellectual creations. By joining Fish's highly committed ideal readers, on the other hand, we may ultimately include ourselves among the ranks of the saved. Or, with Stavely, we may use modern psychosocial assumptions to expose Milton's supposedly more pretentious millennialist ones. But none of these approaches directly confronts Milton's penchant for purveying affective power as moral truth. Neither do they account for the sudden rhetorical shifts from Milton's imagery back to his rational argument, away from which, whether willingly or reluctantly, we have permitted ourselves to be seduced.

Not that we ought to resist the seduction. In fact, I suggest that our experience with the rhetoric of the antiprelatical tracts is not unlike Milton's own. Writing these tracts is a Milton who, at this stage in his literary career, quite ingenuously equates moral conviction with affective intensity; a Milton who, in his poetic and religious desire to realize Truth as it were on the pulses, finds the cool rationality of his intended polemical task too enervating for such realization. Rhetorically speaking, the fundamental impulse in the antiprelatical tracts is neither against the prelates nor in favor of the presbyterians, but toward the linguistically and affectively sensuous. For Milton, at this point, there lies Truth.

But even if we accept the equating of sensuousness with Truth, there remain rhetorical anomalies in the antiprelatical tracts. Occasionally, Milton's impulse toward the sensuous so intrudes upon the rational argument that it inconveniences the author himself. Something like this happens when, in *Of Reformation*, he confronts the historical fact of martyrdom in the persons of Bishops Cranmer, Latimer, and Ridley: Milton's ill-timed pejoratives clash with inopportune historical facts to produce a virtual tug-of-war for affective precedence. As a responsible historian, Milton must acknowledge the fact of the bishops' martyrdom, which he does. But once this is admitted into the argument, rhetorical difficulties arise. For, almost uniquely among Milton's historical facts, the fact of martyrdom has potential affective power. We find that power operating even in Milton's own attempt at a casual dismissal: "What then? . . . He is not therfore above all possibility of erring, because hee burnes for some Points of Truth." This statement, instead of diminishing, actually elucidates martyrdom's stark drama: the meticulousness of Milton's sarcastic "some Points" contrasts with and intensifies the resonant, graphic "hee burnes." Thus a fact like martyrdom subtly intrudes upon the affective phase of Milton's impeachment of the bishops. In effect, the rhetoric of history actually competes here with the affective appeal of Milton's rhetoric of Truth. So Milton's rhetorical task becomes twofold: he must somehow diffuse the affective power of the bishops' martyrdom, and, at the same time, he must find new terms for dealing with these people whose recorded history militates against his predisposition to reduce them by his imagery to a caricature of their moral failings. This accomplished, he is free to unleash a sensuously compelling display of conviction: the passage on the bishops eventually develops into one of the most stunning scenarios in the tract.

All of this comes about through a complicated series of maneuvers. The passage begins early in *Of Reformation* as Milton's historical investigation finds the bishops personally responsible for the wrongs they have participated in or condoned:

And for the *Bishops*, they were so far from any such worthy Attempts, as that they suffer'd themselvs to be the common stales to countenance with their prostituted Gravities every Politick Fetch that was then on foot, as oft as the Potent *Statists* pleas'd to employ them. . . . if a Toleration for *Masse* were to be beg'd of the King for his Sister MARY . . . who but the grave Prelates *Cranmer* and *Ridley* must be sent to extort it from the young King? . . . When the Protectors Brother, Lord *Sudley*, the Admirall through private malice, and mal-engine was to lose his life, no man could bee found fitter then Bishop *Latimer* (like another Doctor *Shaw*) to divulge in his Sermon the forged Accusations laid to his charge thereby to defame him with the People. (Pp. 530–33)

Considering that he is arguing here on the historical level, Milton's language is surprisingly vivid ("common stales . . . prostituted Gravities . . .

Potent *Statists*"), inferring the kind of affective intensity that character-izes his moral sphere. Indeed, as the investigation continues, we discover that this language and its intensity depend on Milton's narrowly limiting the selection of historical materials. In purely historical terms, such anomalies as time-serving prelates who also happened to become mar-tyrs are humanly credible. But this kind of ambiguity makes indifferent imagery; conversely, Milton's facile caricature of the bishops as "com-mon stales" with "prostituted Gravities" cannot sustain the contradictory extra dimension implied by their martyrdom. Therefore, as soon as the bishops' martyrdom is admitted onto the scene, Milton hastens to ex-plain it away with a digression on the meaning of martyrdom. By the end of this, Cranmer, Latimer, and Ridley have been transformed from corrupt and powerful historical figures into mere puppets, while the en-tire burden of culpability is shifted from the bishops to a rhetorically more convenient abstraction — "episcopacy." The shift begins with the mention of the bishops' martyrdom:

But it will be said, "These men were *Martyrs*: What then? Though every true Christian will be a *Martyr* when he is called to it; not presently does it follow that everyone suffering for Religion, is without exception. Saint *Paul* writes, that *A man may give his Body to be burnt . . . yet not have Charitie*: He is not therfore above all possibility of erring, because hee burnes for some Points of Truth.

Witness the *Arians* and *Pelagians* which were slaine by the Heathen for *Christs* sake; yet we take both these for no true friends of *Christ*. If the *Martyrs* (saith *Cyprian* in his 30. Epistle) decree one thing, and the *Gospel* another, either the *Martyrs* must lose their Crowne by not observing the *Gospel* for which they are *Martyrs*; or the Majestie of the *Gospel* must be broken and lie flat, if it can be overtopt by the *novelty* of any other *Decree*. (Pp. 533–35)

Milton impugns martyrdom on doctrinally valid grounds: martyrs don't make Truth, they only witness it. And as the passage continues, he makes it clear that it is only man's idolatry that would limit Truth to such "igno-minious bondage," the witness of the historical martyr. But martyrdom's proper place in Christian doctrine is here only a secondary concern. More pressing is Milton's need to weaken the affective impact of the martyr-dom of Cranmer, Latimer, and Ridley. Therefore, instead of simply dis-missing the bishops' martyrdom as he had seemed about to do ("What then?"), Milton awkwardly belabors the issue, attenuating martyrdom's emotional appeal by conjuring up the disreputable Arians and Pelagians, by reductively labeling martyrdom a "novelty," and then by quoting Gospel and also, interestingly, Cyprian — himself of course a bishop, and a martyr. Finally (somewhat desperately?), Milton undercuts the presumed sanctity of the martyr's witness (the Greek stem μαρτυρ means "witness") by arrogating to himself the ultimate witness:

And heerewithall I invoke the *Immortall* DEITIE *Reveler* and *Judge* of Secrets, That wherever I have in this BOOKE plainely and roundly (though worthily and truly) laid open the faults and blemishes of *Fathers, Martyrs,* or Christian *Emperors;* or have otherwise inveighed against Error and Superstition with vehement Expressions: I have done it, neither out of malice, or list to speak evill, nor any vaine-glory; but of meere necessity, to vindicate the spotlesse *Truth* from an ignominious bondage, whose native worth is now become of such low esteeme, that shee is like to finde small credit with us for what she can say, un-lesse shee can bring a Ticket from *Cranmer, Latimer,* and *Ridley;* or prove her selfe a retainer to *Constantine,* and wears his *badge.* More tolerable it were for the *Church* of GOD that all these Names were utterly abolisht, like the *Brazen Serpent;* then that mens fond opinion should thus idolize them, and the Heav-enly *Truth* be thus captivated. (P. 535)

Aside from overriding the authority of the martyr's witness, Milton's lin-guistic act of invocation automatically subverts whatever vestige may re-main of the morally neutral terms of historical argument. Any words that are to be witnessed by "the *Immortall* DEITIE *Reveler* and *Judge* of Secrets" will necessarily conform to the moral polarities of a theocentric universe. Conveniently, this shift of rhetorical level also facilitates for Milton the kind of "surgical" prodecure that is ordinarily the prerogative of the satirist: he can now "[lay] open the faults and blemishes of *Fa-thers, Martyrs,* or Christian *Emperors.*" That is, moral errors will hence-forth be treated as if they were the bishops' corporeal flaws, abscesses rather than integral qualities of character. This is the sort of physical assault on a moral problem that almost viscerally satisfies in the imagerial realm, while in Milton's historical realm it would be ludicrous. Here, the "surgery" is made possible because the invocation simply cancels the claims of the historical realm. We see no more a world of men and events, but of abstractions. Error and Superstition are the new objects of Mil-ton's wrath, while the bishops become mere traffickers in spiritual com-modities: "Truth . . . is like to finde small credit with us for what she can say, unlesse shee can bring a Ticket from *Cranmer, Latimer,* and *Ridley.*" By the final sentence of the paragraph, these three have been reduced to no more than verbal signs of themselves, "Names": "More tolerable it were for the *Church* of GOD that all these Names were ut-terly abolisht, like the *Brazen Serpent;* then that mens fond opinion should thus idolize them, and the Heavenly *Truth* be thus captivated." Already distanced as offstage ticket dispensers, the bishops are now fairly obliterated by the prominent and opposing images of the Brazen Serpent, and Heavenly Truth in captivity.

With the end of the digression on martyrdom the historical argument resumes, and as it does, we find it divested of all its troublesome affective properties, whether good or evil. This reassertion of moral neutrality in the historical realm not only conserves affective resources for the imagery ahead, but for Milton's purposes it now sufficiently dissociates the bishops from the epithets they had acquired ("common stales . . . prostituted Gravities") in the rather less strategical earlier passage. This makes them presently available to new, quite contrary definitions in Milton's realm of Truth:

> Now to proceed, whatsoever the *Bishops* were, it seemes they themselves were unsatisfi'd in matters of *Religion*, as they then stood, by that Commission granted to 8. *Bishops*, 8. other *Divines*, 8. *Civilians*, 8. *common Lawyers*, to frame *Ecclesiasticall Constitutions;* which no wonder if it came to nothing; for (as *Hayward* relates) both their Professions and their Ends were different. Lastly, we all know by Examples, that exact *Reformation* is not perfited at the first push, and those unweildy Times of *Edward 6.* may hold some Plea by this excuse. (Pp. 535–36)

The rational detachment Milton now brings to the historical realm virtually absolves the bishops of the moral responsibility he had once been so concerned to lay upon them. "Whatsoever the *Bishops* were" declares, in effect, that neither historical nor moral evidence for or against the bishops has any bearing on the question: it would have been nearly impossible for them to succeed with church reformation anyway — the times were difficult, the task onerous. Only as Milton's rhetoric begins to shift once more from the historical to the moral and affective level do we discover that he has actually redirected his attack. As the paragraph moves forward, historical events become gradually more vague and generalized, while the moral and spiritual dimension expands and polarizes. Accelerated references to "*Episcopacie*" identify and call attention to the new enemy, while the bishops reemerge from their historical obscurity as reconstituted but radically simplified beings:

> Now let any reasonable man judge whether that *Kings Reigne* be a fit time from whence to patterne out the Constitution of a *Church Discipline*, much lesse that it should yeeld occasion from whence to foster and establish the continuance of Imperfection with the commendatory subscriptions of *Confessors* and *Martyrs,* to intitle and ingage a glorious *Name* to a grosse *corruption.* It was not *Episcopacie* that wrought in them the Heavenly Fortitude of *Martyrdome;* as little

is it that *Martyrdome* can make good *Episcopacie:* But it was *Episcopacie* that led the good and holy Men through the temptation of the *Enemie*, and the snare of this present world to many blame-worthy and opprobrious *Actions*. (P. 536)

From the historically tangible setting defined by morally neutral language — the "constitution of a *Church Discipline*" in the reign of Edward VI — the scene broadens through polarities ("glorious *Name* . . . grosse *corruption*," "Heavenly Fortitude . . . temptation of the *Enemie*") to a dualistic universe, abstract and morally absolute. "Episcopacy" is the primary agent now, while the bishops themselves are mindless followers, men "good and holy," but apparently innocent of exercising individual will or moral choice. Evil acts are "many," "blameworthy and opprobrious," but unidentified. Sensuous detail, completely severed from the empirical moorings of historical checks and specificity, finds in this abstract moral realm a freedom and independent vitality that enable it to build to the startling climax:

And it is still *Episcopacie* that before all our eyes worsens and sluggs the most learned, and seeming religious of our *Ministers*, who no sooner advanc't to it, but like a seething pot set to coole, sensibly exhale and reake out the greatest part of that zeale, and those Gifts which were formerly in them, settling in a skinny congealment of ease and sloth at the top: and if they keep their Learning by some potent sway of Nature, 'tis a rare chance; but their *devotion* most commonly comes to that queazy temper of luke-warmnesse, that gives a Vomit to GOD himself. (P. 536–37)

"Before all our eyes" is exactly where Milton's affective rhetoric can flourish. By subordinating the rational claims of the historical argument to the suprarational claims of his polarized and theocentric moral universe, Milton once more creates a sensory apprehension of Truth. Instead of historical bishops engaged in historically verifiable acts, the sensuous details achieve something closer to what Milton argues are the products of episcopacy: manipulable, "lukewarm" bishops. Yet sensuous as are its details, the scene never becomes only these. It is simultaneously abstract and concrete, *"Episcopacie"* and "before all our eyes." Reiterated sibilants and rhymes reinforce this simultaneity: "seeming religious" and "seething pot," "reake out" and "zeale," "skinny congealment" and "ease and sloth." Finally, the most familiarly homely concrete detail is juxtaposed with the most exalted abstraction. And that which forces juxtaposition of these extremes is the image of Milton's episcopized ministers, whose consequent "luke-warmnesse . . . gives a Vomit to GOD himselfe." The final image elicits from Milton's readers an interesting complex of responses, as attested by the range of comments in the critical canon. At once we feel embarrassment for a multilevel breach of decorum: it startles every sublime image we have of God to find him not only in the kitchen but sick there; and it further unnerves our sense of literary propriety for a great poet to create such a scene. At the same time as the image offends, however, it compels with its sensuous pleasurability. It is richly iconoclastic, grossly humorous, memorable. It may be that the decorum appalled is the idolatrous decorum of the lukewarm bishops. If so, it is an effect the iconoclast in Milton could only relish.[18]

The image of God vomiting is clearly a *succès de scandale:* more than any other, it is this scene that critics refer to when they protest Milton's scurrility — a fact clearly anticipated by Milton, since he prepares for it with the disclaimer in the "invocation" that precedes it. This apologetic passage — really an oath — is often (dubiously) cited by critics as Milton's attempt to justify his strong language. Perhaps Milton liked to believe that it did justify him, but the critical reception suggests that the expedient failed. Moreover, Milton's singleminded pursuit of linguistic sensuousness in the present passage suggests that he didn't much care whether his readers accepted the self-justification or not. We have seen that he went to a good deal of trouble to make the conditions right for creating the image of God retching over the bishops — that, having prematurely caricatured Cranmer, Latimer, and Ridley in a manner that would prove inconsistent with some of the facts yet to be treated, Milton found himself obliged to reshuffle his moral charges in the interest of an even better caricature. If this is indeed what happened, we may well ask, why did Milton make such an injudicious move in the first place? Why did he proceed with name-calling that he later would only have to retract, or at least cover for? And I think the most plausible answer is that he simply couldn't resist. His desire was to create what felt like Truth, and at the moment he wrote of the bishops' "prostituted Gravities," that image fulfilled his desire. As the disjointed argumentative levels of the antiprelatical tracts show, Milton's rhetorical concern here is with local effects. When he discovers an occasion for inserting or developing a rich image, he exploits it with little regard for its rhetorical connections before and after. If this results in contradictions, as it does in his treatment of the bishops, so be it. His instinct for forceful expression of conviction leads him indiscriminately to accept forcefulness as a test of validity: if it feels strong, it must be True.

But championship of such a Truth has its risks. If Milton's animus against the bishops is so intense that it spontaneously manufactures occasions to break forth, we might surely expect the same of his passion for the cause he favors. But we cannot. For instance, Milton's effort to portray the millennial certitude of modern-day saints is as troubled a passage as can be found anywhere in the antiprelatical tracts. It occurs in *Animadversions*, whose contentious evocation of a grimy polemical present points up the difficulty of realizing and maintaining millennial vision. In his desire to reify this eternal and theocentric ideal, Milton detaches his argument from its historical context — only to find himself casting about for ways to explain reformation's present failure.

Milton's opponent, the self-styled Humble Remonstrant, has tried to dismiss reformist objections to episcopacy as newfangled querulousness: "They cannot name any man in this Nation that ever contradicted *Episcopacie*, till this present Age" (p. 703). A statement like this challenges the millennialist where in chiliastic terms he ought to be strongest, but where in temporal and historical terms he clearly can become vulnerable. To evaluate any thought or action, the millennialist refers automatically to revelation. The Remonstrant and his cohorts, on the other hand, refer to history. With the two sides thus speaking, in effect, two different languages, the possibilities for discourse are curtailed. Therefore, Milton's rebuttal of the Remonstrant's charges must simultaneously engage the temporal "enemy" — that, after all, is the purpose of the tract — and operate as if, in the ultimate scheme of things, he doesn't matter. The contradictoriness of Milton's position is borne out in the ensuing passage.

First he must defend the millenarian reformers against the implication that they themselves, no less than the episcopists, are merely historical entities instead of chosen instruments of God:

What an over-worne and bedrid Argument is this, the last refuge ever of old falshood, and therefore a good signe I trust that your Castle cannot hold out long. This was the plea of *Judaisme*, and Idolatry against *Christ* and his *Apostles*, of *Papacie* against Reformation: and perhaps to the frailty of flesh and blood in a man destitute of better enlight'ning, may for some while bee pardonable; for what has fleshly apprehension other to subsist by then Succession, Custome, and Visibility, which onely hold if in his weaknesse and blindnesse he be loath to lose, who can blame? but in a *Protestant* Nation that should have thrown off these tatter'd Rudiments long agoe, after the many strivings of Gods Spirit, and our fourscore yeares vexation of him in this our wildernesse since Reformation began, to urge these rotten Principles, and twit us with the present age, which is to us an age of ages wherein God is manifestly come downe among us, to doe some remarkable good to our Church or state, is as if a man should taxe the renovating and re-ingendring Spirit of God with innovation, and that new creature for an upstart noveltie; yea the new Jerusalem, which without your admired linke of succession descends from Heaven, could not scape some such like censure. (P. 703)

Milton seizes the Remonstrant's term, "present age," and employs it as a cutting edge to radically separate the Remonstrant's realm from that of the millenarians. Whereas the "present age" for the Remonstrant is simply the current experience of a continuing history, the millennialists' "present age" is a fulfillment of prophecy, an age "*which is to us* an age of ages wherein God is manifestly come downe among us" (my emphasis). The moral and rhetorical alignment of these two realms Milton makes readily apparent: on the side of the Remonstrant we have falsehood, Judaism, Idolatry, Papacy, flesh and blood frailty, fleshly apprehension, Succession, Custom, Visibility, weaknesse, blindnesse, tatter'd Rudiments, rotten Principles. On the side of the millennialists are Christ and his Apostles, Reformation, Protestant Nation, Gods Spirit, God manifest, remarkable good, renovating and re-ingendring Spirit of God, new Jerusalem, Heaven. In an illuminating discussion of *The Reason of Church-Government*, Stanley Fish shows how the judgment implicit in such opposing lists pressures the reader to align himself with the millenarian reformists. In fact, Fish accommodates the recurrent disjunctions between the two rhetorics of the antiprelatical tracts by brilliantly finessing the tedious historical and rational argument over to the side of the prelates, leaving the spiritual rectitude of Milton's imagery of Truth to be embraced by the self-redeeming reader. Fish's strategy is appropriate, because that is precisely what Milton himself does here. But the present passage also exposes a difficulty. The reader may well reject, as Milton does, the cumbersome and static rational argument, but that action does not automatically entail rejection of the prelates; there are, after all, prelates on both of Milton's argumentative levels, and we have seen that the force of their presence depends on the rhetorical use Milton wishes to make of them. In Milton's realm of Truth, the prelates may be manipulable, but they are not dispensable: the polarized dynamic that vitalizes Milton's sensuous imagerial realm requires an enemy. To see why this should be so, we need only read again through the opposing lists gleaned from *The Reason of Church-Government* and set forth by Stanley Fish. First, on the side of the prelates:

gross, patched, varnished, embellishings, veil, sumptuous, tradition, show, visibility, polluted, idolatrous, Gentilish rites, ceremonies, feather, bravery, hide, deformed, plumes, pomp, flesh, outward, ceremonial law, delusions, particolored, mimic, custom, specious, sophistical, names, fallacy, mask, dividing, schismatical, forked, disfigurement, Egyptian, overcloud, scales, false, glitter, beads, art, sweet, dim, reflection, fleshly wisdom, garb, defaced, overcasting, copes, vestures, gold robes, surplices, adorn, corporeal resemblances, clothing, maskers, gaudy glisterings, delude, carnal, high, sensual, fermentations, worldly, external, flourishes, counterfeit, crafty, artificial, appearance, outward man, skin, defile, ignorance, pride, temples, carpets, tablecloth, slimy, confections, profane, faulty, false-whited, gilded, vanities, dross, scum, luggage, infection, formal outside, greasy, brazen, temporal, oil over, besmear, corrupt, shadow, darkened, obscured.

And now, on the side of the reformists:

plainly, clearness, eternal, invariable, inspired, open, spiritual eye, inward, plain, clear, evident, pure, spiritual, simple, lowly, internal, faith, homogeneous, even, firm, united, truth, steadfastness, perfection, unity, seamless, unchangeable, constancy, light, sacred, illumination, luster, inspiration, revelation, eye-brightening, inward prompting, divine, bright, belief, common sense, simplicity, clear evidence, naked, inward holiness, inward beauty, bareness, lowliness, purity of Doctrine, wisdom of God, glory, enlightened, true knowledge, holy, cleansed, health, purge, God's word.[19]

Of the two lists, we have no doubt that the second is the one with which we are supposed to align ourselves. But it is the first that is interesting to read. Indeed, the elements of list number two are so spiritual, so abstract and ineffable, that their rhetorical effectiveness depends on juxtaposition with their worldly, fleshly opposites in list number one. An exhortation toward list two without an attendant warning away from list one would make pallid oratory. In contrast with the haphazard human and institutional alliances of Milton's historical realm, the self-polarizing elements of his moral realm absolutely require one another, both for definition and for affective intensity. Thus, to affirm Milton's Truth is really to affirm the polarities that bring it to life — that is, to affirm *both* lists. And as the polarities are formulated entirely in sensory rather than rational terms, the verities they so affirm are not rational but affective. In other words, what the "self-redeeming" reader embraces in the antiprelatical tracts is the entire panoply of sensuous language — here, Milton's Truth is his carnal rhetoric.

    To some degree, of course, this is Milton's point: it is precisely because our eyes are darkened and our sensibilities are fallen that the Word's only access to us is through our carnal apprehension. But that premise, as we find on returning to *Animadversions,* has a double edge. If a sensuous apprehension of Truth requires that the reader — or the author — be compelled to enlist himself among the adherents to one side of a set of oppositions, it will clearly be necessary to keep both sides in view. So long as Milton keeps a sharp eye on prelatical evil, his sense of conviction maintains its impetus: whatever it is he believes in, it visibly cannot be *that.* For some Milton scholars, most notably Thomas Kranidas and Kester

Svendsen, the strength of Milton's pejorative imagery is in its capacity to imply its opposite even where the positive vision is wanting: from disease, we are to infer health; from disproportion and disorder, order and unity; and so forth.[20] As a general principle for assessing Milton's moral polarities, this works quite well, though in the local instance we may be hard pressed to imagine the opposite of a bishop-sick God. But as Fish's study shows, we need not speculate about Milton's positive vision—the language is there. It's just that, as we've seen, such language gives us almost nothing to look at. So, sensibilities earthbound, ever carnal, we are apt to forget. And in our carnality we are not alone. As Milton works his way into the millennial vision of *Animadversions*, his effort to relinquish the supporting carnal rhetoric of antiprelatical imagery leads him anxiously to appeal for a more and more concrete, sensuously apprehensible response from God.

In his contemptuous rejoinder to the Remonstrant ("What an overworne and bedrid Argument is this"), Milton shows no sign of recognizing that a world bereft of prelates might turn out to be less than stable. But there are hints nevertheless. Between and around the self-polarizing elements that make up the two lists in this passage—falsehood, idolatry, Custome, as against Christ, remarkable good, new Jerusalem—there lie other elements that resist easy alignment. If contrary interpretations of "the present age" measure the moral and rhetorical distance between "you," the Remonstrant, and "us," the reformists, who is responsible for "our fourscore years' vexation of him [Gods Spirit] in this our wildernesse"? Does this "our" refer to the same group of people as those who "should have throwne off these tatter'd Rudiments long agoe," the citizens of "a *Protestant* Nation"? Perhaps Milton's shift in pronouns for the Remonstrant ("*your* Castle . . . *his* weakenesse and blindnesse . . . *your* admired linke of succession" [my italics]) should warn us against too rigorous an assignment of responsibilities, but it is hard not to see in "our fourscore years' vexation of him" implicit chastising of the reformers themselves. Indeed, once Milton dismisses the Remonstrant, he turns a more critical eye toward the reformers. But in dismissing the Remonstrant Milton does more than just quit an adversary: he openly abandons the already segregated ("the present age") temporal level of discourse. Polemical debate is reduced to a circuit of petty quarrelsomeness—"If you require a further answer . . . in stead of other answer . . . not caring otherwise to answer this un-Protestantlike Objection"; and the Remonstrant is left solidly in the middle of it—"leaving this *Remonstrant* and his adherents to their owne designes."

Theoretically, all that should be left to do is evoke the alternative: the millenarian's eternal realm of Truth, populated by the enlightened, "every true protested *Brittaine*." At first, it looks like that is what Milton is going to do, as he further illuminates the reformist interpretation of "the present age":

in this Age, *Brittains* God hath reform'd his Church after many hundred yeers of *Popish* corruption; in this Age hee hath freed us from the intolerable yoke of *Prelats*, and *Papall* Discipline; in this age he hath renewed our *Protestation* against all those yet remaining dregs of superstition: Let us all goe every true protested *Brittaine* throughout the 3. *Kingdoms*, and render thanks to God the Father of light, and fountaine of heavenly grace, and to his son CHRIST our Lord; leaving this *Remonstrant* and his adherents to their owne designes. (P. 704)

"*Brittains* God hath reform'd . . . hee hath freed . . . he hath renewed." These lines clearly express the conviction that God is present, working now among the faithful. But it should be noted, too, that these confident lines are spiked with "*Popish* corruption," "the intolerable yoke of *Prelats*," "*Papall* Discipline" and "dregs of superstition." Still, as the faithful depart to render thanks for God's favor, they leave all this behind. What follows, we may presume, should be the promised hymn of praise. It does not. Instead, there follows a more painstaking rehearsal of these acts of Britain's God, this time without the easy targets of pope and prelate:

Let us recount even here without delay the patience and long suffering that God hath us'd towards our blindnesse and hardnes time after time. For he being equally neere to his whole Creation of Mankind, and of free power to turne his benefick and fatherly regard to what Region or Kingdome he pleases, hath yet ever had this Iland under the speciall indulgent eye of his providence; and pittying us the first of all other Nations, after he had decreed to purifie and renew his Church that lay wallowing in Idolatrous pollutions, sent first to us a healing messenger to touch softly our sores, and carry a gentle hand over our wounds: he knockt once and twice and came againe, opening our drousie eye-lids leasurely by that glimmering light which *Wicklef*, and his followers dispers't, and still taking off by degrees the inveterat scales from our nigh perisht sight, purg'd also our deaf eares, and prepar'd them to attend his second warning trumpet in our Grandsires dayes. How else could they have been able to have receiv'd the sudden assault of his reforming Spirit warring against humane Principles, and carnall sense, the pride of flesh that still cry'd up Antiquity, Custome, Canons, Councels and Lawes, and cry'd down the truth for noveltie, schisme, profanenesse and Sacriledge: when as we that have liv'd so long in abundant light, besides the sunny reflection of all the neighbouring Churches, have yet our hearts rivetted with those old opinions, and so obstructed and benumm'd with the same fleshly reasonings, which in our forefathers soone melted and gave way, against the morning beam of *Reformation*. (Pp. 704–05)

By the end of this recapitulation of God's works among the faithful, we find that the very faults hitherto charged against the prelates are now brought to bear on the reformers themselves. Now it is "*our* blindnesse and hardnes," *our* nation's church "wallowing in Idolatrous pollutions," the "inverterat scales" cover *our* sight, *our* ears are deaf; despite the best examples of neighboring churches, we "have yet *our* hearts rivetted with those old opinions," those same "humane Principles, and carnall sense, the pride of flesh that still cry'd up Antiquity, custome, Canons, Councels and Lawes"; we yet remain "obstructed and benumm'd with the same fleshly reasonings" (my emphasis throughout). Fleshly reasonings, old opinions, pride of flesh, human principles — all are "the same." But without the prelates, the rhetorical effects of these charges are not the same. For, it seems, Milton's true protested Britons are favored by a patient and long-suffering God: they are watched by his "speciall indulgent eye"; idolatrous pollutions are transformed by a "healing messenger" into "sores . . . wounds"; it is possible that our nigh perished sight may be due merely to "drousie eye-lids." This mitigating of charges, however salutary for the reformers, weakens the impetus of Milton's affective rhetoric. For, instead of building toward a display of millennial conviction, such as his attacks on the prelates have always produced, Milton's critique of the reformers practically leaves his millennial vision in shreds. Everywhere else in *Animadversions*, Milton's references to "we" the reformers implies a cohesive body of like-minded visionaries. But without the prelatical foil, the reformist "we" disintegrates under Milton's scrutiny: if fleshly reasonings gave way so readily in our forefathers, he asks, how can we, in light of their example, remain so hardened? Have we, who are to fulfill their expectations, so much less virtue than they? *Are* we what we claim?

If God hath left undone this whole worke so contrary to flesh and blood, till these times, how should wee have yeelded to his heavenly call, had we beene taken, as they were, in the starknes of our ignorance, that yet after all these spirituall preparatives, and purgations have our earthly apprehensions so clamm'd, and furr'd with the old levin. O if we freeze at noone after their earely thaw, let us feare lest the Sunne for ever hide himselfe, and turne his orient steps from our ingratefull Horizon justly condemn'd to be eternally benighted. (P. 705)

What had started out to be a prayer of thanks has evolved through critical self-examination into an increasingly anxious questioning of the reformists' capacities to sustain their millennial expectations. We may recall the triumphant voice with which Milton had initially turned away from his opponent:

If you require a further answer, it will not misbecome a Christian to bee either more magnanimous, or more devout then *Scipio* was, who in stead of other answer to the frivolous accusations of *Petilius* the *Tribune; This day Romans* (saith he) *I fought with* Hanibal *prosperously; let us all goe and thank the gods that gave us so great a victory.* (Pp. 703–04)

But by the time Milton actually begins to frame his address to God, his tone has altered considerably: his prayer takes the form not of praise and gratitude, but of entreaty. By Milton's own analysis, the frivolous accusation of the Remonstrant could be right on target: the millennialists might well be "justly condemn'd to be eternally benighted." From this prospect he recoils violently: "Which dreadfull judgement O thou the ever-begotten light, and perfect Image of the Father, intercede may never come upon us." Then his language begins, at first tentatively ("as we trust thou hast"), then with gradually increasing assurance ("thou hast open'd . . . and given us . . . thou has done justice"), to piece together the fragile elements of his vision of the millennium. But at the same time — as perhaps we might have anticipated — his gradual movement toward positive vision is accompanied by the return of an increasingly palpable, clearly nonreformist, enemy:

Which dreadfull judgement O thou the ever-begotten light, and perfect Image of the Father, intercede may never come upon us, as we trust thou hast; for thou hast open'd our difficult and sad times, and given us an unexpected breathing after our long oppressions; thou has done justice upon those that tyranniz'd over us, while some men waver'd, and admir'd a vaine shadow of wisedome in a tongue nothing slow to utter guile, though thou hast taught us to admire onely that which is good, and to count that onely praise-worthy which is grounded upon thy divine Precepts. Thou hast discover'd the plots, and frustrated the hopes of all the wicked in the Land; and put to shame the persecutors of thy Church; thou hast made our false *Prophets* to be found a lie in the sight of all the people, and chac'd them with sudden confusion and amazement before the redoubled brightnesse of thy descending cloud that now covers thy Tabernacle. (P. 705)

The already weakened charges against the reformers are now further diffused in the context of "our difficult and sad times," then excused by recalling "our long oppressions" under "those that tyranniz'd over us." A residue of reformist error may be admitted in the words "while some men waver'd . . . though thou hast taught us to admire onely that which is good." But with resurrection of the enemy (oppressors, tyrants, a tongue uttering guile, plotters, the wicked, persecutors, false Prophets), the reformists can once more be unambiguously aligned on the side of God, whose accomplishments can also therefore be celebrated with renewed vigor: "Thou hast discover'd the plots, and frustrated the hopes of all the wicked . . . put to shame the persecutors . . . thou hast made our false *Prophets* to be found a lie . . . chac'd them with sudden confusion and amazement." In Milton's initial recapitulation of God's works among the English reformers, millennial vision had been threatened by historical fact: recollection of Wickliff and his followers had put present-day reformers to shame; presumption of God's constant reforming activity had been baffled by the apparent blindness and hardness of protestant hearts. But as the return of an external enemy once more permits moral polarities, historical reality is left behind, and God's works among men may be conceived in more and more absolute terms: from the uncertainty of "while some men waver'd," the assertions progress to God's unqualified discovery and frustration of "*all* the wicked in the land," his finding false prophets a lie "in the sight of *all* the people" (my emphasis). Because the absolute terms of a polarized moral realm have been reestablished, Milton's vision is now freed to see what it needs must — a glimpse of the apocalypse, extracted from Revelation:

Who is there that cannot trace thee now in thy beamy walke through the midst of thy Sanctuary, amidst those golden *candlesticks*, which have long suffer'd a dimnesse amongst us through the violence of those that had seiz'd them, and were more taken with the mention of their gold then of their starry light; teaching the doctrine of *Balaam* to cast a stumbling-block before thy servants, commanding them to eat things sacrifiz'd to Idols, and forcing them to fornication. (Pp. 705–06)

"Who is there that cannot trace thee now"? Clearly the reformers of the historical critique could not; neither could the partisan polemicist who examined them — "O if we freeze at noone after their earely thaw, let us feare lest the Sunne for ever hide himself." Only in reaction against a well-defined enemy, capable of being charged with the reformists' failures, can Milton propel his rhetoric toward a vision of Truth.

But even this hard-won vision cannot sustain itself alone — it yearns to be reified. The entire argument of *Animadversions* (as of all the antiprelatical tracts) rests on the implicit assumption that Milton's cause is identical with God's cause, that the prelatical enemy is felt by God to be exactly what Milton feels it to be. What Milton asks, then, is for God to justify this assumption — he asks God, in other words, for concrete proof that Milton is right. And he sees to it that, should Milton turn out to be wrong, God knows very well whose fault that would be:

Come therefore O thou that hast the seven starres in thy right hand, appoint thy chosen *Preists* according to their Orders, and courses of old, to minister be-

fore thee, and duely to dresse and powre out the consecrated oyle into thy holy
and ever-burning lamps; thou hast sent out the spirit of prayer upon thy servants
over all the Land to this effect, and stirr'd up their vowes as the sound of many
waters about thy Throne. Every one can say that now certainly thou hast visited
this land, and hast not forgotten the utmost corners of the earth, in a time when
men had thought that thou wast gone up from us to the farthest end of the
Heavens, and hadst left to doe marvelously among the sons of these last Ages.
O perfect, and accomplish thy glorious acts; for men may leave their works unfinisht, but thou art a God, thy nature is perfection; shouldst thou bring us thus
far onward from *Egypt* to destroy us in this Wildernesse though wee deserve;
yet thy great name would suffer in the rejoycing of thine enemies, and the deluded hope of all thy servants. (P. 706)

With these words Milton makes the most extraordinary claim in the antiprelatical tracts, although it is only a logical inference from his basic
premise: if Milton's cause is neither more nor less than God's cause, then
failure of that cause will make God suffer much the way Milton would.
A more transparently self-serving piece of anthropomorphism would be
hard to find. Yet Milton seems oblivious to the solecism, and with good
reason. This God who must look after his reputation among men is the
direct product of Milton's own rhetorical requirements. Only after visual-
izing God casting down the prelatical enemy can Milton work up a por-
trait of the cohesiveness and faith of the reformers: "Who is there that
cannot trace thee *now* . . . Every one can say that *now* certainly thou
hast visited" (my emphasis). Yet God would not, for all that, suffer failure precisely as Milton would. God's case would be worse, since he would
have to put up not just with the jubilant enemy but with the resentment
of his disappointed followers as well: "thy great name would suffer in
the rejoycing of thine enemies, and the deluded hope of all thy servants."
Furthermore, the enemy is no longer "ours" but thine," for in revitaliz-
ing the polarities of his realm of Truth, Milton has shifted entire responsibility for the English Reformation from off the unsound shoulders of
the reformers and onto God: "men may leave their works unfinisht, but
thou art a God, thy nature is perfection." This leaves the newly unified,
though quite ineffectual, reformers with nothing to do but applaud. And
interestingly, once the reformers are safely out of the enemy's clutches,
the enemy can again be acknowledged as "ours":

When thou hast settl'd peace in the Church, and righteous judgement in the
Kingdome, then shall all thy Saints addresse their voyces of joy, and triumph
to thee, standing on the shoare of that red Sea into which our enemies had almost driven us. And he that now for haste snatches up a plain ungarnish't present as a thanke-offering to thee, which could not bee deferr'd in regard of thy

so many late deliverances wrought for us one upon another, may then perhaps
take up a Harp, and sing thee an elaborate Song to Generations. (P. 706)

Milton's pledge of a millennial "Song to Generations" hints toward a poetic unattainable in a hectic polemical world. But aside from that, since
Milton has just remonstrated with God for neglecting his credit among
men, the promise of an elaborate song oddly resembles a bribe. With other
antiprelatical tracts, Milton's argument culminates in rewards for the
faithful and punishment for the prelatical enemy; but in this unique attempt to derive millennial vision from history, such polarities break down.
Here the reformers look little better than the prelates: the enemy may
still triumph, the faithful may deserve abandonment. Therefore, responsibility for "the present age" is taken out of men's hands. And so is Milton's own rhetorical task, that of fully defining "the present age," whose
opposed meanings (historical versus prophetic) he had delineated but
could not sustain. Rewards, punishments, millennial vision, rhetorical
task — all causes as well as consequences — are in the end left solely to God.
In a different rhetorical context, perhaps, such a resolution would be appropriate for an absolute Calvinist God. But that is not the God Milton
sets forth in this passage. Here Milton's God is alternately apparent and
elusive, finally provoking Milton to urge him with something like a threat.
When Milton at last defers to God his own task of illuminating the true,
the prophetic, meaning of "the present age," he implores God to show
not just the enemy, but to show, concretely, *visibly*, the faithful as well.
Even the Holy Spirit becomes a material entity, actually divisible into
portions, as Milton's own yearning for sensory gratification of a spiritual
need fills the passage:

In that day it shall no more bee said as in scorne, this or that was never held so
till this present Age, when men have better learnt that the times and seasons passe
along under thy feet, to goe and come at thy bidding, and as thou didst dignifie
our fathers dayes with many revelations above all the foregoing ages, since thou
tookst the flesh; so thou canst vouchsafe to us (though unworthy) as large a portion of thy spirit as thou pleasest; for who shall prejudice thy all-governing will?
seeing the power of thy grace is not past away with the primitive times, as fond
and faithless men imagine, but thy Kingdome is now at hand, and thou standing
at the dore. Come forth out of thy Royall Chambers, O Prince of all the Kings
of the earth, put on the visible roabes of thy imperiall Majesty, take up that
unlimited Scepter which thy Almighty Father hath bequeath'd thee; for now the
voice of thy Bride calls thee, and all creatures sigh to bee renew'd. (Pp. 706–07)

In the opening paragraphs of his first antiprelatical tract, *Of Reformation*, Milton alludes contemptuously to the superstitious man, the

atheist *manqué* who "all in a pudder shuffles up to himselfe such a *God*, and such a *worship* as is most agreeable to remedy his feare, which feare of his, as also is his hope, fixt onely upon the *Flesh*, renders likewise the whole faculty of his apprehension, carnall." Clearly, Milton's own fears and hopes lie not in the fleshly dimension dreaded by the man of crude superstition. Rather, the rhetorical ambivalences of the antiprelatical tracts argue a different order of carnal apprehension — an affective intensity capable not only, to use K. G. Hamilton's phrase, of "swamping the argument," but of seducing, deluding, and finally defeating the arguer. For Milton, however, the issue goes beyond mere style. The antiprelatical tracts document the way in which Milton's vision of the millennium depends on a self-generated and self-sustained structure of rhetoric. When in *Animadversions* Milton shuffles up such a God as will remedy his own fear and answer to his own hopes, it is one who can remove from his shoulders more than just the unwanted burden of his present battle with the prelates. Milton would be relieved as well of the agonizing possibility that his most fundamental assumptions about God and God's cause may be in error.

Ithaca College

NOTES

1. Joan Webber, *The Eloquent "I": Style and Self in Seventeenth Century Prose* (Madison, 1968), p. 207.

2. *Complete Prose Works of John Milton*, 8 vols., ed. Don M. Wolfe et al. (New Haven, 1953–82), vol. I, p. 536–37. All quotations from Milton's prose are from this edition and volume, and subsequent page references will appear in the text.

3. See Thomas Kranidas, "Milton and the Rhetoric of Zeal," *TSLL*, VI, no. 4 (Winter, 1965), 423–32.

4. French's article, "Milton as Satirist," is in *PMLA*, LI (1936), 414–29. Critics who share French's perspective on Milton as a satirist include Edward LeComte, "Milton as Satirist and Wit," *Th'Upright Heart and Pure*, ed. Amadeus P. Fiore (Pittsburgh, 1967), pp. 45–59; and Joel Morkan, "Wrath and Laughter: Milton's Ideas on Satire," *SP*, LXIX (1972), 475–95.

5. K. G. Hamilton, "The Structure of Milton's Prose," in *Language and Style in Milton*, ed. Ronald David Emma and John T. Shawcross (New York, 1967), p. 329. Hamilton's comment is anticipated by Fred Emil Ekfelt in "The Graphic Diction of Milton's English Prose," *PQ*, XXV (1946), 66: "There are long concrete passages which not only do not advance the argument but often conceal it."

6. Stanley Fish, *Self-Consuming Artifacts* (Berkeley and Los Angeles, 1972), p. 283.

7. Keith Stavely, *The Politics of Milton's Prose Style* (New Haven, 1975), p. 33.

8. Ibid., pp. 33, 10.

9. French, "Milton as Satirist," p. 429.

10. Stavely, *The Politics of Milton's Prose Style*, pp. 23, 28.

11. See Fish, *Self-Consuming Artifacts*, p. 290 et passim.

12. Ibid., 301–02.

13. See LeComte, "Milton as Satirist and Wit," p. 51. The phrase characterizing Milton's stance is from Fish, *Self-Consuming Artifacts*, pp. 298–99: "Rather than proclaiming (and documenting) his fitness for the task at hand, Milton declares that the business at hand is beneath him, because it is beneath the capacities he has been given by God. It is a kind of arrogant humility, in which the emphasis is not on his powers but on their source in divine inspiration."

14. Fish, *Self-Consuming Artifacts*, p. 302.

15. In his detailed analysis of comparable imagerial progressions in *The Reason of Church-Government*, Stanley Fish calls this the "zoom lens effect," *Self-Consuming Artifacts*, pp. 265–302.

16. Richard M. Weaver, *The Ethics of Rhetoric* (Chicago, 1953), p. 158, has noted that Milton's "frequent use of pairs of words . . . give the impression of thickness, which is in turn the source of the impression of strength . . . what the pairs create is the effect of dimension."

17. Thomas Kranidas has argued that the image of the "radiant singing body" is one of the great unifying metaphors that give coherence to Milton's seemingly disparate prose. See *The Fierce Equation* (The Hague, 1965), Chapter 2 et passim.

18. See Kranidas, *The Fierce Equation*, for a definition of "decorum" rich enough to embrace such images as the foregoing.

19. Fish, op. cit., 290–91.

20. Kester Svendsen, *Milton and Science* (Cambridge, 1956), p. 223 et passim; Kranidas, *The Fierce Equation*, p. 52 et passim.

MILTON'S USE
OF RABBINIC MATERIAL

Golda Werman

T HE INFLUENCE of Midrash (rabbinical exegesis of the Bible) on
Paradise Lost was noted by scholars of Judaica long before literary
critics became aware of Milton's debt to rabbinic sources.[1] Miltonists
were generally not acquainted with the Hebrew midrashic literature;
they believed that all the embellishments to the biblical story which could
not be traced to either Christian sources or to classical Greek and Roman
works were invented by the poet. The publication of Louis Ginzberg's
seven volume *Legends of the Jews* in English (Philadelphia, 1909–38),
which first gave non-Hebrew readers access to the full scope of the rich
rabbinic literature, enabled critics to see for themselves the affinity of
Paradise Lost to the treatment of the Genesis story in Midrash;[2] exegetical materials in the poem which were neither Christian nor classic often
had their counterparts in the Jewish legends. Excited by their discovery,
critics began to publish examples of these parallels in the 1920s.

An early seminal article on this subject by Edward C. Baldwin (1929)
pointed to more than thirty instances of Milton's use of midrashic material in *Paradise Lost*, mostly from Ginzberg.[3] Some of the midrashic ana-
logues cited by Baldwin are strikingly similar to passages or ideas in
Paradise Lost which were hitherto thought to be Milton's inventions;
others are more tangential, but the number and quality of correspondences support the thesis that Milton must have drawn on Jewish sources.
Baldwin does not, however, attempt to explain how Milton overcame
the enormously difficult linguistic and methodological barriers that this
extensive literature presents to the nonscholar; he simply, and untenably,
extended the poet's ability to read the Hebrew Bible, a skill taught to
every university student of that day, to a scholarly mastery of rabbinics.[4]
Ginzberg's monumental work, which translates, summarizes, and orga-
nizes hundreds of separate legends into narrative patterns, and which
provides a scholarly apparatus and bibliography as well, may have given
Baldwin the false impression that this is an easily accessible literature.
In Milton's time, however, a very high level of expert knowledge would
have been required even to locate these intricate texts which are dispersed
throughout numerous unrelated volumes.

Other early critics, notably Harris F. Fletcher and Denis Saurat, also assumed that Milton was an accomplished Judaic scholar, despite the absence of any biographical evidence to substantiate this view.[5] They were convinced that Milton's wide erudition included the languages (Hebrew and Aramaic) and methodology of rabbinics, unaware of the difficulties that rabbinic texts pose to the reader who has not devoted years to their study. Variously, critics have credited the poet with a first-hand knowledge of talmudic works: the *Midrash Rabbah* and other early midrashic collections, the pseudepigraphic writings, the mystical *Zohar*, and the medieval Bible commentaries, especially those of Rashi.[6] In their concentration on Milton as a Semitic scholar, critics have overlooked the obvious: Milton made use of translations, just as they did.

The seventeenth century was an age of Hebrew erudition among Christian scholars, and much midrashic material was translated into Latin by Christian Hebraists for the benefit of interested Christians who were not trained in rabbinics.[7] Milton could choose from an extensive literature in Latin which illuminated both the Old and the New Testaments with Jewish laws, customs, and legends extracted from the Mishnah, the Talmud, and midrashic collections; often portions of the original Hebrew texts were printed alongside the Latin version.[8] In addition, a multitude of Latin monographs based on rabbinic texts were written by Christian Hebraists to provide material for Protestant dogmatics.[9] These new Protestant translations were, in many cases, generated by a scholarly love of learning for its own sake rather than for polemical attacks against the Jews or for apologetic purposes, as had been the case with earlier Catholic translations of rabbinic materials.[10]

In addition, theologians of the Reformation leaned heavily on Jewish exegesis to fill in the gap left by the Protestants' rejection of Catholic tradition and authority. Of particular interest to Puritans were the ancient Jewish explications dealing with religious and public institutions of the Bible because they, like the Rabbis before them, believed in the possibility and virtue of reestablishing a contemporary religious order and political system based on Scriptures. Both maintained that the Bible, properly understood, contains the answers to all of life's problems, personal and civil as well as theological. Furthermore, it was important for the Protestants to demonstrate that Jewish exegesis, some of which was, according to tradition, as ancient as Scripture itself, sided with them rather than with the Catholics. It was therefore not unusual for Protestant theologians of Milton's time to punctuate their writings and sermons with rabbinic quotations, usually derived from secondary sources.

Among the basic scholarly books produced by Protestants, to which

Puritans could turn for translated rabbinical materials, were: the elder Johannes Buxtorf's *Lexicon Chaldaicum Talmudicum et Rabbinicum*, published by his son in 1640, which contains learned articles on rabbinic subjects; Christopher Cartwright's *Mellificum Hebraicum*, 1649, which glosses the Old Testament, the New Testament, and the Apocrypha with both exegetical and homiletic midrashim; and John Lightfoot's *Horae Hebraicae et Talmudicae*, published over a score of years beginning in 1658, which glosses books of the New Testament with extracts from the Jerusalem and Babylonian Talmuds, Rashi, the Tosafot, and Maimonides.[11]

In the perspective of this Protestant theological *Zeitgeist*, Milton's use of rabbinic materials in his prose is not especially remarkable; nor does it indicate a profound knowledge of Semitics. Milton's Hebraic learning was not exceptional for a university-educated person of his day: he could read the Hebrew Bible, including the Aramaic sections, and he may have studied the Targums (the Aramaic translations of the Bible). These tools, as I have pointed out, are not sufficient of themselves for reading rabbinic texts whose compressed style and difficult methodology require years of practice to decipher. Since there is no evidence, either in his writings or in the biographical material available, that he ever undertook an intense study of rabbinics, or that he had the slightest interest in such a time-consuming pursuit, we must conclude that Milton made use of the same translations and lexicons which other Protestants of his day utilized.

Those of Milton's readers who have either persuaded themselves,[12] or allowed themselves to be persuaded,[13] that the poet was at home in the world of rabbinic literature and read the original works with ease have also lost sight of Milton the polemicist. In the disputatious style of the prose tracts, Milton cites talmudic passages and uses technical masoretic terms, as if he is quoting from the original texts.[14] This has led some readers to assume that he had no need of secondary sources. A close inspection of Milton's use of this material, however, demonstrates that he had such a narrow understanding of the principles he cites that he could not have used the original sources: the painstaking effort involved in studying the Hebrew/Aramaic texts would inevitably have led to a more profound knowledge than we find.

A passage in the *Apology for Smectymnuus* (1642) illustrates Milton's method in using Jewish materials. He appears to quote directly from the most complex of rabbinic texts, the Talmud, and also cites the masoretic rule of *Qere* (to be read) and *Ketiv* (for what is written), implying that he had an extensive knowledge of the Masorah, the tradition which establishes the correct reading of the Bible:

Turne then to the first of Kings where God himselfe uses the phrase; *I will cut
off from Iereboam him that pisseth against the wall.* Which had it beene an un-
seemly speech in the heat of an earnest expression, then we must conclude that
Ionathan, or *Onkelos the Targumists* were of cleaner language then he that made
the tongue; for they render it as briefly, *I will cut off all who are at yeares of
discretion*, that is to say, so much discretion as to hide nakednesse. Whereas God
who is the author both of purity and eloquence, chose this phrase as fittest in
that vehement character wherein he spake. Otherwise that plaine word might
have easily bin foreborne. Which the *Masoreths* and Rabbinicall *Scholiasts* not
well attending, have often us'd to blurre the margent with *Keri*, instead of *Ketiv*,
and gave us this insuls rule out of their *Talmud*, *That all words which in the
Law are writ obscenely, must be chang'd to more civill words.* (*YP* I, 902–03)[15]

The instructions of *Qere* and *Ketiv*, which are found in the margins of
Hebrew Bibles, denote the correct readings of those words which were
regarded as deviating from the original biblical text: incorrect grammatical forms, textual errors, misspellings, faulty vocalizations, omissions,
and, only rarely, euphemisms. For his own polemic reasons Milton emphasizes the least frequent use of the *Qere*, euphemistic substitutions, as
if this were the only application of the rule.[16] Such a distortion can only
be attributed to a superficial knowledge of the masoretic materials. Milton even offers his own apparently expert opinion on the rule of *Qere*;
he declares the Rabbis' use of it stupid.

    Judging by the number of errors in this passage alone, however, Mil-
ton is not qualified to evaluate the rule. In treating the *Qere* and *Ketiv*
as if they deal with euphemisms exclusively he misconstrues the tradition. He is mistaken in thinking that there is a Targum Onkelos on Kings;
there is none. Nor is there a *Qere* on 1 Kings XIV, 10 for "he pisseth against
the wall." The parallel phrase in 1 Samuel XXV, 34 has no *Qere* either.
Milton misunderstands the Targum: the "cleaner language" he finds so
objectionable is intended to be interpretive, not delicate. None of the chief
commentators of the Rabbinic Bible attempt to employ a more euphemistic phrase for "him that pisseth against the wall," and the Talmud
employs this very phrase as a legal prooftext (TB Bava Batra 19b).[17] The
false delicacy with which Milton invests the Rabbis does not exist in the
sources, not even in the very sources which he cites to make his point.

    Milton does not stop at using this bit of knowledge concerning the
Qere in the above passage in the *Apology* alone. He repeats his restricted
understanding of the rule as applying only to euphemistic changes and
expresses his annoyance with it several times throughout his career, over-
working a minor point of masoretic erudition. In the *Areopagitica* (1644)
Milton returns to the subject: "and ask a Talmudist what ails the mod-

esty of his marginal *Qere*, that Moses and all the prophets cannot persuade him to pronounce the textual *Ketiv*" (*YP* II, 517). And again, eleven years later, in his *Defense of Himself* (1655), he writes:

Not the writings of Solomon the Elegant will escape you as censor, nor will those of the prophets evade your censure of unseemliness, yea sometimes of obscenity, as often as to the Masorets and Rabbins it is pleasing to set down their Keri, for that which is written plainly. As for me, I confess I prefer to be plain of speech with the sacred writers than speciously decent with the futile Rabbins. (*YP* IV, pt. 2, 745)

This passage is a striking example of Milton's misuse of the masoretic rule. The biblical verse on which it is based (Num. xxv, 8) describes the priest Phinehas's spearing of the Midianite princess, Cosbi, and the Jew, Zimri, during their public orgy. In his reading of the verse, in which Phinehas "thrust both of them through, the man of Israel and the woman through her belly (*qabatah*)," Milton thinks that the Hebrew word *qabatah* means something more explicit than belly ("Moses . . . speaks without reserve, as he often does throughout, but especially when he tells in what place the spear of Phinehas transfixed the woman").[18] He is also under the impression that there is a Qere to change the reading. Milton is mistaken. There is no *Qere* for *qabatah*. The Targum of Onkelos does not change the word. The Targum of Pseudo-Jonathan goes into great detail, describing Phinehas carrying the couple aloft, alive and naked, through the camp after driving his iron lance through them both, but the sexual organs are not mentioned. The Targum Yerushalmi renders the term "through the body."

Rashi, whose exegetical commentary is found in the Rabbinic Bible, does state that the lance was driven through the sexual organs of both the man and the woman. But Milton need not have consulted Rashi for this interpretation since it was also available in at least two Latin books which were important to him: the younger Johannes Buxtorf's Latin translation (Basel, 1629) of Moses Maimonides' *Guide for the Perplexed* and William Vorstius's Latin translation (Leiden, 1644) of the eighth-century Midrash *Pirkei de-Rabbi Eliezer*. The *Guide for the Perplexed* points out that "the Hebrew language has no special name for the organ of generation in females or in males . . . and only describes them in figurative language. . . . The female organ is called *Kobah* (Num. xxv, 8), from *Kebah* (Deut. xviii, 3), which denotes 'stomach'."[19] In its explication of Numbers xxv, 8, the *Pirkei de-Rabbi Eliezer*, which in Vorstius's Latin translation is the probable source of many of the midrashic elements in *Paradise Lost*, also includes the idea of piercing the sexual organs: "manu Mosis lanceam, & postillos currens transfodit posticam foederis ejus (membri circumcisi), atque transiit lancea in ventriculum mulieris."[20] This may indicate that Milton had the Vorstius translation as early as 1655.

Milton's narrow understanding of the masoretic terms suggests that he derived his knowledge from an essay on the subject in a language he knew well. An abridged guide such as the elder Johannes Buxtorf's Latin supplement to his widely read Rabbinic Bible (1618–19), the *Tiberius Masorethicus* (Basel, 1620), would have enabled Milton to skim some useful information without studying the subject in depth. Milton appears to be unaware of the errors he makes; if he intentionally misread the evidence for his polemic purposes, he chose the wrong verses to make his point.

Even Milton's citations from the Talmud in the *First Defense*, which have been used as evidence of his superior accomplishments in Hebrew and rabbinics since Fletcher first brought his views to the attention of Milton's readers, are based on Latin translations.[21] They offer no more proof of his ability to handle Hebrew and Aramaic sources than do his statements in the same work from the Jewish authorities, Philo and Josephus, who wrote in Greek. As Secretary of Foreign Languages, it was Milton's duty to refute the learned arguments against regicide presented by the celebrated French scholar, Salmasius, in his *Defensio Regia pro Carolo I* (1649). Milton's method of disputation is to repeat his opponent's arguments in order to ridicule them or to prove them false; this includes the citations from TB Sanhedrin 20b and TB Sanhedrin 18a, culled by Salmasius from a Latin secondary source and used in his *Defensio Regia* (pp. 33, 36). Milton echoes these passages in the *First Defense* (*YP* IV, pt. 1, 353, 355).

Although he castigates Salmasius for quoting from glossaries and anthologies instead of from the original works (*YP* IV, pt. 1, 338), Milton does not expect his adversary to use the Talmud in the original. Quite the opposite; Milton so readily accepts his opponent's use of a Latin compendium for talmudic quotations that he reproaches him for not expressing gratitude to the translator: "That Hebrew kings can be judged and even condemned to the lash is shown at length by Sichard from the rabbinical writings; and it is to him that you owe all this matter, though you are not ashamed to howl against him" (*YP* IV, pt. 1, 355). An intermediate source for rabbinic materials was apparently considered an indispensable and legitimate aid and constituted a different category from the glossaries which Milton found so objectionable. Indeed, for his own rabbinic information, Milton made use of the very same intermediate source, William Schickhard's *Jus Regium Hebraeorum* (Strasbourg, 1625).

He refers to this work three times in the *First Defense* (*YP* IV, pt. 1, 350, 355, 356) and noted in his Commonplace Book: "the King of the Hebrews was not free from obedience to the laws. see Schickard, jus regium, Theor. 7" (*YP* I, 460).[22] Hebrew scholars might be expected to understand the original rabbinic sources; others, Milton and Salmasius included, used the translations which were provided by Christian Hebraists.

The inapt and contradictory criticism of talmudic material in the *First Defense* reveals Milton's limited grasp of rabbinics. He speaks of the "rabbis" (*YP* IV, pt. 1, 344) for instance, as if the talmudic sages represented a single body of agreement on theological and political issues, apparently unaware that the Talmud records the varied and often conflicting opinions of many Rabbis on numerous subjects, including that of kingship, under discussion in the *First Defense*. Had Milton been able to read the Talmud he might have found that many rabbis agreed with him on the limited rights of kings. Furthermore, his use of the phrase "swindling rabbis" (*YP* IV, pt. 1, 344) should not be taken as a judgment which is based on serious reflection upon the sources; it is a rhetorical device designed to reflect doubt on Salmasius who has used quotations from the talmudic Rabbis in support of regicide. As a polemicist Milton is not fastidious; if the ammunition appears propitious, he fires.

The talmudic citations in the *First Defense* are brief. Milton quotes more extensively from books he has read in the original and can appreciate firsthand: the Hebrew Old Testament and the Greek works of the historian Josephus (Flavius Josephus, 38–100 A.D.), *Antiquities of the Jews* and *Against Apion*, and of the philosopher Philo (20 B.C.–40 A.D.), the *Legum Allegoria* and *De Specialibus Legibus*.[23] These Jewish authors, who write in a language he knows well, earn Milton's respect; he contrasts them with the "rabbis" for whom he expresses contempt, although he knows their writings only from brief translated passages. Josephus, states Milton, is "an excellent interpreter of his people's laws . . . and far superior to a thousand of those swindling rabbis" (*YP* IV, pt. 1, 344); Philo is "a writer of weight and a contemporary of Josephus, who wrote a lengthy commentary on all the Mosaic law and was most learned in its lore" (*YP* IV, pt. 1, 344).

Milton's prejudice against the Pharisees, whose legal discussions comprise the Talmud, is so fixed that he rejects their midrashic material almost on principle. Yet when he comes across the same midrashic material in Josephus, he finds it interesting enough to copy. In the *First Defense* Milton speaks derisively of an *aggadah* (midrashic legend) from TB Sanhedrin 19a and b quoted by Salmasius via Schickhard, which gives an account of the Rabbis of the Sanhedrin ordering the king, Alexander

Yannai, to stand while giving testimony, and their consequent execution
by the angel Gabriel.[24] Milton refers to this *aggadah* as an "old wives'
tale or even worse, being but a rabbinical fable" (*YP* IV, pt. 1, 355). Yet
at another point in the same essay Milton repeats a different version of
the legend, with a rational explanation, which he has from Josephus' *Antiquities* (XIV, 9.3); it speaks of "those 800 Pharisees whose crucifixion
Alexander ordered" (*YP* IV, pt. 1, 410). This version of the midrash is
also found in the Talmud (TB Sanhedrin 107b, uncensored version, ms.
Munich).

Milton sometimes cites rabbinic material inadvertently in his quotations from Josephus, unaware that the historian sprinkled his writings
liberally with midrashim. An example of this can be found in the *Reason
of Church Government* where Milton, borrowing from Josephus, un-
knowingly paraphrases a well-known midrash on God's use of gentle persuasion rather than coercion in winning obedience:

Moses therefore the only Lawgiver that we can believe to have been visibly taught
of God, knowing how vaine it was to write lawes to men whose hearts were not
first season'd with the knowledge of God and of his workes, began from the book
of Genesis, as a prologue to his lawes; which *Josephus* right well hath noted.
That the nation of the Jewes, reading therein the universall goodnesse of God
to all creatures in the Creation, and his peculiar favour to them in his election
of *Abraham* their ancestor, from whom they could derive so many blessings upon
themselves, might be mov'd to obey sincerely by knowing so good a reason of
their obedience. (*YP* I, 747)[25]

Another *aggadah*, which Milton has taken from Josephus and used
in *Eikonoklastes*, demonstrates that the king is stronger than wine but
that woman is stronger than the king and, finally, that truth is strongest of all:

It happn'd once, as we find in *Esdras* and *Josephus*,[26] Authors not less beleiv'd
than any under sacred, to be a great and solemn debate in the Court of *Darius*,
what thing was to be counted strongest of all other. He that could resolve this,
in reward of his excelling wisdom, should be clad in Purple, drink in Gold,
sleep on a Bed of Gold, and sitt next *Darius*. None but they doubtless who were
reputed wise, had the Question propounded to them. Who after some respit
giv'n them by the King to consider, in full Assembly of all his Lords and gravest Counselors, return'd severally what they thought. The first held that Wine
was strongest; another, that the King was strongest. But *Zorobabel* Prince of
the Captive Jewes, and Heire to the Crown of Judah, being one of them, proov'd
Women to be stronger then the King, for that he himself had seen a Concu-
bin take his Crown from off his head to set it upon her own: And others beside
him have lately seen the like Feat don, and not in jest. Yet he proov'd on, and

it was so yeilded by the King himself, & all his sages, that neither Wine nor Women, nor the King, but Truth, of all other things was the strongest. (*YP* III, 582–583)

Milton's reference to Josephus and Esdras acknowledges his debt to two authors whose aggadic legends he finds attractive and which he uses proudly. But the same *aggadah* also appears in rabbinic works he disdains: *Josippon*,[27] a depository of "useless Pharisaic maxims" and lies, according to the *First Defense* (*YP* IV, pt. 1, 409), and the Talmud,[28] which houses the "rabbinical fables" he finds so distasteful. Had Milton first come across this midrash in either of these sources, or even in a secondary source which cites Josippon or the Talmud, his bias might well have precluded using the legend in *Eikonoklastes*.

On the other hand, when filtered through the Greek writings of Josephus and Philo which he admires, Milton is willing to accept even explicitly labeled Pharisaic material. In the *Tetrachordon* he writes: "This the Pharisees held, that for every cause they might divorce, for every accidental cause, any quarrell or difference that might happ'n. So both *Josephus* and *Philo*" (*YP* II, 646). The ruling is based on the Mishnah Gittin (9.10), the Rabbinic legal code which outlines the grounds for divorce: "Bet Hillel says, Even if she has spoiled his food. . . . Rabbi Akiba says, Even if he finds another woman more beautiful than she is." Apparently Milton is willing to suspend his usual negative judgment of rabbinics in this case, not only because the rabbinic decision coincides with his own ideas concerning the indignity of continuing a loveless marriage, but also because it has the imprimatur of authors whom he respects and whose treatment makes the material comprehensible to him.

Milton can only understand rabbinic material that is placed in a context which elucidates it, such as Schickhard's essay on kingship or Josephus' discussion of marriage and divorce. In the *Antiquities* Josephus summarizes the laws which govern Jewish family life and lists the regulations dealing with marriage, with children's duties to their parents, with neighbors to each other, with a man who has violated a virgin, and with divorce. Milton quotes only a portion of the passage from the *Antiquities* (IV, viii, 23): "He that desires to be divorced from his wife for any cause whatsoever," but he has also read its continuation, "let him in writing give assurance that he will never use her as his wife any more; for by this means she may be at liberty to marry another husband." Divorce in Judaism, Milton learns, was instituted as a protection for the woman, making it possible for her to remarry and establish a new life after a failed marriage.

Had Milton come across a single line from the Mishnah such as "a man may divorce his wife even if she has merely spoiled his food," out of context, he might easily have mistaken its intent and seen it as a sign of frivolousness in the Rabbis. Josephus' interpretation puts the statement into focus: when the spiritual communion between husband and wife ceases, any reason, including a burnt dinner, is an adequate cause for divorce. Milton understands, agrees, and quotes the material in his prose. The laconic style of rabbinic writings assumes a common, rich background of understanding on the part of the reader; without the luminescence of either long familiarity with the materials, or of a commentary which clarifies the rabbinic statements, rabbinic literature often sounds like so much disconnected nonsense, interspersed with an occasional pretty story.

Milton's superficial understanding of the rabbinic material in the prose tracts does not support the position of the critics who believe that he could read and comprehend original rabbinic works. On the contrary, the evidence indicates that Milton derived his midrashic material by way of casual gleanings from secondary works in translation rather than from a deep study of the sources.

Is Milton, then, pretentiously sciolistic in affecting a competence in rabbinics that he did not have? Perhaps he is, in part. But we must not forget his objective: Milton was an official government spokesman, commissioned to write polemical tracts in defense of his country's political position. In these, as well as in the treatises which proclaim his personal views alone, he took certain liberties, including that of citing rabbinic material as if he were quoting from the original Hebraic texts. Credulous readers, beginning with Fletcher, were so impressed by Milton's display of learning that they uncritically accepted his ability to handle the Hebraic rabbinic sources.

Other readers, George Conklin and Robert Adams in particular, were skeptical.[29] They correctly perceived that Milton could not have read the original Hebrew/Aramaic texts. But Fletcher and his followers were correct, too, in recognizing rabbinic material in Milton's works. Now we have an explanation for this seeming paradox: though original rabbinic texts were incomprehensible to him, Milton did read rabbinic works in translation and some of this material found its way into the poetry as well as into the prose.

Milton is particularly attracted to *aggadah*, the legendary material in rabbinic literature that has much in common with poetry. In *Paradise Lost* Milton utilizes *aggadah* to enhance and develop the biblical story, weaving legends from the long narrative Midrash, *Pirkei de-Rabbi Eliezer* (in the 1644 Latin translation by the Arminian, Willem Vorstius)[30] so artfully into the epic's pattern that they appear to be part of the original

Genesis story rather than extrabiblical material. Other midrashic works in translation, including the *Avot de-Rabbi Nathan* in the Latin edition by Francis Tayler (London, 1651 and 1654), and the Latin works mentioned in this essay, could well have been used by Milton in the same way; investigation of them might uncover more sources of nonbiblical Jewish material in Milton's works.

Tel Aviv University

NOTES

1. Among the Hebraists who mention Milton's use of Midrash in their English works are: Richard Laurence, in the introduction to his translation of the apocryphal *Ascension of Isaiah* (Oxford, 1819), pp. 164–67; Moses Gaster, in the introduction to the translation of the *Chronicles of Jerahmeel* (1899; rpt. New York, 1971), p. lix; Isidore Epstein in the introduction to the *Midrash Rabbah*, trans. Harry Freedman and Maurice Simon (London, 1939), p. xxi.

2. Only a small number of individual midrashic works had been translated in the past.

3. "Some Extra-Biblical Semitic Influences upon Milton's Story of the Fall of Man," *JEGP*, XXVIII (1929), 366–401. Baldwin's examples are mainly taken from Ginzberg's *Legends*, and are credited as such.

4. E.g., p. 397: "That Milton's linguistic equipment for reading the rabbinical books was entirely adequate is a matter of common knowledge." Baldwin claims that the poet read many of the apocryphal and pseudepigraphical books in the original, as well as the *Midrash Rabbah* and the cabbalistic *Zohar* (written in an invented derivative of Aramaic), which even Hebraic scholars cannot read without specialized training. Baldwin's evidence for this extravagant claim is the poet's own testimony in "Ad Patrem" and other works that he learned Hebrew along with Latin, Greek, French, and Italian. But Baldwin fails to distinguish between biblical and rabbinical Hebrew. A knowledge of rabbinical Hebrew and methodology would have been as exceptional for a Christian in Milton's day as it is in ours; a knowledge of biblical Hebrew was not unusual. According to editors Edwin R. Bevan and Charles Singer in *The Legacy of Israel* (1927; rpt. with corrections, Oxford, 1969), p. 316, Hebrew became one of the three languages which educated men studied with the advent of the New Learning in the fifteenth century. The *trilinguis eruditio* in Becket's day meant a knowledge of Latin, French, and English; by the time of Erasmus the three languages were Latin, Greek, and biblical Hebrew.

5. Harris F. Fletcher, *Milton's Semitic Studies* (Chicago, 1926), and *Milton's Rabbinic Readings* (Urbana, 1930). Denis Saurat, "Milton and the Zohar," *SP*, XIX (1922), and *Milton: Man and Thinker* (New York, 1925). But see also Samuel S. Stollman, "Milton's Rabbinical Readings and Fletcher," *Milton Studies*, IV, ed. James D. Simmonds (Pittsburgh, 1972), pp. 195–215, who shows that Fletcher could not handle the difficult Rabbinic Hebrew in the Buxtorf Bible; he mistranslates passages and interpolates nonexistent meanings in the citations he uses as evidence for Milton's use of Buxtorf. Stollman also

suggests, without elaborating, that Milton was even less proficient than Fletcher in the use of Rabbinic Hebrew.

6. Acronym for Rabbi Shlomo Itzhaki of France (1040–1105), author of the best known and most lucid Hebrew commentary on the Bible and the Babylonian Talmud.

7. George F. Moore, "Christian Writers on Judaism," *Harvard Theological Review* (July, 1921), p. 221.

8. The Mishnah is the legal codification of the Oral Law, as distinct from Scripture, or Written Law. Its six tractates, written in Hebrew, were completed about 200 A.D. The Talmud is the collected record of academic discussions, in a combination of Hebrew and Aramaic, based on the Mishnah, by generations of scholars (Rabbis). Two compilations of the Talmud exist: the Babylonian Talmud and the Jerusalem Talmud. Both contain nonlegal, legendary (*aggadah*) digressions combined with legal discussions (*halakhah*). The Babylonian Talmud is more commonly studied. It was completed about 535 A.D., the Jerusalem Talmud about one hundred years earlier.

9. Moore, "Christian Writers on Judaism," p. 215.

10. Ibid., p. 251.

11. The Tosafot are critical and explanatory notes on the Talmud, in Hebrew, by French and German scholars of the twelfth to fourteenth centuries. Maimonides is Moses ben Maimon (acronym Ramban, 1135–1204), philosopher, halakhist, and medical writer. His *Mishneh Torah*, written in Hebrew, is a compendium of the entire *halakhah* of Jewish practice, and his *Guide to the Perplexed*, written in Arabic, is an exposition of the Jewish faith; Milton read the *Guide* in Buxtorf's Latin translation (1629).

12. Fletcher, *Milton's Rabbinic Readings*.

13. James H. Hanford, *A Milton Handbook*, 4th ed. (New York, 1961), pp. 244–45.

14. The Masorah is the body of traditional notes dealing with the correct spelling, writing, and reading of the Old Testament. The notes are found in the margins of Rabbinical Bibles. Also surrounding the biblical text are the commentaries of Rashi and other medieval exegetes, and the Targums.

15. *Complete Prose Works of John Milton*, ed. Don M. Wolfe et al. (New Haven, 1953–82). Unless otherwise noted, Milton's prose is quoted from this edition, hereafter referred to as *YP* and cited parenthetically in the text.

16. See the studies of the Masorah by David Ginsburg, *Introduction to the Massoretico-Critical Edition of the Hebrew Bible* (London, 1897), and Robert Gordis, *The Biblical Text in the Making: A Study of the Kethib-Qere* (New York, 1971), which discuss the infrequent use of the *Qere* for euphemistic changes.

17. The phrase is found in four other places in the Bible: 1 Samuel xxv, 22; 1 Kings xvi, 11; xxi, 21; 2 Kings ix, 8.

18. *Defense of Himself*, *YP* IV, pt. 2, 744.

19. Moses ben Maimon, *Guide for the Perplexed*, trans. Michael Friedlander (1881; 2nd ed. London, 1904). Milton specifically refers to the Buxtorf translation in the *Doctrine and Discipline of Divorce*: "*Maimonides*, famous among the rest in a Book of his set forth by Buxtorfus" (*YP* II, 257).

20. See my article, "Midrash in *Paradise Lost: Capitula Rabbi Elieser*," in *Milton Studies*, XVIII, ed. James D. Simmonds (Pittsburgh, 1983), pp. 145–171, which describes the many structural and narrative elements that the epic borrowed from *Pirkei de-Rabbi Eliezer*. Material formerly thought to have come from *Enoch* and Rashi is found in *Pirkei de-Rabbi Eliezer*. The translation of Vorstius's Latin is: "he took Moses' lance, & ran after him and transfixed him behind, both together (through the circumcised organ), and the lance passed through the belly of the woman."

21. See in particular, Harris F. Fletcher, *Milton's Semitic Studies* (1926; rpt. New York, 1966), pp. 87–88. But see also Leonard H. Mendelsohn, "Milton and the Rabbis: A Later Inquiry," *SEL*, XVIII (1978), 125–35, who argues that Milton could not have used the primary talmudic source because he does not avail himself of immediately adjacent material which would have aided his argument. Mendelsohn, however, does not take into account the parallel sources which Milton might have used which have different adjacent materials. Nonetheless, Mendelsohn's conclusion is correct; Fletcher is mistaken in his assumption that Milton could use original talmudic materials.

22. The editor of *YP* I dates the entry vaguely as "1639–1650 (?)."

23. Milton refers to Josephus four times in the *First Defense: YP* IV, pt. 1, 344, 370, 375, and 409; he refers to Philo once in this work, on page 344.

24. See Mendelsohn, "Milton and the Rabbis," for a discussion of Milton's use of this *aggadah*.

25. In his preface to the *Antiquities of the Jews*, in *Josephus: Complete Works*, trans. William Whiston (Grand Rapids, 1978), p. 24, Josephus states: "Now when Moses was desirous to teach this lesson to his countrymen he did not begin the establishment of his laws after the same manner that other legislators did: I mean, upon contracts and other rites between one man and another, but by raising their minds upwards to regard God, and his creation of the world; and by persuading them that we men are the most excellent of the creatures of God upon Earth. Now when once he had brought them to submit to religion, he easily persuaded them to submit to all other things."

26. Milton quotes from *Antiquities*, XI, iii, 2–6.

27. Josippon, or Josippus, is a pseudonym for Joseph ben Gorion, who wrote a popular chronicle of Jewish history dealing with the period from the return of the Babylonian exile to 70 A.D., concentrating especially on the Hasmonean rulers and the war against Rome. It was widely read by Christians of the sixteenth and seventeenth centuries in the translation by Peter Morvyng, *A Compendious and Most Marveilous History of the Latter Tymes of the Jewes* (London, 1558). The *aggadah* is found in Josippon III, 32–134.

28. A related midrash is found in TB Bava Batra 10a.

29. George K. Conklin, *Biblical Criticism and Heresy in Milton* (New York, 1949); Robert M. Adams, *Milton and the Modern Critics* (1955; rpt. Ithaca, 1966).

30. See note 20.

AREOPAGITICA AND *AREOPAGITICUS:* THE SIGNIFICANCE OF THE ISOCRATIC PRECEDENT

Paul M. Dowling

M ILTON'S *AREOPAGITICA* is of interest to two groups of scholars who come to very different conclusions about the kind of book
it is and thus about what it teaches. Representative of the first group
is Arthur Barker in *Milton and the Puritan Dilemma.*[1] Barker compares
Areopagitica to many other tracts dominated by the ideology of
Puritanism. In this view, Milton's tract argues in favor of Christian liberty in things indifferent for those Puritans attempting to reconcile reformation and liberty in seventeenth-century England. Representative of
the other group is George Sabine in the introduction to his edition.[2] Sabine compares *Areopagitica* to treatises such as Locke's *Letters on Toleration* and Mill's *On Liberty* as statements of the evolving principles
of modern liberalism among the English-speaking people. In this view,
Milton's treatise argues for unlicensed printing for freedom-loving people
in all ages. In the following essay I shall argue by contrast that both these
groups of readers err in trying to fit *Areopagitica* into inappropriate categories which distort our view of the work. The kind of book Milton wrote
becomes clearer when we understand that book with which Milton himself compares his *Areopagitica*, that is, the *Areopagiticus* of Isocrates.

Both Milton's title and a remark in the first paragraph recall the
Areopagitic discourse of this Greek rhetorician. The context of the remark is a discussion of imitation and precedent: Milton notes that Parliament "imitate[s] the old and elegant humanity of Greece, [rather] then
the barbarick pride of a *Hunnish* and *Norwegian* statelines." And, in response to a hypothetical charge that he himself lacks precedent, Milton
says that "if any should accuse me of being new or insolent . . . out of
those ages, to whose polite wisdom and letters we ow that we are not
yet *Gothes* and *Jutlanders*, I could name him who from his private house
wrote that discourse to the Parlament of *Athens*, that perswades them
to change the forme of *Democraty* which was then establisht" (*YP* II,
p. 489). Milton follows the precedent of Isocrates in writing his own *Areopagitica* as a private citizen ("from his private house") to persuade a leg-

islative body. Editors have noted this superficial connection between Milton and Isocrates but have noted so many other differences between the two as to find Milton's drawing attention to Isocrates a problem.[3] The solution to this problem lies in asking ourselves what Milton means when he says that Isocrates' discourse "perswades them to change the forme of *Democraty* which was then establisht."

To answer this question we need to analyze the persuasive character — the rhetoric — of Isocrates' *Areopagiticus*. Let us begin with the speech's historical context and its organization. From internal evidence editors say that Isocrates' speech was written at Athens in the middle of the fourth century before Christ.[4] The end of the previous century had witnessed the complete defeat of Athens in the Peloponnesian War. At the beginning of that war Athens was a limited or even nominal democracy ruled by the statesman Pericles. But Pericles' dependence on naval strategy during that war had the indirect consequence of broadening the franchise at Athens because any poor man who served on an Athenian ship could claim some right to participate in the government of Athens. Despite this increasingly democratic character of Athens, it was the oligarchic party, ruling through the bloody instrument of the Thirty Oligarchs, which first gained power in the city after the defeat. After much bloodshed the Thirty were deposed and the democracy was reestablished in a much more extreme form than had been the case before the war. Under this regime Socrates was condemned to death for corrupting the young and for not believing in the gods the city believed in. And during this time also, Isocrates wrote his *Areopagiticus* addressed to the *ekklesia*, or popular assembly.

The speech is organized into the parts of the classical oration: a proem or exordium, a proposition, a confirmation, a digression, and a peroration.[5] The proem, the first fourteen paragraphs, argues that, despite the prosperity of democratic Athens, the public safety (*hai soteria*) is endangered because we do not have a regime which conducts our affairs well. The proposition states that Isocrates will speak in favor of a return to the "democracy of our forefathers," the "ancestral democracy," which he eventually, if somewhat vaguely, identifies as the Athenian regime of the seventh century associated with Solon and Cleisthenes. The confirmation in the next thirty-five paragraphs describes the advantages of both the political life and the everyday life of this ancient regime. Politically, the ancestors properly understood distributive justice, for they gave to each man according to his merit, they did not elect public officials by lot, and they opened public office only to gentlemen of leisure. In their everyday lives, the ancestors were pious toward the gods, just in their private relations, and moderate in their behavior—especially since the Council of the Areopagus censored and watched over the mores of the citizens. There follows a twenty-paragraph digression responding to an objection and a question. To the objection that this ancestral regime is not democratic, Isocrates responds with a tirade against the oligarchy of the Thirty. To the question, why change our present democracy, Isocrates responds that Athenians should try to live up to their past excellence rather than priding themselves on being better than the Thirty. A brief peroration summarizes and concludes the speech.

Now, although Isocrates never publicly delivered his speech, he composed it in such a manner as to imitate many of the conventions of political speeches of his day. For instance, he pretends at the beginning that he has given formal written notice (*prosodos*) to the *prytaneis* or official of the *ekklesia* and received permission to come forward to speak. But one thing not conventional about this speech is its treatment of the public safety. For speeches arguing a danger to the public safety of the city ordinarily located that danger outside the city in the menace of some foreign enemy. The ordinary internal danger to the public safety was the weakness of the city's armed forces vis-à-vis that foreign menace. But Isocrates locates the danger to Athens' public safety internally and only in the lack of a regime or constitution (*politeia*) which conducts the city's affairs well.[6]

But the unconventional character of Isocrates' speech does not end here. For, although ostensibly Isocrates addresses himself to the democratic many as a fellow democrat, he in fact subtly criticizes his audience. Consider the way the speech begins:

I think many of you wonder whatever is the idea that has led me to come forward to speak concerning the public safety, as if the city were in peril, or its affairs in a dangerous condition, instead of being the owner of more than two hundred triremes, at peace [on land] and mistress of the sea, and still in position to command the support of many allies who will be ready to assist us in time of need, and of a still larger number who pay contributions and obey our orders; while we possess all these [things, someone] would say that we might reasonably be of good courage as being out of reach of [peril], and that it is rather our enemies who ought to be afraid and to take counsel for their own safety. (Freese, 1–2)[7]

In the Greek, Isocrates' first word is "many" (*hoi polloi*), the democratic "many," and the reader is thereby alerted that Isocrates has this audience foremost in his mind as he writes. In fact, a careful analysis of this passage reveals that every detail in it is written with the democratic many in mind. The argument can be reduced to four points: (1) many wonder at my speaking on the public safety; (2) there are two grounds on which I might do so, military peril or the dangerous condition of our affairs (*pragmata*); (3) our military situation is strong; and therefore, (4) someone (*tis*) might say there is no peril to the public safety. Now the first thing to note is that the "someone" who concludes so confidently at (4) has missed the alternatives on which Isocrates says in (2) he might speak on the public safety. Furthermore, Isocrates' description of Athens' military situation in (3) is subtly imbalanced in favor of naval warfare, exactly the situation which the democratic many, who arrived at political power by means of the navy, would favor. For instance, Isocrates mentions particulars of the navy ("more than two hundred triremes") but is silent about details of the army. Again, whereas Athens is "mistress of the sea," she is only "at peace on land." These subtle details fall into a pattern: the "someone" who concludes too easily at (4), misses the alternatives at (2), and presents the democrats' view of the military situation at (3), can be seen as a conventionally-minded representative of the ruling democratic "many," *hoi polloi*, whom Isocrates must initially address. Furthermore, this way of reading the beginning of the speech proves to be one of the keys to its curious rhetorical character: what is said reveals as much about the audience as about the speaker.

Given the rhetorical character of the speech, the reader needs to be alert to the possibility that Isocrates' "ancestral democracy" is called democratic only because the majority of Isocrates' audience is democratic. The question of whether the "ancestral democracy" is truly democratic is answered in the digression of the speech with a tirade against the Thirty, an answer which casts more heat than light and which therefore might arouse the suspicion that Isocrates is hiding something. That suspicion is well founded. When Isocrates first mentions his true subject, for instance, he says that he intends to speak in favor of "that democracy which Solon, the devoted friend of the people, introduced, and which Cleisthenes, who drove out the [tyrants] and restored the rights of the people, reestablished" (Freese, 16). Later in the speech, when Isocrates begins to describe the ancestral democracy, he takes pains to portray the regime as democratic by emphasizing the basic role of election and audit which the *demos* fulfilled and by deemphasizing the role of holding office and governing which the propertied gentlemen alone fulfilled:

In short, they had made up their minds that the people, like an absolute master, ought to control the public offices, punish offenders and settle disputed points, and that those who were able to enjoy ease and possessed sufficient means should attend to public affairs like servants, and, if they acted justly, should be praised and rest contented with this recognition of their services, while, if they managed affairs badly, they should meet with no mercy, but should be visited with the severest penalties. And how would it be possible to find a democracy more just or more secure than one which set the most influential citizens at the head of public affairs, and at the same time invested the people with sovereign control over these same officials? (Freese, 26–27)

As this and other passages suggest, Isocrates' "ancestral democracy," when stripped of the rhetorical context in which it is presented, is not a true democracy but a mixed regime in which the aristocratic gentlemen hold the balance of power. The regime Isocrates calls the "ancestral democracy" resembles the Roman regime in Shakespeare's *Coriolanus* where, although the plebians have the powers of election and audit, only the patricians can run for office. The ruling patricians or gentlemen in Isocrates' "ancestral democracy" set the tone for life by holding office and by ruling in public, as can be seen in the following passage on equality or justice:

And what chiefly assisted them in managing the state aright was this: of the two recognized principles of equality, the one assigning the same to all, the other their due to individuals, they were not ignorant which was the more useful, but rejected as unjust that which considered that good and bad had equal claims, and preferred that which honoured and punished each man according to his deserts; and governed the state on these principles, not appointing magistrates from the general body of citizens by lot, but selecting the best and most capable to fill each office. For they hoped that the rest of the citizens would behave themselves like those at the head of affairs. (Freese, 21–22)

But of course, among ancient democratic cities the democratic principle of equality was to award the same to all and the mode of election was by lot.[8] Isocrates is concealing the extent to which his "ancestral democracy" is dominated by an aristocracy.

One can say, then, that Isocrates' rhetoric is ironic or differential. It addresses two different teachings to two different audiences. Or, more precisely, it disguises Isocrates' true and undemocratic teaching in a deceptive and democratic presentation. In this speech, Isocrates uses the form or the appearance of a conventional political oration on the "public safety" to raise the fundamental issue of the best regime or constitution, to ask (albeit covertly) whether Athens would not be better served with a less democratic, mixed regime where leisured gentlemen rule and set the tone. According to Allan Bloom, this is characteristic of Isocrates' orations as a whole. Isocrates, Bloom claims, "uses the form and subject matter of popular discourse and shows by his use of them that the ordinary sorts of discussions point of themselves to issues more remote and correspondingly more profound."[9] What Isocrates could hope for is that some few among his readers would see that issues which are raised in the popular discourses point to deeper issues addressed by philosophic writers. Even if the few in Isocrates' audience could not change the Athenian regime, they would be made to see both the true issues of their day, as well as how a philosophic view of political questions arises out of practical and popular concerns.

In the light of the preceding analysis of Isocrates' rhetoric, we return to Milton's comment that Isocrates' discourse "perswades them to change the forme of *Democraty* . . . then establisht." Consider the crucial terms "perswades" and "forme." Both are ambiguous. The word "perswades," as the *OED* notes, can mean either successfully persuade or simply make the effort to persuade. More importantly, the term "forme" means either the appearance of a thing or its essence. By using these terms Milton subtly calls attention to the ambiguous character of Isocrates' rhetoric: while Isocrates appears to call for a democratic regime at Athens, in actuality he tries to persuade them to change the essence of that regime.

Of course more evidence is needed to support the contention that Milton understood the precedent of Isocrates as one of ambiguous or ironic rhetoric. But where to find such evidence? No further remarks about Isocrates either in *Areopagitica* or elsewhere in the Miltonic corpus tell us why Milton would title his work after that of Isocrates. The only place to look for such evidence is in Milton's practice of rhetoric in his own *Areopagitica*. Indeed, Milton's comment about Isocrates suggests this very direction for the argument. Milton says that he follows the precedent of Isocrates. To follow the precedent of Isocrates means to imitate Isocrates: Milton must write his own "discourse to the Parlament of [England]" ambiguously, using the form and subject matter of the political discourse of his day, the controversial pamphlet or the speech to Parliament, in order to raise issues more remote from and more profound than those customary to that form.

This Milton does. Milton addresses himself to the English Parliament dominated by Puritans in the way in which Isocrates addresses himself to the Athenian *ekklesia* dominated by the many. To see how this is so, we begin with the *Areopagitica*'s historical context and its organization.

Milton published the *Areopagitica* in 1644, in the midst of the English Civil War.[10] The issues in the war between the forces of Charles I and Parliament were both constitutional and religious. On constitutional grounds some objected to Charles's ruling without calling Parliament for eleven years and to his raising money through taxes which Parliament had not agreed to. On religious grounds, some of the leading members of Parliament objected to the ecclesiastical policies of William Laud, Charles's archbishop of Canterbury. During the Civil War, Milton lived in a London dominated by the Parliamentary and Puritan faction. Although his inmost thoughts during these years are difficult to know, he often appeared in print as a partisan for the faction which dominated London.

Areopagitica first appeared as a forty-page pamphlet arguing for the repeal of Parliament's 1643 Licensing Order, or order for prior censorship of publications. Like Isocrates' *Areopagiticus*, Milton's pamphlet is organized as a deliberative oration of classical rhetoric. The three-page proem or exordium (*YP* II, pp. 486–90) is followed by the proposition, asking Parliament to judge over again or repeal its Licensing Order of 1643 (II, pp. 490–91), and the division outlining the four parts of Milton's argument against licensing: (1) that Roman Catholicism invented licensing; (2) that wide reading unfettered by licensing was favored among the best Christian authorities; (3) that licensing does not achieve its end; and (4) that licensing does real harm. These four arguments take up the next sixteen pages (II, pp. 494–507, 521, 530, 551). The pamphlet ends with a digression (II, pp. 551–60) and a peroration (*YP* II, pp. 560–70).

Areopagitica's subject is Parliament's 1643 Licensing Order, as *Areopagiticus*' subject is the public safety. Milton treats Parliament's understanding of the purpose of licensing as ironically as Isocrates treats the *ekklesia*'s understanding of the threat to the public safety. Initially, Milton quotes the Order and seems to accept Parliament's version of its purpose, to regulate the printing of certain kinds of books. But gradually and subtly Milton moves beyond Parliament's understanding toward a philosophic view of the true issue: the art of legislating morals. This art Milton learns from Plato.

Milton's ironic treatment of his subject can be seen in his treatment of the Licensing Order and its purpose. Early in the speech Milton twice quotes the Licensing Order verbatim, once in the proposition and again in the division. The proposition, where Milton italicized his quotation, asks that Parliament judge "over again that Order which ye have ordain'd *to regulate Printing. That no Book, pamphlet, or paper shall be henceforth Printed, unlesse the same be first approv'd and licenc't by such*, or at least one of such as shall be thereto appointed" (*YP* II, pp. 490–91). The words Milton italicized occur in the second paragraph of the Licensing Order. A quotation from the Order's first paragraph occurs in *Areopagitica*'s division when Milton announces his third argument: "this [Licensing] Order avails nothing to the suppressing of scandalous, seditious, and libellous Books, which were mainly intended to be suppresst" (II, p. 491). This is a clear echo of Parliament's Order: "Whereas divers good Orders have bin lately made by both Houses of Parliament, for *suppress-ing* the great late abuses and frequent disorders in Printing many false forged, *scandalous, seditious, libellous*, and unlicensed Papers, Pamphlets, and Books to the great defamation of Religion and government" (*YP* II, p. 797; italics added).

These exact quotations from the Order occur on pages three and four of the original pamphlet. Some eleven pages later, however, in the con-text of the third argument, Milton begins to move away from Parliament's wording of its Order. This third argument, beginning with the statement that "this order of licencing conduces nothing to the end for which it was fram'd," falls into two parts: the first part takes that end to be reforming "manners" or the national character (*YP* II, pp. 521–28); [11] the second takes the end to be suppressing books which corrupt (II, pp. 528–30). For present purposes we focus only on the argument of the first part where Plato is central.

This argument begins with a restatement of the first argument: "that no Nation, or well instituted State [i.e., no state prior to Roman Catholi-cism] . . . did ever use this way of licencing" (*YP* II, pp. 521–22). Then an objection: "this is a piece of prudence lately discover'd." Not true, re-sponds Milton: for "there wanted not among them long since, who sug-gested such a cours; which they not following, leave us a pattern of their judgement, that it was not the not knowing, but the not approving, which was the cause of their not using it" (*YP* II, p. 522). Then Plato is men-tioned as one from long ago who suggested laws of licensing and two such laws are given as examples. In his *Laws*, Plato seems to tolerate only a smaller body of learning than his own dialogues. Also, he compelled poets to show their writings to judges for approval before reading them to pri-vate men. But, says Milton, Plato meant this law only for the common-wealth described in the *Laws* with all its other rules and circumstances. For if we think to regulate printing, thereby to rectify manners, we must regulate all recreations and pastimes. After showing how futile it would be to attempt to license all recreations in the manner of Plato, Milton concludes that it is inevitable man takes delight in recreations. The wis-dom of a state consists in rendering recreations least harmful, not by li-censing books and recreations, but by "those unwritt'n, or at least un-constraining laws of vertuous education, religious and civill nurture, which *Plato* there mentions, as the bonds and ligaments of the common-wealth" (*YP* II, p. 526).

This argument is subtle and complex both in its treatment of the purpose of the Licensing Order and of Plato. First the Order. When Milton begins the third argument, he rephrases its point by silently dropping mention of the three categories of books the Order intended to suppress. "This order of licencing," he writes, "conduces nothing to the end for which it was fram'd" (*YP* II, p. 521). What that end is he does not immediately say. A page later, however, when he specifies that end, he changes it from suppressing certain categories of books (Parliament's stated purpose) to improving the "manners" of those who read and write the books. "If we think to regulat Printing," he writes, "*thereby to rectifie manners*, we must regulat all recreations and pastimes, all that is delightfull to man" (II, p. 523; italics added). But the term "manners" never appears in the Licensing Order. Milton is attributing to Parliament's Order a purpose or end different from that which the drafters of the Order expressed. Perhaps he does so to suggest what the drafters *should* have intended when they wrote the Order. Milton may be suggesting something along these lines when, at the end of the third argument, he writes, "This is what I had to shew wherein this order cannot conduce to *that end, whereof it bears the intention*" (II, p. 530; italics added).

This possibility becomes more plausible once one grasps the place Plato occupies in this argument. Plato is actually Milton's teacher on legislating the morals of a people. But Milton conceals the extent of his indebtedness to Plato because, as the argument suggests, the Parliamentary licensers would only misunderstand and misuse Plato's teaching. Nonetheless, while appearing to denigrate and reject Plato, Milton actually follows his teaching from the seventh book of the *Laws*. At the same time, Milton satirically depicts a Puritan attempting to follow Plato's censorship in the second and third books of the *Republic*.

To begin with, we note that Milton makes it difficult to see the importance of Plato to this argument. Milton is vague as to which dialogue he alludes, even as he gently mocks the worth of that dialogue. "*Plato*, a man of high autority indeed," he begins, "but least of all for his Commonwealth, in the book of his laws, which no City ever yet receiv'd, fed his fancie with making many edicts to his ayrie Burgomasters, which they who otherwise admire him, wish had bin rather buried and excus'd in the *genial* cups of an *Academick* night-sitting" (*YP* II, p. 522). Other than the ambiguous phrase, "the book of his laws," there is little to indicate that this is the introduction to a number of paraphrases or near quotations from the *Laws* and the *Republic*. And this dialogue is gently mocked by attributing to Plato what Ernest Sirluck calls "an air of vinous irresponsibility" (II, p. 522). What is more, as the argument develops, Plato is made to seem absurdly inconsistent because in this dialogue he tolerates a bulk of learning smaller than his own dialogues as a whole.

Milton's attempts to discourage his reader from taking Plato seriously, however, cannot fully conceal his indebtedness to Plato. His argument, for instance, that Plato intended what he wrote in the *Laws* only for the commonwealth he describes there is more subtle than it first appears. For Milton so limits only the *second* of two Platonic laws to Plato's "fancied republic" — tacitly exempting the first of Plato's censorship laws.[12]

Let us look more closely at the passage. Immediately after apparently denigrating Plato and his *Laws*, Milton writes:

> By which laws he seems to tolerat no kind of learning, but by unalterable decree, consisting most of practicall traditions, to the attainment whereof a Library of smaller bulk then his own dialogues would be abundant. And there also enacts that no Poet should so much as read to any privat man, what he had writt'n, untill the Judges and Law-keepers had seen it, and allow'd it: But that *Plato* meant this Law peculiarly to that Commonwealth which he had imagin'd, and to no other, is evident. (*YP* II, pp. 522–23)

These two periods allude to different laws in separate contexts in Plato's *Laws*.[13] The first Platonic law (*Laws* VII, 811c–812a) concerns learning as a whole ("tolerat no kind of learning"); the second (VII, 801d) concerns only the poets ("no Poet should so much as read").[14] After citing these two laws Milton limits *only the second law* to Plato's imagined commonwealth of the *Laws*: "But that Plato meant *this* Law peculiarly to that Commonwealth which he imagin'd, and to no other, is evident" (*YP* II, p. 522; italics added). And Milton's argument continues with remarks especially aimed at Plato's attraction to poetry and to poets:

> Why was he not else a Law-giver to himself, but a transgressor, and to be expell'd by his own Magistrats; both for the wanton epigrams and dialogues which he made, and his perpetuall reading of *Sophron Mimus*, and *Aristophanes*, books of grossest infamy, and also for commending the latter of them though he were the malicious libeller of his chief friends, to be read by the Tyrant *Dionysius*, who had little need of such trash to spend his time on? (*YP* II, p. 523)

Finally, after speaking of Plato's poetic inclinations as proof of what Plato intended, Milton refers again only to "*this licencing of Poems* [having] reference and dependence to many other proviso's there set down in his fancied republic, which in this world could have no place" (*YP* II, p. 523; italics added).

The silently exempted Platonic law, which occurs at *Laws*, VII, 811c–812a, is the most comprehensive statement on censorship in the dialogue. Here the Athenian Stranger suggests that "the speeches we've been going through since dawn until the present," that is the dialogue as a whole, should become the model for what is tolerated in the education of the future citizens of the commonwealth they are founding:

I don't think I would have a better model than this to describe for the Guardian of the Laws and Educator, or anything that would be better for him to bid the teachers to teach the children, other than these things and things that are connected to them and similar. He should work through the poems of poets, as well as prose writings and things that are simply recited without being written down, and if, as can be presumed, he comes across speeches that are the brothers of these, he should on no account let them pass by but should write them down. Then, in the first place, he should compel the teachers themselves to learn and to praise these writings; if there are any teachers who find the writings unpleasing, he should not employ them as his assistants, but should instead use those who vote with him in their praise. It is to these men that he should give the young, to be taught and educated. (*Laws* 811c–e)

Although no words or phrases from this Platonic passage occur in *Areopagitica*, it fits the description in *Areopagitica* better than does the passage about censoring the poets at *Laws*, VII, 801d. Milton alludes to a Platonic passage "tolerat[ing] no kind of learning," and Plato speaks of censoring "the poems of poets, as well as prose writings and things that are simply recited without being written down." Milton's "unalterable decree, consisting most of practicall traditions" refers to Plato's "speeches we've been going through since dawn," the laws decreed by the dialogue's interlocutors for the founding of their commonwealth. Milton's "Library of smaller bulk then his own dialogues" alludes to the fact that Plato's *Laws* is but one of his dialogues.

In the context of the dialogue itself, this passage suggests that the interlocutors (the Athenian Stranger, Kleinias, and Megillus) are to become founders of the commonwealth in the fullest sense. Their conversation, this dialogue of twelve books, will become a comprehensive statement of the way of life they are founding—a sacred and founding book to which all other learning introduced into their commonwealth at a later time must conform. These founder-legislators are to become like the prophet-founder Minos of Crete, who consulted with Zeus about establishing the laws of his city and whose words then became law in the fullest sense. To use another analogy, these founders and their dialogue are to have the same relationship to their city as Moses and the ten commandments had to the Israelites.[15] By tacitly exempting this first and comprehensive Platonic law from the charge of being limited in application only to the commonwealth described in the *Laws*, Milton suggests that we might think of applying Platonic censorship to the world outside Plato's "fancied republic."

But what does this mean? What happens if a Platonic teaching about comprehensive censoring is applied to this world, that is, to the England of Milton's day? What might happen if the Puritans dominating Parliament attempted to imitate Platonic censorship is suggested in the immediate sequel beginning with Milton's comment, "If we think to regulat Printing, thereby to rectifie manners, we must regulat all recreations and pastimes," and continuing with a discussion of eleven such recreations (*YP* II, pp. 523–26). Here Milton suggests how mistaken it would be to license all recreations and pastimes by saying that the "we" who would imitate Plato must license all of the following: music and song; dancers; lutes, violins, and guitars; airs and madrigals; windows and balconies; bagpipe and rebec; household gluttony; public houses selling drunkenness; wanton garb; conversations of male and female youth; and evil company.

This list is curious. The first two items, music and dance, are indeed regulated by Socrates in his discussion of the education of the warriors in the *Republic*. But most of the items have no clear Platonic source. A number, such as airs and madrigals and bagpipe and guitars, are modern means of recreation Plato could not have known. Several others are clearly identified with modern England, as will be argued below. How to explain this? I would like to suggest that this sequence has been misunderstood by Miltonists, who often interpret it as a reduction to absurdity of Plato's censorship of the arts.[16] The truth is exactly opposite. In actuality, Milton is subtly reducing to absurdity the Puritan licenser's misguided attempt to imitate Plato. Rather than laughing at Plato, Milton laughs with Plato at his contemporaries, using a literary device of parody similar to the one at the beginning of Isocrates' *Areopagiticus*. The "we" whom Milton says would license all these recreations in an attempt to imitate Plato is, like Isocrates' "someone," a misguided representative of the dominant faction in the audience.

One historical observation which makes plausible the suggestion that Milton's "we" is intended to be a Puritan is this: during the seventeenth century the licensing or prohibiting of recreations was an issue which brought to mind the Puritans. For instance, in 1617, James I, in response to Puritan agitation against those taking recreation on Sunday, issued his *Declaration of Sports* in which he allowed that "after the end of Divine Service, Our good people be not disturbed, letted, or discouraged from any lawful recreation; such as dancing, either for men or women, archery for men, leaping, vaulting or other such harmless recreations, nor from having May-Games, Whitson [sic] Ales, and Morris-dances."[17] The Puritan outcry against this *Declaration* was so vehement that James I did not insist upon its public reading by the clergy. His son, Charles I, however, reissued it in 1633, and it became an issue in the Civil War. At the beginning of the Civil War, in 1642, the Puritan-dominated Long Parliament closed the London theater with a statement beginning: "Whereas public sports do not well agree with public calamities, nor public stage-plays with the seasons of humiliation, this being an exercise of sad and pious solemnity, and the other being spectacles of pleasure too commonly expressing lascivious mirth and levity, it is therefore thought fit that while these sad causes and set times of humiliation do continue, public stage-plays cease and be foreborne."[18] And in 1643 the same Parliament passed one ordinance empowering the common hangman to burn all copies of the *Declaration* and another forbidding Sabbath "wrestlings, shooting, bowling, ringing of bells for pleasure or pastime, masque, wake, otherwise called feasts, church-ale, dancing, games, sports or pastime whatsoever."[19] As we shall see, the connections in these documents between lasciviousness and levity on the one hand, and sad piety and war on the other, also characterize Milton's "we," the misguided licenser of the *Areopagitica.*

More particular evidence that Milton's "we" is to be understood as a parody of a misguided Puritan comes to light when we compare particular passages from the *Areopagitica* with passages from Plato's *Republic,* Books II and III, where Socrates discusses the education of the warriors for his just city. Milton calls our attention to this source by mentioning examples of arts which Socrates there regulates, by using specific terms Socrates there uses, and by phrases such as "for such *Plato* was provided of" (*YP* II, pp. 523–24). But this comparison which Milton himself seems thereby to invite reveals a subtle but pervasive pattern of contrasts suggesting that Milton's licenser is puritanical.

His puritanism expresses itself in his insistence upon grave seriousness and upon a purely negative attitude toward the erotic. An example of the first characteristic occurs in what Milton says about licensing the first recreation: "No musick must be heard, no song be set or sung, but what is grave and *Dorick.*" This seems like an echo of the *Republic*'s discussion of censoring song and melody (398c–403c), where Socrates says that the Dorian mode is appropriate to warriors.[20] For the Dorian or Dorick mode, says Socrates, "would appropriately imitate the sounds and accents of a man who is courageous in warlike deeds and every violent work, and who in failure or when going to face wounds or death or falling into some other disaster, in the face of these things stands up firmly and patiently against chance" (*Republic* 399a). Socrates, in other words, wants his warriors to be educated in a music whose mode will foster courage in their souls, will prepare them for the harsh spiritedness required for warlike deeds. The difference between Socrates and Milton's licenser is that the latter puts a double restriction on his music: it must be *grave* and Doric. The two are not the same. Grave is serious, solemn, low in pitch, and deep in tone, whereas the Doric is spirited and lively, perhaps even violent. To overstate the difference here for clarity's sake, one might say that Milton's licenser has turned a spirited military march into a solemn funeral dirge. But is this not what one might expect from Puritans who spoke of the English Civil War as "sad causes and set times of humiliation"? Milton here parodies or plays upon the stereotype of the Puritan who hates levity and play. But such solemnity is foreign to Socrates' notions of warrior education. Indeed, Socrates might worry that overly grave music might remind his warriors of sorrow and death and thus undermine the courage which he is attempting to nurture in them.

There is more evidence of Puritan gravity in what Milton says about musical instruments. He speaks of the need for "twenty licencers to examin all the lutes, the violins, and the ghittarrs in every house; they must not be suffer'd to prattle as they doe, but must be licenc'd what they may say" (*YP* II, p. 524). This again seems to echo Socrates when he limits the just city to the Dorian and Phrygian harmonic modes: he proscribes "many-toned or panharmonic instruments for our songs and melodies," saying, "we'll not support the craftsmen who make lutes, harps, and all the instruments that are many-stringed and play many modes" (*Republic* 399c–d). Now Socrates' purpose here is a positive one: his citizen-warriors who hear only simple, military modes of music will themselves be simple and thereby better able to carry out their single task of guarding the just city. Milton's licenser, by contrast, has a negative purpose: he wants to eliminate music which is frivolous or unserious. Musical instruments "must not be suffer'd to prattle as they doe." Even if the frivolous were eliminated, it is not clear how Socrates' positive purpose in educating his warriors would thereby be addressed.

The other characteristic of the Puritan licenser, a negative attitude toward the erotic, can be seen in Milton's treatment of the art of dance. On this topic Milton says, "There must be licencing dancers, that no gesture, motion, or deportment be taught our youth but what by their allowance shall be thought honest; for such Plato was provided of" (*YP* II, pp. 523–24). Now in a context discussing movements of the human body, the term "honest" means sexually chaste or modest. A contemporary Puritan pamphlet condemning dancing uses the term in this sense: "Maidens and matrons are groped and handled with unchaste hands, and kissed and *dishonestly* embraced: the things, which nature hath hidden, and modesty covered, are then oftentimes by means of lasciviousness made naked, and ribaldry under the color of pastime is dissembled."[21] Milton's licenser, then, is under the impression that he has provided for dancing in the manner of Plato by suppressing the unchaste.

But this is hardly the case. Socrates provides for dancing in the context of a discussion of rhythm (*Republic* 399–401). As in his regulation of the other arts, Socrates wants to nurture good dispositions or virtues: he wants to see "which are the rhythms of an orderly and courageous life" (399e). He is concerned with the overall moral atmosphere in which the warriors are nurtured: "good speech, good harmony, good grace, and good rhythm accompany good disposition, not the folly that we endearingly call 'good disposition,' but that understanding truly trained to a good and fair disposition" (400d–e). Socrates provides for dances, as well as for other arts, in order to encourage a range of good dispositions, such as gracefulness and harmony. He wants the arts censored in order to create an environment in which virtues will be nurtured. He says we must

look for those craftsmen whose good natural endowments make them able to track down the nature of what is fine and graceful, so that the young, dwelling as it were in a healthy place, will be benefitted by everything; and from that place something of the fine works will strike their vision or their hearing, like a breeze bringing health from good places; and beginning in childhood, it will, without their awareness, lead them with fair speech to likeness and friendship as well as accord. (*Republic*, 401c–d)

Socrates' discussion thus includes almost all the arts with a view to their forming an all-encompassing virtuous nurture. As Socrates remarks, "we'll never be musical . . . before we recognize the forms of moderation, courage, liberality, magnificence, and all their kin, and, again, their opposites, everywhere they turn up, and notice that they are in whatever they are in, both themselves and their images, despising them neither in little nor big things, but believing that they all belong to the same art and discipline" (402b–c). Dance as well as the other arts help the warriors recognize and become accustomed to the good dispositions or virtues. By contrast, Milton's Puritanical licenser limits himself to being gravely serious or suppressing the "dishonest" or the unchaste.

At the end of the sequence of recreations Milton concludes that "These things [recreations] will be, and must be; but how they shall be lest hurtfull, how lest enticing, herein consists the grave and governing wisdom of a State." Rejecting licensing, Milton offers in its stead "those unwritt'n, or at least unconstraining laws of vertuous education, religious and civill nurture, which *Plato* there mentions, as the bonds and ligaments of the Commonwealth, the pillars and the sustainers of every writt'n Statute; these they be which will bear chief sway in such matters as these, when all licencing will be easily eluded" (*YP* II, pp. 526–27). Milton here echoes a passage from the seventh book of Plato's *Laws*, the discussion proper of Plato's art of legislating manners.[22]

At the beginning of the seventh book of the *Laws*, the Athenian Stranger discusses what he calls the many "unwritten [*agrapha*] customs" of a people (793b). These customs should not be ordained in written laws, he says, yet they are too important to go unmentioned in his discussion of founding a city. "For there are many little things, not visible to everyone," he says, "which, because of each person's pain, pleasure, and desire, go against the advice of the lawgiver, and would easily make the dispositions of the citizens diverse and dissimilar" (788b). Furthermore he argues that,

these are the bonds [*desmoi*] of every regime, linking all the things established in writing, and laid down, with the things that will be set forth in the future, exactly like ancestral and in every way ancient customs; if nobly established and made habitual, they provide a cloak of complete safety for the later written laws, but when they perversely stray from the noble they are like props [*epeismata*] of the walls of houses which buckle in the middle and cause the whole edifice to fall, one part under another, the parts that were later constructed in a fine way collapsing after the props themselves, the ancient thing, have collapsed. (*Laws* 793c)

Beside the general idea that written laws are founded on customs, Milton echoes specific words from this passage: *agrapha* . . . unwritten; *desmoi* . . . bonds and ligaments; *epeismata* . . . the pillars and the sustainers.

The argument in the *Laws* to which Milton alludes focuses on the Platonic art of legislating morals or manners, an art, it must be emphasized, entirely different from modern censorship as practiced by the English Parliament of Milton's day. Modern censorship tries to shape morals or manners by laws. Plato, by contrast, understood that written laws must be founded securely upon the manners of a people, upon their many unwritten customs. That is to say, the manners of a people suggest how laws are to be drafted, to what they should appeal in a given people, and how far such laws can go in transforming a people. As the Athenian Stranger in the *Laws* says, these unwritten customs "provide a cloak of complete safety for the later written laws" like "props of the walls of houses."

An example of what the Athenian Stranger means would be helpful here. In his commentary on this point, Thomas Pangle refers to passages of Jean-Jacques Rousseau's *Letter to D'Alembert on the Theatre* as a modern restatement of this Platonic art.[23] Rousseau exemplifies this art in a critique of the efforts by the French government to outlaw dueling. Rousseau notes that dueling existed in France because of a strong public prejudice, an "unwritten custom," in favor of it as the honorable means by which gentlemen redressed offenses and gave satisfaction for an affront. This public prejudice concerning the preeminence of honor must become the foundation for laws and institutions against dueling. For instance, Rousseau argues that the Tribune charged with regulating dueling should have been called the "Court of Honor" and it should have used as punishment only disgrace, with no hint of physical force in any of its dealings. Again, "to uproot the public prejudice" in favor of dueling, "judges of great authority" should have presided in such a court, "old soldiers laden with honorable titles" who have "proved a hundred times at the cost of their blood that they are not unaware when duty demands that it be spilled" (Rousseau, p. 68). The decisions of this court should have been placed above those of even the sovereign himself, so as to give it an especially honorable position in France. These stipulations by Rousseau suggest how Plato's art of legislating morals works: the "unwritten customs" of a people shape the laws and institutions.

Rousseau's discussion makes clear the wrong-headedness of the licenser in Milton's *Areopagitica*. As the licenser regulated printing in order to rectify some manners, so he would regulate all recreations in order to rectify all the manners of the English nation. But this is to get it backward. The licenser fails to understand that he must allow the nation's manners to shape any laws or institutions he hopes to establish concerning the nation's recreations and pastimes. The licenser who tries to regulate recreations without first considering manners will fail. Judging from comments Milton makes in his sequence of recreations, the English nation as a whole seems decidedly un-Puritan. The English are not puritanically somber or grave about their music: "all the lutes, the violins, and the ghittarrs . . . must not be suffer'd to prattle *as they doe*" (italics added). There may even be a hint of the erotic in English enjoyment of music: "all the airs and madrigalls, that whisper softnes in chambers." The English youths are accustomed to conversation with the opposite sex: "Who shall regulat all the mixt conversation of our youth, male and female together, *as is the fashion in this Country*" (italics added). Lastly they openly indulge their enjoyment of food and drink: "What more Nationall corruption, for which England hears ill abroad, then household gluttony." But the Puritan licenser cannot simply remake England in his own mode, cannot become a totally new founder in the manner of the interlocutors in Plato's *Laws* or *Republic*. If he ever hopes to influence the many ways Englishmen take delight and pleasure, he must cease to think merely of passing laws to regulate manners and must begin to use those manners as the foundation of any laws or institutions he might establish. In fine, the Puritans must learn about licensing from Milton's teacher Plato.

Milton's understanding of the Isocratic precedent, then, is the key to the kind of book *Areopagitica* is as well as to what it teaches. Milton treats Parliament's understanding of licensing as ironically as Isocrates treats the *ekklesia*'s understanding of the public safety. First, he subtly changes licensing's purpose to improving "manners." Then, while appearing to denigrate Plato's censorship edicts in the *Laws* as utopian, Milton silently exempts from denigration the most comprehensive of these edicts. But by a parodic sequence he suggests what might happen if a Puritan licenser attempted to censor all recreations in a misguided attempt to imitate Plato's *Republic*. Finally, Milton says that the true purpose of licensing should be achieved by the art of legislating morals discussed in Plato's *Laws*. In short, Milton's book combines "polite wisdom and letters," as Milton says of Isocrates' *Areopagiticus*, in a blend which eludes our categories. In order to understand this book, we need to reconsider Milton's lifelong fascination with "the polite wisdom and letters" of "the old and elegant humanity of Greece."

Canisius College

NOTES

An earlier version of the material on Isocrates was written for a 1982 NEH Summer Seminar given by Professor Stanley Fish at Johns Hopkins University.

   1. Arthur Barker, *Milton and the Puritan Dilemma: 1641–1660* (Toronto, 1942), pp. 63–97, esp. 96–97. Listing all the citations from either group would be impractical. Worth especial note, however, is A. S. P. Woodhouse, "Milton, Puritanism, and Liberty," *UTQ*, III (1935), 483–513, an early and seminal argument that Milton's pamphlets need to be read in the context of mid-seventeenth-century Puritan pamphleteering. This is the view taken in Ernest Sirluck's volume of the *Complete Prose Works of John Milton*, ed. Don M. Wolfe et al. (New Haven, 1953–82), vol. II, pp. 163, 170–178, esp. 176; hereafter cited in the text as *YP* by volume and page.
   2. George Sabine, "Introduction," *Areopagitica and Of Education* (New York, 1951), pp. vii–x. See also George Sabine, *A History of Political Theory* (New York, 1961),

pp. 508–12 and C. E. Vaughan, *Studies in the History of Political Philosophy Before and After Rousseau* (New York, 1960), vol. II, p. 232.

3. Joseph Anthony Wittreich speaks of "violent discrepancies in style and aim" between the two Areopagitic discourses in "Milton's *Areopagitica:* Its Isocratic and Ironic Contexts," in *Milton Studies*, VI, ed. James D. Simmonds (Pittsburgh, 1972), p. 102. See also Sirluck's remark that Milton's choice of titles is "rather curious" (*YP* II, p. 486) and Hales's remark that between the two Areopagitic speeches "there is clearly but a slight resemblance" in his edition of *Areopagitica* (Oxford, 1874), p. xxxi. The root of the problem is the following perception of the two speeches: "Isocrates implores the General Assembly to restore controls to the Court of the Areopagus, while Milton nervously pleads with Parliament to lift controls" (Wittreich, p. 102; see also Hales, p. xxxi and *The Prose of John Milton*, ed. J. Max Patrick [Garden City, 1967], p. 269). It would be more accurate to say that both wish to arrange exterior conditions so as to increase interior freedom or virtue. For instance, Milton wants licensing lifted so that "the true warfaring Christian" can attain a "pure" rather than "a blank virtue," "can apprehend and consider vice" (*YP* II, pp. 514–16). See my "The Scholastick Grosnesse of Barbarous Ages: The Question of the Humanism of Milton's Understanding of Virtue," *Milton and the Middle Ages*, ed. John Mulryan (Lewisburg, 1982) pp. 67–68.

Some argue Milton's true precedent is St. Paul's Areopagitic discourse recorded in *Acts* xvii, 18–34. See Sirluck, *YP* II, p. 486 and Wittreich, pp. 111–12. But this alternate is less plausible than the Isocratic possibility. Milton's one allusion to St. Paul's Areopagitic discourse makes no claim for it as a precedent because Milton's rhetorical situation is almost the reverse of St. Paul's. Milton faces a Christian audience which wants to limit books and ideas by licensing. St. Paul faces a philosophical audience of Stoics and Epicureans (*Acts* xvii, 18) who are avid for new teachings and doctrines (xvii, 21). Milton's argument was rejected (in part) because it was too learned and too remote from the workaday concerns of Parliament (Barker, p. 88), St. Paul's because it seemed absurdly irrational to his philosophical audience (Acts xvii, 31–32).

4. Some useful information is contained in the introduction and notes to Isocrates, *The Orations of Isocrates*, trans. J. H. Freese (London, 1894); hereafter cited in the text as Freese by paragraph numbers used in standard editions. Bracketed words in quotations from Isocrates are my translations of the Greek available in *Isocrates* (London, 1929), vol. II, pp. 100–57. A summary of the history of Athens is in J. B. Bury and Russell Meiggs, *A History of Greece* (New York, 1975), pp. 245–322. A discussion of the powers of the *ekklesia* in the radical democracy after the Peloponnesian War is in Charles Hignett, *A History of the Athenian Constitution* (Oxford, 1952), pp. 232–44.

5. For the arrangement of the classical oration, see Aristotle, *Rhetoric*, III, 13–19, whose rules of rhetoric Milton recommends in *Of Education* (*YP* II, p. 402). Useful as commentary is Larry Arnhart, *Aristotle on Political Reasoning: A Commentary on The "Rhetoric"* (DeKalb, 1981), pp. 177–82.

6. For a discussion of the conventions of Athenian oratory, see Hignett, pp. 242–43. For the requirements of a political speech on the public safety, see Aristotle, *Rhetoric*, I, 4–8. Arnhart makes clear that conventional political oratory must *serve* the regime in power, not argue *against* it (pp. 71–72).

7. My understanding of Isocrates is indebted to Allan Bloom, *The Political Philosophy of Isocrates* (Ph.D. diss., University of Chicago, 1955). Milton's references to Isocrates are more compatible with Bloom's philosophical interpretation than with the oratorical one in R. C. Jebb, *The Attic Orators from Antiphon to Isaeus* (London, 1893), vol. II, chapters xii–xviii. In *Areopagitica* Milton links "wisdom and eloquence" and "po-

lite wisdom and letters" in speaking of Isocrates. And in *Of Education* Milton places Isocrates with philosophic thinkers such as Pythagoras, Plato, and Aristotle rather than with political orators such as Demosthenes and Cicero (*YP* II, pp. 407, 401).

8. Aristotle, *Politics*, VI, 1, esp. 1317b17–23. Hignett, pp. 214–15, argues that Aristotle's description of a radical democracy is largely a reproduction of the characteristic features of the Athenian democracy of his own (and Isocrates') day.

9. Bloom, *Political Philosophy of Isocrates*, p. 19.

10. Sirluck's introduction (*YP* II, pp. 1–136) summarizes the historical background. See also George Macauley Trevelyan, *History of England: The Tudor and The Stuart Era* (Garden City, 1953), pp. 168–98. For *Areopagitica*'s rhetorical organization, see Sirluck (*YP* II, pp. 170–71).

11. In the seventeenth century, as the *OED* makes clear, "manners" referred to customary or habitual modes of behavior, especially in reference to their moral aspect. Perhaps "mores" or "national character" are our closest approximations. Above all, "manners" did not have the twentieth century sense of superficial politeness with no relation to morals. At the end of *Areopagitica* Milton suggests something of the power of this term when he says he would not tolerate anything "which is impious or evil absolutely either against faith or maners" (*YP* II, p. 565), for this would undermine those supports which religion and moral character give to England's laws. For an argument on this passage, see my "Milton's Use (Or Abuse) of History in *Areopagitica*," in *Cithara: Essays in the Judaeo-Christian Tradition*, vol. XXIII (1983), 33.

12. Failing to note that Milton discusses two censorship laws, Irene Samuel misses this point in *Plato and Milton* (Ithaca, 1947), pp. 59–63.

13. *The Laws of Plato*, trans. Thomas L. Pangle (New York, 1980); hereafter cited in the text as *Laws* by Stephanus pages used in standard editions of Plato. Bracketed words in quotations transliterate the Greek available in *Plato: The Laws* (Cambridge, Mass. 1926), vol. X–XI.

14. Although there is some agreement among commentators that the second of these laws of censorship is a paraphrase of *Laws* VII, 801d, I have seen no one identify correctly the source of the first law as *Laws* VII, 811c–812a. Only Patrick (p. 293) gives separate annotations for the two different passages from *Laws* VII, but he gives no precise source for the first.

15. Here I follow Thomas Pangle's "Interpretive Essay," pp. 490–91, included with his translation of *Laws*.

16. Sirluck (*YP* II, p. 524) and Patrick (p. 294). But the list contains recreations which it is not ridiculous for governments to regulate (e.g., the hours public drinking houses remain open and the clothing worn in public). Also, government regulation of recreations was considered normal in Milton's day. See Marcia Vale, *The Gentleman's Recreations: Accomplishments and Pastimes of the English Gentleman: 1580–1630* (London, 1980), pp. 4–6.

17. Quoted in Robert W. Henderson, "The King's Book of Sports in England and America," *Bulletin of the New York Public Library*, vol. LII (1948), 540. Milton's attitude towards sports and recreations was not Puritanical. Although he made a disparaging reference to James's Declaration in 1641 in order to criticize the Bishops (*Of Reformation*, *YP* I, p. 589), a year later he suggested that the civil magistrate take charge of "our publick sports, and festival pastimes, that they may be . . . such as may inure and harden our bodies by martial exercises to all warlike skil and performance, and may civilize, adorn and make discreet our minds by the learned and affable meeting of frequent Academies, and the procurement of wise and artfull recitations sweetned by eloquent and gracefull

inticements to the love and practice of justice, temperance, and fortitude" (*Reason of Church-Government*, *YP* I, p. 819). Milton's discussion of recreations and sports in *Of Education* is similarly positive in tone (*YP* II, pp. 409–10). See Samuel, pp. 50–59.

18. Quoted in Samuel R. Gardener, *History of the Great Civil War* (New York, 1965), vol. I, pp. 14–15.

19. Quoted in Henderson, p. 545.

20. *The Republic of Plato*, trans. Allan Bloom (New York, 1968); hereafter cited in the text as *Republic* by Stephanus pages used in standard editions. Bloom's commentary on the warriors' education (pp. 337–65) has been especially helpful. Hales, p. 105, was the first to cite this passage from the *Republic* as Milton's source. Sirluck, on the other hand, attributes all the Platonic allusions to the *Laws*. But a computer-generated index reveals, for instance, that Milton's term *Doric* (*Doreus*) does not appear in *Laws* VII, where the other Platonic echoes are found (Leonard Brandwood, *Word-Index to Plato* [Leeds, England, 1976]); it is used in the *Laws* in connection with music only at II, 670b. Furthermore, at the end of the sequence of recreations Milton alludes to the *Republic*: "To sequester out of the world into *Atlantick* and *Eutopian* polities, which never can be drawn into use, will not mend our condition" (II, 526). "*Atlantick*" has been cited as an allusion to Plato's *Timaeus* (Jebb, p. 86), to the *Critias* (Sirluck), or more loosely to Plato's version of the story of Atlantis (White, p. 85; Patrick, p. 295). It has not been noted that the *Timaeus* and the *Critias* are connected with the *Republic* by their dramatic settings. They are continuations of the *Republic*, in which the interlocutors try to draw the *Republic*'s best city (its "Eutopian" polity) into use by means of the story of Atlantis. See Seth Benardete, "On Plato's *Timaeus* and Timaeus' Science Fiction," *Interpretation: A Journal of Political Philosophy*, vol. II (1971), 21–22.

21. Quoted in Vale, p. 93 with italics added.

22. The following argument, especially in such details as Milton's echoing of specific Platonic terms, benefitted from Brandwood's index as well as from Pangle's literal and readable translation. Commentators point to other places in Plato, such as *Republic* IV (Hales, p. 110), *Laws* I, 643–44 (Sirluck), and both of these (Patrick, p. 296). But neither of these passages discusses the priority of custom over written law, nor are there such detailed echoes of particular Platonic terms, as is the case in *Laws* VII, 793c.

23. Pangle, "Interpretive Essay," pp. 477–78. See Rousseau, *Politics and the Arts: Letter to M. d'Alembert on the Theatre*, trans. Allan Bloom (Glencoe, 1960); hereafter cited in the text as Rousseau. Bloom's introduction has been helpful also, esp. pp. xxiv–xxv.

MILTON'S THEOLOGICAL VOCABULARY
AND THE NICENE ANATHEMAS

Michael E. Bauman

Throughout the history of western Christianity, a major stumbling
block has been agreement upon the definition of certain terms.[1]
— William B. Hunter, Jr.

FOR MORE than a century and a half since the publication in 1825
of his long-lost, systematic theology, *De doctrina christiana*, John
Milton's interpreters have been struggling, with Milton and one another,
to determine into which school of Trinitarian or anti-Trinitarian thought
he ought to be enrolled. They have "matriculated" Milton into the schools
of Servetus, Socinus, and Ochino, as well as pre-Nicene subordinationism, Unitarianism, Arianism and orthodoxy.[2] While some of these arguments appear more compelling than others, no one view has been able
to capture a lasting scholarly consensus. If a majority opinion exists today,
it is probably that which labels Milton an orthodox subordinationist.[3]
In order to correct the series of philological and theological misconcep-
tions entailed by this widely held view, I shall elucidate the content of
Milton's theological vocabulary, on the one hand, and demonstrate the
comprehensive affinity of his anti-Trinitarian views to the Arian tenets
condemned at the Council of Nicea, on the other.

I. MILTON'S THEOLOGICAL VOCABULARY

A. "Substantia"

Those who classify John Milton as either an "orthodox Trinitarian"
or a "subordinationist" do so because they have misunderstood the meaning of "substantia." According to some Miltonists, substantia is a quality
shared by Father and Son, which unites them in deity and which Milton
employs as the equivalent of the Nicene terms οὐσία or ὑπόστασις.
Hunter, for example, states that, "in Milton's view, then, the Trinity may
be defined as either three essences or three hypostases in one substance
which is derived from the Father."[4] He thus makes it appear that by the
term "substantia" Milton denotes that self-existent, eternal, infinite, and

71

indivisible yet communicable οὐσία peculiar to the tripersonal godhead. Such a view is mistaken in two ways: first, it ignores Milton's repeated explicit denials of a multipersonal godhead; and second, it confuses Milton's metaphysical materialism with orthodox Trinitarianism.

First, Milton vehemently opposes any three-in-one formula of divinity. Contrary to some critics' assertions that he holds to multiple essences within the godhead, Milton explicitly states that "God is one being, not two. One being has *one* essence" (*YP VI*, 212; italics added). He repeatedly insists upon the absolute singularity of the godhead. According to Milton, God is one person, no more. To support this notion, he cites St. Paul's words in 1 Corinthians viii, 4–6:

> we know that an idol is nothing in the world, and that there is no other God but one: for although there are those that are called Gods both in heaven and earth (for there are many Gods and many Lords), nevertheless for us there is one God, the Father, from whom all things are and in whom we are, and one Lord Jesus Christ, through whom all things are and through whom we are.

As Milton himself construes this passage:

> Here, *there is no other* or *second* God, *but one*, excludes not only a second essence but any second person whatsoever [non essentiam solum sed personam alterum quamcunque excludit]. For it is expressly stated, viii. 6: *the Father is that one God;* therefore there is no *other* person, but one only. There is no other person, that is, in the sense in which Church divines usually argue that there is when they use John XIV. 16 as proof of the existence of the Holy Spirit as a person. Again, the single *God, the Father from whom all things are* is numerically opposed to *those that are called Gods both in heaven and earth*, and *one* is numerically opposed to *many*. (*YP* VI, p. 216)[5]

To strengthen his case, Milton then turns to Ephesians iv, 4–6:

> there is one body and one spirit, just as you are called in one hope of your calling: one Lord, one faith, one baptism; one God and Father of all, who is above all and through all and in you all.

From these verses Milton deduces that:

> there is one Spirit and one Lord, but that one is the Father. Thus he is the one God in the same sense as that in which all the other things mentioned are one, that is, numerically, and therefore also one in person [et ita unus Deus, quemadmodum caetera illa omnia una sunt, id est numero adeoque ipsa persona]. (*YP* VI, p. 217; *CW* XIV, p. 206)

In fact, Milton flatly maintains that the Bible does not say "a single word" about the Trinity (*YP* VI, p. 420).[6] Plainly, any interpretation of Milton that posits a multipersonal godhead is mistaken.

Not only does Milton deny a multipersonal deity, but the term "substantia," as he employs it, does not denote that unique, constitutional οὐσία of deity to which the immutable and inalienable attributes of God attach. To Milton, substantia is not the substratum peculiar to deity, as is the Nicene term οὐσία. Unlike those who possess the Nicene οὐσία, those who possess Milton's substantia are not necessarily God, because in Milton's universe *all beings whatsoever* share the same generic substantia. Within the orthodox Trinitarian scheme, however, the divine οὐσία is unequivocally the possession of the godhead only, and is in no way common to beings not themselves absolutely divine.[7]

Milton's conception and use of substantia is that of modified Aristotelianism and, in Milton's hands, has a unique dual nature.[8] Sometimes Milton speaks of substantia in its primitive unarticulated mode as the substratum of all existence. At other times he alludes to its individuated mode, as when he speaks of single subsistences or beings. In either case, Milton speaks of the same substantia. What differs is not the substantia itself, but the mode or expression of existence bestowed upon it by God when he grants it a hypostasis or essence.

In Milton's view all beings, God included, are comprised of the same original substantia — the substance of God. Consequently, everything is of the same genus — "God-kind."[9] This does not mean, however, that God is everything or that everything is God. Milton is no pantheist. He merely denies that material existences arise out of nothing (*ex nihilo*), an idea he considers an impossibility — even for Omnipotence. As Milton explains:

not even God's virtue and efficiency [virtus et efficientia divina] could have produced bodies out of nothing (as it is vulgarly believed he did) unless there had been some bodily force in his own substance, for no one can give something he has not got [nemo enim dat quod non habet]. (*YP* VI, p. 309; *CW* XV, p. 24)[10]

Thus, what most Genesis commentators classify as the *product* of creation, Milton sees as the *material* of it. That is, in its unarticulated mode Milton's substantia is the underlying substratum of all existences. All beings — God and creatures alike — share it. Unlike possession of the Nicene οὐσία, possession of Milton's substantia entails, of itself, no special metaphysical status. To Milton, substantia is but the necessary stuff, or matrix, of existence without which nothing can or does exist. Contrary to what some scholars contend, substantia, in Milton's system, is not the infallible hallmark of true divinity. While each of the innumerable existences in Milton's universe possesses the same substantia, only the Father is fully divine.

In its primitive state, substantia is the passive material cause of all existence and, because God himself is material, it constitutes the passive dimension in God. Substantia remains in this condition until God essentiates or individuates it — that is, constitutes it as an "essentia" independent of himself. Until it has received this individuation, this substantia is without essentia proper.[11]

In its articulated mode, substantia sometimes denotes a class of being or genus within nature. Once articulated, substantia becomes an independent essentiation assuming its own proper level or rank within the "great chain of being." Within this "chain" God ranges all the various subsistences, from the grosser forms (like rocks) up to the pure, ethereal, "intelligential substances" (like angels). In other words, once articulated, this previously unformed matrix of existence, the substantia underlying all beings, admits varying degrees of refinement or disposition.

One very important theological deduction must be made, therefore, regarding Milton's alleged Trinitarianism. Because creation is fundamentally an act of circumscription and articulation out of the preexistent matter constituting the passive, material aspect of God,[12] because all beings whatsoever arise from this "one first matter," and because Milton's deity is not multipersonal, then merely sharing in that substantia does not involve a being in any special metaphysical or theological status. One cannot say, as Hunter does, that Milton's "thought here was guided by the fact that both Son and Spirit are derived from the divine substance and are thus themselves divine" (*Bright Essence*, p. 41), because being derived from the substantia of God does not confer divinity on a being, only existence. Absolutely all beings (Satan included) have the substantia of God, yet none of them but the Father has the attributes of God — which inhere not in Milton's term "substantia," but in his term "essentia," which, as we will see, Milton deems an utterly incommunicable property.

B. "Essentia" and "Hypostasis"

Because Milton is a materialist, he cannot distinguish beings merely by their substantia. Because all existences from God downward are of one substantia, he distinguishes them the only way a materialist can — by the essentia or hypostasis granted to their substantia by God.

According to Milton, "essentia" and "hypostasis" are identical, one being the Latin, the other the Greek, term for the same concept. That the terms are interchangeable for Milton is amply clear. As he himself teaches,

the essence of God, since it is utterly simple, allows nothing to be compounded with it, and . . . the word *hypostasis*, Heb. i.3, which is variously translated *substance, subsistence,* or *person,* is nothing but that most perfect essence by which

God exists from himself, in himself, and through himself. For neither *substance* nor *subsistence* can add anything to an utterly complete essence [essentiae absolutissimae], and the word *person*, in its more recent use, means any individual thing gifted with intelligence, while *hypostasis* means not the thing itself but the essence of the thing in the abstract. *Hypostasis*, therefore, is clearly the same as essence [hypostasis ergo plane idem quod essentia est]. (*YP* VI, pp. 140–42; *CW* XIV, p. 42)[13]

By saying that the divine essentia is that principle of being within God whereby he is self-existent and perfect, as well as "immense," "infinite," "eternal," "immutable," "incorruptible," omnipresent, "omnipotent," and "one" (*YP* VI, pp. 142–46), Milton closely aligns his terminology with the Nicene usage. Whereas to the Nicene fathers, ὑπόστασις equals οὐσία, as terms signifying the divine nature, for Milton hypostasis equals essentia, as terms signifying the divine nature. What Nicea means by οὐσία or hypostasis, Milton means by essentia or hypostasis.[14]

Milton, however, claims that the divine essentia permits absolutely no communication. Only the Father possesses it. By contrast, the Nicene formulation posits a Father and Son who equally share a common οὐσία. Milton deems this idea of a multiplicity of persons in the divine essentia an absurdity which has engendered disastrous effects upon the Christian faith:

This doctrine turns the Christian religion completely upside down [Quae quidem religionem Christianam funditus evertit]. The usual reply is that, while one person can only be of one finite essence, many people [personas] can be included in an infinite essence. This is ridiculous [ridiculum est]. For the very fact that the essence is infinite is an additional reason why it can include only one person. Everyone acknowledges that both the essence and the person of the Father are infinite: therefore the essence of the Father cannot be communicated to another person [communicari igitur Patris essentia personae alteri non potest], otherwise there might be two or, indeed, a million infinite persons.[15]

In other words, as Lewalski aptly explains, "God's essence, always equated by Milton with the divine nature itself, is radically incommunicable to any other because it can pertain only to one hypostasis or person, the Father, and because its attributes such as Unity and Infinity can in no sense be shared" (*Brief Epic*, p. 144). On this point Milton is clear and emphatic. For example, he states and then refutes some of the retorts he imagines his orthodox readers will make. Says Milton:

In spite of the fact that we all know there is only one God, Christ in scripture is called not merely *the only begotten Son of God* but also, frequently, *God.* Many people, pretty intelligent people in their own estimation, felt sure that this was inconsistent. So they hit upon the bizarre and senseless [ratione alienissima] idea that the Son, although personally and numerically distinct [numero alterum], was nevertheless essentially one with the Father, and so there was still only one God.

The numerical significance of "one" and of "two" must be unalterable and the same for God as for man. It would have been a waste of time for God to thunder forth so repeatedly that first commandment which said that he was the one and only God, if it could nevertheless be maintained that another God existed as well, who ought himself to be thought of as the only God. Two distinct things cannot be of the same essence. God is one being, not two [unum ens, non duo]. One being has one essence, and also one subsistence—by which is meant simply a substantial essence. If you were to ascribe two subsistences or two persons to one essence, it would be a contradiction in terms. You would be saying that the essence was at once one and not one. If one divine essence is common to two components, then that essence or divinity will be in the position of a whole in relation to its parts, or of a genus in relation to its several species, or lastly of a common subject, in relation to its non-essential qualities. If you should grant none of these, there would be no escaping the absurdities which follow, as that one essence can be one third of two or more components of an essence. (*YP* VI, pp. 212, 213)[16]

From this radical differentiation in essentia between the Father and all other beings, Milton draws the only possible anti-Trinitarian conclusion: "he who is not essentially one with God the Father cannot be the Father's equal" (*YP* VI, p. 222; *CW* XIV, p. 214). Any other conclusion he considers irrational:

God imparted to the Son as much as he wished of the divine nature, and indeed of the divine substance . . . But do not take *substance* to mean total essence. If it did, it would mean that the Father gave his essence to his Son and at the same time retained it, numerically unaltered, himself. That is not a means of generation but a contradiction of terms. (*YP* VI, pp. 211–12)[17]

In summary, Milton used the term "substantia" to mean that material "stuff" of which all things without exception are composed. Substantia does not confer divinity on a being, only existence. All beings have it but only one of them is fully God. What is peculiar to God, and utterly incommunicable, is the divine essentia or hypostasis, in which the attributes of deity inhere. No person other than the Father possesses this essentia because, for Milton, the Deity is not multipersonal, and because the divine essentia is incommunicable. God the Father is the only true God, and he has no equal.

C. "Beget" or "Generate"

In Milton's view God has both an internal and an external efficiency. That is, his sphere of operation is both intrinsic and extrinsic to his being. His decrees are intrinsic and the execution of his decrees extrinsic, with the extrinsic including such external activities as "generation, creation and the government of the universe" (*YP* VI, pp. 153, 205).[18]

While no orthodox Trinitarian would do so, Milton categorizes the Son's generation as one of God's "external efficiencies." To Milton, the Son is utterly distinct from the Father and is other than fully God. This whole scheme sets him over against orthodoxy, which identifies the Son's generation as an example of the Father's internal efficiency.[19] The orthodox can hold this tenet because they believe the divine οὐσία is communicable, and therefore subject to possession by the various persons of the godhead equally.

Milton's delineation of the Son's generation varies from the orthodox view in at least four other ways. First, Milton denies the orthodox concept of eternal generation: "not a scrap of real evidence for the eternal generation of the Son can be found in the whole of scripture" (*YP* VI, p. 206). Biblical texts like John I, 1, Colossians I, 15 and Hebrews I, 2 do not demonstrate the Son's eternity, merely his priority with regard to the rest of creation. To Milton, such "passages prove that the Son existed before the creation of the World, but not that his generation was from eternity" (*YP* VI, p. 206; see also *YP* VI, p. 210). Milton also undercuts the Son's eternal generation by comparing the concept of generation to the logically and chronologically antecedent concept of decree: "God begot the Son as a result of his own decree. Therefore it took place within the bounds of time [in tempore], for the decree itself must have preceded its execution" (*YP* VI, p. 209).[20]

Second, unlike the orthodox, Milton denies that the Son's generation is necessary. To him, the Father "begot his Son not from any natural necessity but of his own free will" (*YP* VI, p. 209). In Milton's scheme the Son owes his being solely to the will of the Father. While the Nicene divines conceive of an eternally and necessarily generative divine οὐσία, Milton believes that "God could certainly have refrained from the act of generation and yet remained true to his own essence, for he stands in no need of propagation. So generation has nothing to do with the essence of deity" (*YP* VI, p. 209; *CW* XIV, p. 186).

Third, Milton does not accept the Nicene notion that the Son was "begotten not made." For him, the terms are frequently interchangeable.[21] To Milton, the concept of begetting entails two aspects: the one is production or creation, which he calls the literal meaning of the term, and the other is exaltation or elevation, which is its metaphorical meaning. The first refers to calling the Son into existence, the second to bestowing upon him "the name which is above every name." As Milton explains: "In scripture there are two senses in which the Father is said to have begotten the Son: one literal, with reference to production [producendo]; the other metaphorical [metaphorico], with reference to exaltation" (*YP* VI, p. 205). While the orthodox accept Milton's second sense of the word, they deny his first. Begetting, they insist, does not involve production. Milton thinks otherwise: "if one in fact begets another being, who did not previously exist, one brings him into existence" (*YP* VI, p. 211). While the Arians and Milton speak thus of the Son, the orthodox do not.

These factors all combine to lead inevitably to the fourth way in which Milton's view of the Son's generation differs from the orthodox — his assertion that begottenness prohibits divinity. Milton reasons that if a being is begotten, it is not eternal, not of necessary existence, not uncaused, uncreated, or unproduced. In short, a begotten being is not God. To Milton, the conclusion seems inescapable: "It is quite clear that the Father alone is a self-existent God [unum Patrem a seipso esse Deum]: clear, too, that a being who is not self-existent cannot be a God" (*YP* VI, p. 218).[22]

The doctrinal significance of this aspect of Milton's theological vocabulary must not be overlooked. According to the distinguished Patristic scholar, J. N. D. Kelly, Arianism was notable for two prominent features: "its exaggerated emphasis on *agennesia* [unbegottenness] as the indisputable characteristic of Deity, and its rejection of the idea that the Godhead can communicate its essence" (*Early Christian Doctrines*, p. 230). As we have seen, both of these Arian tenets are also salient features in Milton's theology. Thus, if what Kelly says is true concerning the distinctive features of the ancient heresy, and if Milton affirms them both, he is already largely Arian. What differences may lie between Milton and the Arians are less than fundamental because Milton affirms those very points that render Arianism theologically distinct and aberrant. Nevertheless, Milton's affirmation of these two fundamental tenets, as we shall see, does not begin to exhaust the extent of his Arianism.

II. MILTON AND THE NICENE ANATHEMAS

"But as for those who say, There was when He was not, and, Before being born He was not, and that He came into existence out of nothing, or who assert that the Son of God is of a different hypostasis or substance, or is created, or is subject to alteration or change — these the Catholic Church anathematizes."

— The anathemas appended to the Nicene creed[23]

So far I have been showing what Milton is not. He is not orthodox. It now remains to state more fully why Milton should be labeled an Arian, first by comparing his views on the Son with those Arian tenets condemned at Nicea, and then by contrasting them with the views of orthodox Reformed divines.

A. *"There was when He was not, and, Before being born He was not"*

Milton, like the Arians, denied the Son's eternity. His position was based upon three considerations: first, what Milton perceived as the impossibility of a subsistence being both begotten and eternal; second, the Second Person's sonship; and third, the fact that decrees necessarily antedate their execution. Concerning the first consideration, Milton explains:

Indisputably the Father can never have begotten a being who was begotten from eternity. What was made from eternity, was never in the process of being made. Any being whom the Father begot from eternity, he must still be begetting, for an action which has no beginning can have no end. If the Father is still begetting him, he is not yet begotten, and is therefore not a Son. It seems, then, utterly impossible that the Son either should be or was begotten from eternity. If he is a son, then either he was once in the Father and proceeded from him, or else he must always have existed, as now, separate from the Father, with a separate and independent identity. If he was once in the Father but now exists separately, then he must once have undergone a change, and is therefore mutable. If he has always been separate from the Father, how is he *from* the Father, how *begotten*, how a *Son* and how, lastly, is he separate in subsistence unless he is separate in essence too? (*YP* VI, pp. 261–62; *CW* XIV, p. 308).[24]

Milton's second reason for denying the Son's eternity springs from the fact that the Son was *son*. By claiming that the Second Person was simultaneously a begotten son *and* eternal, the orthodox, Milton believed, led themselves into many logical dilemmas:

The name "Son," upon which my opponents chiefly build their theory of his supreme divinity, is in fact itself the best refutation of their theory. For a supreme God is self-existent [Summus enim Deus a seipso est], but a God who is not self-existent, who did not beget but was begotten, is not a first cause but an effect, and is therefore not a supreme God [non igitur summus Deus]. Moreover it is obvious that anyone who was begotten from all eternity, has existed from all eternity. But if a being who has existed from all eternity has also been begotten, why should not the Father have been begotten, and have had a father? (*YP* VI, pp. 263–64; *CW* XIV, p. 312)[25]

Third, Milton denies the Son's eternity because he believes that a decree must be logically and chronologically prior to its execution. Milton is clear that the Son owes his existence to a divine decree: "God's first and most excellent SPECIAL DECREE [decretum . . . speciale] of all concerns HIS SON" (*YP* VI, p. 166).[26] And because Milton believes that the execution of a decree can occur only after the decree itself, he believes that the Son cannot be eternal.[27] In Milton's view, there was first a decree, next a begetting resulting from the decree; only afterward was there a Son who resulted from the begetting.

By denying the eternal generation of the Son, Milton stands with the Arians in opposition not only to Nicene orthodoxy, but also to the standard Reformed divines. For example:

Perkins: "The Son is . . . begotten of the Father from all eternity."
             "he is the eternal Son of his Father."
Wollebius: "The Son . . . is begotten by the Father from eternity."
Ursinus: "the eternal Father, who from eternity begat the Son."[28]

In his effort to refute them, Ursinus enumerates the various objections raised by the heretics against orthodox Trinitarianism and, with reference to the Son's eternity, says the heretics reason that "He that has a beginning is not eternal. The Son has a beginning. Therefore he is not that eternal Jehovah who is the Father."[29] This reasoning precisely parallels Milton's.

Predictably, Milton believes his view is the only truly biblical one, and in support of it he advances such passages as Colossians I, 15–17, which asserts that the Son is the firstborn of all creation. Such statements mean that "he was the first of created things [rerum creatarum primum fuisse], and that through him all other things, both in heaven and earth, were afterwards made" (*YP* VI, p. 206). According to Milton, the Bible is utterly devoid of evidence supporting the orthodox view of the Son's eternal generation (*YP* VI, p. 206).

Scholars opposing the identification of Milton's view with Nicene Arianism sometimes try to drive a wedge between them by contending that Milton believed the Son was created in time and that Arius did not. The two positions, they maintain, are therefore at variance. But here they err. Milton, unlike most Renaissance biblical commentators, does not believe time began with the creation of the world in Genesis I, 1.[30] His view of conditions before our world began is not without time. Indeed, there was real time, to which Milton repeatedly refers. It is celestial time. In *Paradise Lost*, for instance, Milton actually invents a heavenly mechanism for measuring it:

> There is a cave
> Within the mount of God, fast by his throne,
> Where light and darkness in perpetual round
> Lodge and dislodge by turns, which makes through heaven
> Grateful vicissitude, like day and night.   (*PL* VI, 4–8)[31]

Since, in Milton's scheme, time is "the duration of things past, present and future" and since sequence and duration could be measured "long before the creation of the world,"[32] then the Son, because he was begotten subsequent to a decree, was born in time.

Arius, by comparison, carefully avoided using the word "time" in relation to the Son's generation.[33] He did so because he adopted Plato's view which sees time as dependent upon the movement of the heavenly bodies. Since the heavenly bodies were not yet in existence when the Son was generated, Arius cannot claim that the Son was begotten in time. Nevertheless, while maintaining that his generation was not in "time," Arius plainly denies that it was from eternity. He conceives of it as an event of a particular moment, concerning which there was a "before," "during," and "after"[34] — concepts which to Milton mean "time." In other words, while the two men define the word "time" differently, neither affirms the Son's eternity. Both Arius and Milton conceive of the Son's generation in terms of sequence and duration. For the one, this implies time, for the other it does not. For neither does it imply eternity. Thus, their differences are cosmological and linguistic, not theological; they pertain to the cosmos and to language, not to the Son. Both Milton and Arius would adhere equally to the anathematized view that "There was when He was not." On this point, Milton is a Nicene Arian.

B. "He came into existence out of nothing"

By this anathema the orthodox intended to condemn any notion that the Son was creaturely or that he was alien to the divine οὐσία. As such, it stands somewhat as a parallel to the anathema which follows it. The orthodox strenuously denied that the Son stood on the creaturely side of the line dividing God from creation. Of course, if the Son was made ἐξ οὐκ ὄντων (from nonbeing) as the Arians insisted, he could not be fully divine because he did not share in the divine οὐσία, and hence in the divine attributes. Milton, as a thoroughgoing materialist, does not subscribe to the idea that the Son, or *any* being, came from nothing. Quite the contrary; all beings, from God the Father down to the lowest link in "the great chain of being," share a common material substratum (see above, sections IA and IB). This fact, however, should not be taken to mean that Milton is at odds with the anathematized position or that he is in agreement with the intention which condemned it. Milton's materialism is not a factor to be interjected by literary critics into his views on the Trinity. By advocating materialism Milton is not thereby elevating the metaphysical status of the Son. The Son is not more divine for having this substantia, because, in Milton's scheme, such substantia does not confer divinity on a creature, only existence. No entity whatsoever exists without that substantia, and by it alone none of them is made God. One must not posit a Trinity of substantia, as C. A. Patrides does.[35] If Patrides were correct, we would each of us be divine, for we, too, all derive from the same divine substantia as the Son and the Spirit. To step outside the bounds of Arianism on this point, Milton would need to assert that the Son was generated from the divine essentia, an assertion that he never makes. Milton's materialism does not render a *trinity* of substantia but, rather, an uncounted multitude, for who could calculate the number of beings or individual entities, from the inanimate to the angelic and beyond, which partake of the divine substantia? Obviously, such participation does not make a being God. Patrides has mistakenly interjected Milton's materialism as the basis for his alleged Trinitarianism. But God may grant as much as he pleases of the divine substantia to a being without granting him the essentia of divinity. As I have already shown, for Milton, the attributes of deity attach to the essentia of God, not to the substantia (see above, section IB).

Put another way, those who argue that Milton is not Arian because he does not subscribe to the anathematized view that the Son was created out of nothing are mistaken because the orthodox themselves would not subscribe to Milton's opposite view — that the Son was created out of matter. The theological antithesis of ἐξ οὐκ ὄντων is not materialism, it is ὁμοούσιον τῷ πατρί (of the same οὐσία as the Father). That is, it is orthodoxy. None of the orthodox Fathers at Nicea were materialists, nor were they opposing people who were. Materialism is not a Nicene or anti-Nicene consideration. At issue is the Son's connection to, or division from, the Father's οὐσία. What the orthodox affirm of the Son's derivation with regard to the Father's οὐσία, both Milton and the Arians deny. Milton's materialism does not make him more orthodox or less Arian. Materialism is not a Nicene Trinitarian stance and it cannot be used to link Milton with orthodoxy or to separate him from heterodoxy. The point at issue here is the essential distinction which exists between Father and Son, not the common fabric of materiality underlying the entire universe. The difference between Arius and Milton on the issue of the Father and Son's common substantiality lies in the province of metaphysics and not Trinitarianism. Simply because Milton says that the Son shares in the Father's substantia, we cannot align him with the orthodox, or thereby set him against the Arians. Milton's sense of consubstantiality does not render the Son equal to the Father; it makes him like all other creatures — precisely the notion the orthodox so strenuously opposed. Milton's is an Arian Son.[36]

C. *"the Son of God is of a different hypostasis or substance"*

In discussing earlier his theological vocabulary, I have shown that Milton's equivalent for the Greek word οὐσία, (translated here by J. N. D. Kelly as "substance") is the Latin essentia. I have also shown that unlike the orthodox, and like the Arians, Milton considered the concept of a multipersonal essentia a contradiction in terms because the divine essentia was utterly incommunicable and could not be subject to generation. Milton considered such views not only unscriptural but also illogical, because, (1) those who differ numerically, as do the Father and Son, differ in essence; (2) those who differ in causation differ in essence; and (3) those who have a different will differ in essence. But even all this does not exhaust the differences between Milton and orthodoxy.

First, the Father and Son differ in essence because the Father's essentia is utterly simple, incommunicable, and not subject to begottenness. The Son, therefore, could not possibly have the same essentia as His Father. Says Milton:

If he did derive his essence from the Father, let my opponents prove how that essence can be supremely divine or, in other words, one with and the same as the Father's essence. For the divine essence, which is always one [cum divina essentia quae una semper est], cannot possibly generate or be generated by an essence the same as itself. Nor can any subsistence or person possibly act or be acted upon in this way, without its whole essence also acting or being acted upon in a similar way. Now generation produces something that is and exists apart from its generator. Therefore God cannot generate a God equal to himself, because he is by definition one and infinite. Since therefore the Son derives his essence from the Father, the Son undoubtedly comes after [posterior] the Father not only in rank [ordine] but also in essence [essentia]. (*YP* VI, p. 263; *CW* XIV, p. 310, 12)

Second, because he does not share in the divine essentia, Milton's Son does not have necessary existence. Milton believes that the Father could have remained true to his own divine essence and nature without ever having generated the Son. The Father is under no necessity to propagate. He did so only as a free act of His own will (*YP* VI, p. 209; *PL* VIII, 419ff.). Because the Son exists solely on account of the Father's decree, which was made in "ABSOLUTE FREEDOM: that is, not forced, not impelled by any necessity [nulla necessitate impulsus]" (*YP* VI, p. 154), he does not have necessary existence. A being that does not exist necessarily is not God. This also means that God is not a Father by necessity or from eternity. God is Father "primarily by virtue" of this particular decree (*YP* VI, p. 166). In all this, Milton stands over against Nicene orthodoxy.

Not only is Milton's view unorthodox by comparison with the Nicene creed, it is heterodox when set against the views of those orthodox Reformed divines who assert that the divine *essentia*, because it can be shared, permits a multiplicity of persons in the godhead:

Ursinus: "Essence, from the Greek οὐσία . . . may be communicated."
"He is the true, proper, and natural Son of God, begotten from the essence of the Father . . . the same is, therefore, communicated to him whole and entire, since the divine essence is infinite, indivisible and not communicated in part."

Wollebius: "The Trinity of persons does not destroy the unity of the essence: there are three persons but one God."
"The unity of the three persons of the Sacred Trinity consists of identity of essence."
"By equality of persons is meant that the three persons of the Godhead are equal in essence, attributes, essential actions, glory, and honor."

Perkins: "Neither can they [i.e., the persons of the Trinity] be divided, by reason of the infinite greatness of that most simple essence, which one and the same is wholly in the Father, wholly in the Son and wholly in the Holy Ghost, so that in these there is a diversity of persons, but unity in essence."[37]

In order to refute them, Ursinus also lists a number of the fallacies upon which the heretics base their beliefs, some of which are readily recognizable as Miltonic:

A most simple essence cannot be the essence of three persons. God is a most simple essence.

The divine essence is not begotten. But the Son is begotten. Therefore he is not [of] the divine essence which the Father is.[38]

D. "or is created, or is subject to alteration or change"

According to Milton, the Son was subject to metaphysical and moral change. That is, he was subject to change in his being and in his character.[39] In the first place, the Son's existence is derived and temporal, not necessary and eternal. As we have seen already, "there was when He was not." The move from nonexistence to existence is, of course, the most profound of metaphysical changes. All the Son has or is, he owes to the will and grace of the Father. His qualities, even his existence, he received. Obviously, derivative created existence and attributes signify mutability and contingency. Unlike his Father, the Son possesses acquired, not natural, qualities and titles, and these, because they are acquired, are not eternal or unchangeable. Because none of the Son's attributes are eternal, they came into being at some point, and coming into being entails radical change. Milton stridently affirms the Son's metaphysically derivative character:

the Son himself reports that he received from the Father not only the name of God and Jehovah [nomen Dei et Iehovae], but also whatever else he has. The apostles, later, bear witness to the same fact: that he received from the Father his individuality, his life [vitam] itself, his attributes [attributa], his works [opera], and, lastly, his divine honor [honorem . . . divinum]. (*YP* VI, p. 259; *CW* XIV, p. 302)[40]

The Son's metaphysical contingency renders him different from and inferior to the eternal, unchanging Father, whose being and attributes are perfect and immutable. Whatever the Son has, whatever he is, is temporal, not eternal, and derivative, not natural or immutable. In Milton's Arian view, the Son's being is distinctly inferior to the Father's. As he explains:

the Son's divine nature [is] something distinct [distincta] from and clearly inferior [plane minore] to the Father's nature. For to be with God, πρὸς θεὸν, and to be from God, παρὰ θεῷ; to be God, and to be in the bosom of God the Father; to be God, and to be from God; to be the one, invisible God, and to be the only begotten and visible, are quite different things [aspectabilem disparata sunt] — so different that they cannot apply to one and the same essence. The fact that he derived his glory, even in his divine nature [divina natura], before the foundations of the world were laid, not from himself but from the Father, who gave it because he loved him, makes it obvious that he is inferior to the Father. (*YP* VI, p. 273; *CW* XIV, pp. 336–38)

Ursinus, rehearsing the theological machinations of the heretics so he can refute them, says: "He who has all things from another is inferior to him from whom he has them. The Son has all things from the Father. Therefore, he is inferior to the Father."[41] Once again, this argument precisely parallels Milton's heretical reasoning.

Milton arrives at the Son's mutability by two other routes. First, as he sees it, the doctrine of the Father's immutability or incorruptibility is deduced from, and dependent upon, his eternity (*YP* VI, pp. 143–44). Because the Son is not eternal, he can be neither immutable nor incorruptible. Second, the Son's mutability is verified by his historical incarnation, which, as Milton conceives it, requires divesting, or emptying, oneself of various qualities. God the Father, because he is incapable of such change, is incapable of incarnation as well. As Milton reasons:

a God who is infinite can no more empty himself than contradict himself, for infinity and emptiness are mutually exclusive terms. But since he [i.e., the Son] emptied himself of that form [forma] of God in which he had previously existed, if the form of God were to be taken to mean the essence of God, it would prove that he had emptied himself of the very essence of God, which is impossible [non potest]. (*YP* VI, p. 275; *CW* XIV, p. 342) [42]

The Son can undergo incarnation because he can undergo the change required for such a process. That he can do so proves, on the one hand, that he lacks "the very essence of God," and, on the other hand, that he is of a different (and lesser) essentia than the Father:

the essence of the Son is not the same as the essence of the Father [essentiam filii non esse eandem cum essentia Patris] . . . For if it were the same the Son could not have coalesced [coalescere] in one person with man, unless the Father had also been included in the same union — unless, in fact, man had become one person with the Father as well as with the Son, which is impossible. (*YP* VI, p. 425; *CW* XV, p. 272)

Put another way, because the Son was incarnated, one may conclude that he emptied himself and, therefore, is subject to change. One may also conclude, with reference to an earlier anathema, that the Son's essentia is different from the Father's.

In Christian theology, the Son became incarnate in order to play the role of mediator between man and God. According to Milton, the fact that the Son was a mediator proves that he was both inferior to the Father and subject to change:

But I maintain that he could not have been a mediator, nor could he have been sent by or obedient to God, unless he was by nature less than God and the Father [nisi natura minor Deo et Patre]. So even when he has stopped playing the part of a mediator, however great he may be in the future or may have been in the past, he must still be subject to God and the Father. (*YP* VI, p. 243; *CW* XIV, p. 262)

Because he is subject to change, the Son is distinct from the Father and inferior to the Father. He both assumes and discards the role of mediator and he has a "greatness" that is subject to enhancement or diminution. Milton, therefore, adamantly contends that the Son's incarnation and his role as mediator separate Him from the Father's immutable essentia. If they did not, one could not avoid the conclusion that the eternal, unchangeable Father had himself died as a man on the cross, an idea both impossible and heretical. As Milton explains, "if the Son is of the same essence as the Father, and if the same Son, after a hypostatical union [post unionem hypostaticam], coalesces in one person with man, I do not see how to avoid the conclusion that man, also, is the same per-

son as the Father—a conclusion which might produce quite a few paradoxes!" (*YP* VI, p. 264; *CW* XIV, p. 312). Put another way, the role of
mediator entailed an incarnation. The incarnation entailed, among other
changes, death. The unchangeable God can never die. The Son died. He
is not, therefore, the unchangeable God. By way of corollary, Milton further argues that if one maintains that the Father and Son share a common *essentia*, then one is led inescapably to the heresy of Patripassion-
ism, the belief that the Father himself suffered on the cross. Milton's
adversaries try to wiggle out of this dilemma by distinguishing between
the Son's divine and his human nature, but to no avail:

> my opponents . . . use the two natures of Christ, and their conjunction in the
> office of mediator, as a convenient little device for evading any arguments brought
> against them, with the result that they are more difficult to pin down than Ver-
> tumnus. They apply what scripture says about the Son to either the Son of God
> or the Son of man separately, as it suits them—now to the mediator as God, now
> as man, and sometimes as both together. *But . . . he receives everything from
> the Father: everything—not only what belongs to him as mediator, but also what
> belongs to him as Son. If he is not still the same God after being made mediator,
> then he was never the supreme God.* (*YP* VI, pp. 259–60, my italics; *CW* XIV,
> p. 302)

In other words, the orthodox are forced to discard either the Son's media-
torial incarnation or his full deity. Because the Son became a mortal man,
Milton argues, he is neither immutable nor the Father's equal.

With regard to the Son's mutability, then, Milton reasons that the
eternal unchangeable God cannot undergo an alteration in existence.
The Son, however, is not so. He was begotten subsequent to a decree and
thereby moved from nonexistence into existence. Milton also believes that
the eternal immutable God cannot divest himself of his attributes in order
to assume flesh, because that process entails radical change. Because the
Son did exactly that, he is other than God, less than God, and mutable.
Furthermore, while a man, the Son suffered and died. This, Milton says,
the Son underwent as one complete person, and not in his human nature
only. To suffer and die is to sustain profound change. The Son died and
therefore is not immutable. Immutability is not subject to suffering because immutability entails impassibility.[43] Much less does it tolerate death.
As the mediating third party between God and man, the Son became
incarnate, suffered, died, and rose again. The Nicene creed notwithstand-
ing, one can conclude only that the Son is not the immutable God. According to Milton, the Arians were right.

Whether we evaluate Milton's doctrine in the light of his theological vocabulary, or whether we examine his position in the light of the Nicene anathemas, we discover that Milton occupies a position either identical with or similar to that of the Arians. By comparison, his views do not align with the orthodoxy of his own or earlier eras. By any honest reckoning, Milton is an Arian.

Northeastern Bible College

NOTES

1. W. B. Hunter, C. A. Patrides, and J. H. Adamson, *Bright Essence* (Salt Lake City, 1971), p. 15.

2. On Servetus, see Martin A. Larson, "Milton and Servetus: A Study in the Sources of Milton's Theology," *PMLA*, XLI (1926), 891–934. On Socinus, see George Newton Conklin, *Biblical Criticism and Heresy in Milton* (New York, 1949), and J.-P. Pittion, "Milton, La Place, and Socinianism," *RES*, XXIII (1972), 138–46. On Ochino, see Louis A. Wood, *The Form and Origin of Milton's Anti-Trinitarian Conception* (Ontario, 1911). Hunter, Patrides, and Adamson, *Bright Essence*, argue for pre-Nicene subordinationism. The claim for Unitarianism is made by William E. Channing, "Remarks on the Character and Writings of John Milton," *The Works of William E. Channing, D.D.* (Boston, 1886), and H. John McLachlan, *The Religious Opinions of Milton, Locke and Newton* (University of Manchester, 1941). The argument for Milton's Arianism may be traced chronologically through Maurice Kelley, *This Great Argument* (Princeton, 1941); John A. Clair, "A Note on Milton's 'Arianism,'" *Essays and Studies in Language and Literature*, V (1964), 44–48, ed. Herbert H. Petit; Barbara Kiefer Lewalski, *Milton's Brief Epic: The Genre, Meaning, and Art of "Paradise Regained"* (Providence, 1966), pp. 133–63; Stella Purce Revard, "The Dramatic Function of the Son in *Paradise Lost*: A Commentary on Milton's 'Trinitarianism,'" *JEGP*, LXVI (1967), 45–58; H. R. MacCallum, "'Most Perfect Hero': The Role of the Son in Milton's Theodicy," *"Paradise Lost": A Tercentenary Tribute*, ed. Balachandra Rajan (Toronto, 1969), pp. 79–105; Maurice Kelley, "Milton and the Trinity," *HLQ*, XXXIII (1970), 315–20; Maurice Kelley, introduction and notes to *Christian Doctrine* in *The Complete Prose Works of John Milton*, ed. Don M. Wolfe et al. (New Haven, 1953–82), vol. VI (cited hereafter as *YP* VI). For the fullest argument for Milton's Arianism to date, see my "Milton's Arianism: 'Following the way which is called Heresy'" (Ph. D. diss., Fordham University, 1983). Arguments for the orthodoxy of Milton's thought may be found in Joseph W. Morris, *John Milton: A Vindication Specially from the Charge of Arianism* (London, 1862); Sister Miriam Joseph, C.S.C., "Orthodoxy in *Paradise Lost*," *Laval Theologique et Philosophique*, VIII (1952), 243–84; and James H. Sims, "*Paradise Lost*: Arian Document or Christian Poem?" *Etudes Anglaises*, XX (1967), 337–47.

3. This view originated with Hunter's seminal article, "Milton's Arianism Reconsidered," *HTR*, LII (1959), 9–35, which he later amplified in "Some Problems in John Milton's Theological Vocabulary," *HTR*, LVII (1964), 353–65.

4. *Bright Essence*, p. 18. The same position is advanced in chart form by C. A. Patrides, *Bright Essence*, p. 5. For criticism of Patrides's chart, see Dayton Haskin, "Mil-

ton's Strange Pantheon: The Apparent Tritheism of *De Doctrina Christiana*," *Heythrop Journal*, XVI (1975), 129–48.

5. For Milton's Latin text, see *The Works of John Milton*, ed. Frank Allen Patterson et al., (New York, 1931–38), vol. 14, p. 202 (cited hereafter as *CW*).

6. See *CW* XV, p. 262. To Milton, Father and Son are "one" only in the sense that they "speak and act as one." Their oneness is "not in essence but in love, in communion, in agreement, in charity, in spirit, and finally in glory." *YP* VI, p. 220. For other views that Milton rejects the three-in-one formula, see Haskin, "Strange Pantheon," pp. 137, 144–45; Lewalski, *Brief Epic*, pp. 138, 143; and Stella Purce Revard, review of *Bright Essence*, *JEGP*, LXXII (1973), 129–30.

7. As J. N. D. Kelly, *Early Christian Doctrines* (New York, 1958), p. 235 says, by affirming that the Father and Son are of the same οὐσία, the orthodox demonstrated "their conviction that the Son was fully God, in the sense of sharing the same divine nature as His Father."

8. For Milton's view of substantia, see also John Peter Rumrich, "Milton's Concept of Substance," *ELN*, XIX (1982), 218–33.

9. Ibid., p. 230. Substantia is that "one first matter" of which Milton speaks in *Paradise Lost*, V, 472ff. See also J. B. Leishman, *Milton's Minor Poems*, ed. Geoffrey Tillotson (London, 1969), p. 221, and Lewalski, *Brief Epic*, p. 140.

10. Elsewhere Milton says, *YP* VI, p. 310: "God produced all things not out of nothing but out of himself." Milton's belief that God is material and that matter is not something fundamentally extrinsic to him is based on his infinity. In the same place Milton explains: "I do not see how God can truthfully be called infinite if there is anything which might be added to him. And if something did exist, in the nature of things, which had not first been from God and in God, then that might be added to him."

11. This is the case in *Paradise Lost* II, 439, where chaos is spoken of as "*unessential night.*" Chaos indeed has substantia, but because it is unarticulated matter, it lacks essentia. The same principle is alluded to in *PL* VII, 233. See also the explanation in A. S. P. Woodhouse, *The Heavenly Muse: A Preface to Milton* (Toronto, 1972), p. 149.

12. This circumscription in no way entails a "reduction" of the infinite matter in God. There is not less of it in him after creation than before. Because God is inifinite, "subtraction" from him still renders him infintely unreduced. See Rumrich, "Substance," p. 226.

13. In reviewing here the various translations of the term "hypostasis," Milton is referring to, but not necessarily endorsing, the translations of theologians like William Ames, *The Marrow of Theology*, trans. John Dykstra Eusden (Boston, 1968), pp. 83, 84, and Johannes Wollebius, *Compendium Theologiae Christianae*, in *Reformed Dogmatics*, ed. and trans. John W. Beardslee III (Oxford, 1965), p. 41. My point is advanced also by Woodhouse, *Heavenly Muse*, p. 171, and Haskin, "Strange Pantheon," p. 164. This synonymity is widely accepted and allows little, if any, debate.

14. According to J. N. D. Kelly, *Early Christian Creeds* (New York, 1972), p. 241, "the terms *hypostasis* and *ousia* are employed as equivalents."

Although Milton's use of "hypostasis" and "essentia" is largely uniform, he does allow himself some latitude of usage. That Milton generally intends the divine "nature" by the term "essentia" is clear from many passages. For example, he states: "Nature . . . can only mean either the essence itself or the properties of that essence . . . nature can mean nothing in this context except the essence itself. . . . It follows that the union of two natures in Christ was the mutual hypostatic union of two essences . . . the union of two natures, that is, of two essences" (*YP* VI, p. 423). When Milton says, a little later, that there is, in Christ, "a mutual hypostatic union of two natures, or in other words of two essences, of two substances and consequently of two persons" (*YP* VI, p. 424), he employs the term "substantia" to mean a "substantial essence," that is, substance which has been hypostasized, or essentiated. Patrides, *Bright Essence*, p. 4, wrongly contends that Milton's system attaches true divinity to substantia and not to essentia. In support of this he quotes Milton's words that the Father "imparted to the Son as much as he pleased of the *divina natura*, nay of the *divina substantia*." Patrides then says that "the Son is made expressly of the Father's *substantia*, as is the Holy Spirit." But this argument will not do because (1) "natura" equals "essentia," and (2) for Milton, true divinity is neither "imparted" nor subject to communication. Deity is natural, eternal, inalienable, and immanent. Neither can a being who is "made" be God, as Patrides confesses Milton's version of the Son and Spirit are. Furthermore, Patrides's view ignores the fact that Milton denies that the godhead is multipersonal and that every being whatsoever, animate or inanimate, shares a common substantia.

15. *YP* VI, 225. *CW* XIV, 220–22. See also John Reesing,"The Materiality of God in Milton's *De doctrina christiana*," *HTR* L (1957), 161 n. 3.

16. For an example of these "absurd" ideas (as Milton calls them), concerning the multiplicity of persons in a single essence, see William Perkins, *The Work of William Perkins*, ed. Ian Breward (England, 1970), p. 181. With such reasonings Milton, of course, does not agree. He says "the essence of God, since it is utterly simple, allows nothing to be compounded with it." *YP* VI, 140. See also *YP* VI, 264.

17. Thus, Hunter's belief (*Bright Essence*, pp. 18, 25), that Milton is in agreement with the Nicene "homoousios" and the creed of 381 is wide of the mark. Milton's position is opposed also to that of the standard Reformed divines; see Wollebius, *Compendium*, pp. 44, 45; Perkins, *Work*, p. 203; Ames, *Marrow*, p. 88; and Zacharius Ursinus, *The Commentary of Dr. Zacharius Ursinus on the Heidelberg Catechism* (Columbus, 1852; rept. Grand Rapids, 1956), pp. 130, 133, 193, 196. Note, too, that Milton's use of the term "essentia" as the equivalent of the Nicene οὐσία parallels that of these Reformed divines. His theology differs, not his language.

18. See also Hunter, *Bright Essence*, p. 49; Haskin, "Strange Pantheon," pp. 138–39; Lewalski, *Brief Epic*, p. 140; and *YP* VI, p. 299 n. 1.

19. For instance, Perkins, *Work*, p. 182: "the Father begot the Son, not out of himself, but within himself."

20. This contrasts with the standard Puritan divines like Perkins, *Work*, p. 182: "The Father [has been] from all eternity begetting the Son."

21. Hunter, too, has noticed Milton's equation of begetting or generating with creation. As he explains, *Bright Essence*, p. 40: "Milton seems to confuse these and similar terms deliberately when he says that 'God of his own will created [creavit], whether he generated [generavit] or produced [produxit], the Son' . . . likewise the Holy Spirit 'was created [creatum], that is, produced [productum]' from the divine substance." Of course, beings who are "created" or "produced" are not part of the Trinity, to Milton or to an orthodox theologian.

22. Milton's conclusion is antithetical to that of the orthodox Reformed divines, who, like Perkins, *Work*, p. 182, assert: "Although the Son is begotten of his Father, yet nevertheless he is of and by himself very God." Or, as Revard, "Dramatic Function," pp. 47, 48, aptly explains, "The primary distinction, according to Milton, then, between the Father and Son is this. The Father is an uncreated being—a being that has existed from all eternity . . . The Son is a created being. The word "begotten" is used of him only to distinguish him from all others of God's creatures. The Son is superior to all other beings. . . .

Nevertheless, although he is higher than all other creatures, he is not therefore the same as the Father . . . . By nature, the Son is neither coeternal, coessential, nor coequal." See also her further comments, review of *Bright Essence, JEGP*, LXXII (1973), 131.

23. Translation by J. N. D. Kelly, *Early Christian Creeds*, p. 216.

24. This passage also bears heavily upon Arian considerations other than the Son's temporality, such as his separation from the Father, his mutability, and his creatureliness, which I will consider below.

25. Also, *YP* VI, p. 209: "a real son is not of the same age as his father." His position is exactly that of the Arians, as described by G. L. Prestige, *God in Patristic Thought* (London, 1952), p. 147: "They asked, for instance, how the Son could always have existed with the Father; sons never are as old as their fathers; a father is thirty years old when he begets his son; it is true of every son that 'he was not, before his generation' . . . the Arians pressed the metaphor of paternity and sonship as rigorously as it was possible to press the statements of Scriptures."

26. Also, *YP* VI, pp. 167, 208: "it appears that the Son of God was begotten by a decree of the Father . . . however the Son was begotten, it did not arise from natural necessity [non necessitate naturae], as is usually maintained, but was . . . a result of the Father's decree and will [decreto et volundate Patris]." This last passage also contradicts the orthodox view that the Son has necessary existence.

27. See *YP* VI, p. 209; *YP* VI, p. 166 n. 42; and Woodhouse, *Heavenly Muse*, p. 169.

28. Perkins, *Work*, p. 182; Wollebius, *Compendium*, p. 41; Ursinus, *Commentary*, p. 124.

29. Ursinus, *Commentary*, p. 200.

30. For Milton's view of time, see Arnold Williams, "Renaissance Commentaries on Genesis: Some Elements of the Theology of *Paradise Lost*," *PMLA*, LVI (1941), 151–64; and Laurence Stapleton, "Milton's Conception of Time in *The Christian Doctrine*," *HTR*, LVII (1964), 9–21.

31. Technically, although there is no time in Chaos (*PL* II, 891ff.), the fallen angels spent nine days plummeting through it. By comparison, Milton does believe there is time in Hell (*PL* I, 50ff.).

32. Stapleton, "Time," pp. 11, 14.

33. For Arius's view of time, see G. C. Stead, "The Platonism of Arius," *Journal of Theological Studies*, XV (1964), 16–31.

34. Ibid., p. 26. This point is also underscored, Stead says, by Arius's repeated use of the aorist tense.

35. *Bright Essence*, pp. 4–5.

36. For the views of other critics who support my position, see MacCallum, "Perfect Hero," p. 89; Lewalski, *Brief Epic*, pp. 145, 146; and Woodhouse, *Heavenly Muse*, p. 196.

37. Ursinus, *Commentary*, pp. 129, 193. See also pp. 132, 133, 196; Wollebius, *Compendium*, pp. 44, 45. See also pp. 38–41. Perkins, *Work*, p. 181.

38. Ursinus, *Commentary*, pp. 138, 200.

39. The Son's capacity for moral or character development is especially prominent in *Paradise Lost* and I have treated it at length in "Milton's Arianism," pp. 163–80.

40. Milton also says, *YP* VI, 261: "the Son . . . receives his very being from the Father." This fact leads inescapably to the Son's mutability. According to Wollebius, *Compendium*, p. 39, derivative beings "have a changeable and borrowed life."

41. Ursinus, *Commentary*, p. 195.

42. As Revard, "Dramatic Function," p. 50, observes: "Unlike the Father, the Son is mutable . . . only the Father is changeless."

43. As Prestige, *God in Patristic Thought*, p. 156, explains: "behind all expression of Arian thought lay the hard and glittering syllogism that God is impassible; Christ, being γεννητός, was passible; therefore Christ was not God."

THE DEMONIC BACCHUS
IN SPENSER AND MILTON

Joan Larsen Klein

I N T H E Middle Ages, writers included drunkenness in the sin of gluttony and associated gluttony with lechery because both sins were,
as Gregory the Great said, the "vitia carnalia" — "Ventris Ingluvies" and
"Luxuria." Chaucer's Parson told his companions that "After glotonye
thanne comth lecherie" and the Pardoner used holy writ to prove that
"luxurie is in wyn and dronkennesse."[1] Spenser shows "lustfull *Lechery*"
riding after "loathsome *Gluttony*" in his parade of sins (*The Faerie
Queene*, I, iv, 21–26) and seems to intend Gluttony to anticipate the false
Genius in the luxurious Bower of Bliss. In the House of Pride, "exces-
siue *Gluttonie*," like the false Genius in the Bower of Bliss, is the "Steward . . . That of his plenty poured forth to all" (I, iv, 43). As Comus
urges the Lady to make her beauty "current," she, like Guyon, repudiates the invitation to lust partly because she sees in it "swinish gluttony."[2]

When Spenser and Milton created figures signifying gluttony and
lust, they adapted not only medieval but also Renaissance versions of
these sins clothed in classical garb. Bacchus came to be identified with
gluttony because he was portrayed most often as the drunken wine
god, was associated with the libidinous Venus, and was served by wild
bacchantes — although early mythographers and emblematists rarely connected him with the seven deadly sins. In his parade of sins, however,
Spenser conflates a medieval Gluttony and a Renaissance Bacchus and
links both to Lechery. Spenser's false Genius looks like the young and
handsome Bacchus, and his attractions mirror those of Excesse, however
much his intents remind of us Archimago's. Milton's Comus embodies
(quite literally because he is the son of Bacchus and Circe) many Renaissance associations of Bacchus, especially those which link him to Venus.

Although Spenser seems to have created his bacchic figures in terms
of Renaissance mythologies and emblem books, Milton seems to have
created Comus in terms of the male, sometimes hermaphroditic, often
bacchic, and certainly demonic tempters found in the first three books
of *The Faerie Queene*. But, as Milton resolves the conflict between Comus
and the Lady, that is, between demonic lust and the virtuous soul, he

93

rejects many of the resolutions reached by Spenser in the later books of
The Faerie Queene. Like Spenser himself, Milton rejects the vision of the
hermaphroditic union of Amoret and Scudamore that ends the first version of the poem. He also rejects the political and historical implications
of the marriage of Britomart and Artegal envisioned in the Temple of
Isis. Milton repudiates the progressively more worldly concerns of the last
three books of *The Faerie Queene* in order to focus on the spiritual nature of the struggle between vice and virtue and the spiritual consequences
of the Lady's victory over Comus. In the process, however, Milton implies that his new achievement in *A Mask* may be only a pastoral prelude
to the epic struggle between God and Satan in *Paradise Lost.*

I

Early in *The Faerie Queene* Spenser makes it clear that the pagan
pastoral world of nature to which Bacchus was usually linked can be used
as an instrument of "Eternall prouidence" (I, vi, 7). This occurs when
the traditional associates of Bacchus, "a troupe of *Faunes* and *Satyres*"
(and later Bacchus's teacher, "old *Syluanus*") rescue Una from Sansloy's
ravening lust (I, vi, 7, 16). Bacchus himself, however, appears only allu-
sively in this episode as the wine which Sylvanus wrongly thinks has excited his troupe ("*Bacchus* merry fruit" [I, vi, 15]) and thus seems to be
deliberately excluded from her rescue. Spenser goes on to imply, moreover, that the old world of the woodland gods, gladdened though it is
by the sight of Una's grace and truth, remains invincibly ignorant, a world
to be left behind.

Spenser also suggests, however, that when these same pagan gods
and demigods are dissociated from the natural world, they function as
attributes of demonic evil. A fallen Bacchus, or a figure like him, takes
part in the parade of sins and functions allegorically as Gluttony. Spenser emphasizes the divorce of sin from the natural world by presenting
the parade of sins in emblematic rather than narrative terms. The entire
parade, as A. C. Hamilton notes in his edition (p. 67), forms one of the
more important emblems in Book I, the beast with seven heads. Each
individual sin is also fashioned as an emblem and given the tripartite structure of name, picture, and interpretation which Alciati popularized.[3]
Spenser establishes the emblematic nature of Gluttony by naming him
and then picturing him, first as a medieval Gluttony on a pig, whose
"belly" was "vp-blowne with luxury" (I, iv, 21), and second, as a figure
not unlike the naked, fat, and sweating Bacchus found among other places
in Alciati's picture of the statue of Bacchus in the *Diverse Imprese.* Spenser's Gluttony is clad "In greene vine leaues" "And on his head an yuie

girland had" (I, iv, 22). Alciati and his commentators, however, did not see in Bacchus the sin of gluttony.[4] It was England's Whitney in *A Choice of Emblemes* who connected Alciati's picture of Bacchus with gluttony in language which anticipates Spenser's:

> The timlie birthe that SEMELE did beare,
> See heere, in time howe monsterous he grewe:
> With drinkinge muche, and dailie bellie cheare, . . .
> Which carpes all those, that loue to much the canne,
> And dothe describe theire personage, and their guise:
> For like a beaste, this doth transforme a man.[5]

The diction Spenser uses to interpret his own picture of bacchic Gluttony recalls Whitney's and comes to the same moral conclusion. In addition, it looks ahead to that one figure in the Bower of Bliss who permanently abandons manhood in order to persist in sin, the "hoggish"-minded Grill (II, xii, 86–87):

> Still as he rode, he somewhat still did eat,
> And in his hand did beare a bouzing can,
> Of which he supt so oft, that on his seat
> His dronken corse he scarse vpholden can,
> In shape and life more like a monster, then a man.   (I, iv, 22)

Spenser makes the usual medieval association between Gluttony and Lechery when he places Lechery after Gluttony in the parade of sins. But Spenser's male Lechery does not anticipate Acrasia or anyone else in the Bower of Bliss, as his readers might have expected. Instead Lechery, holding in his hands a "burning hart," anticipates Busirane in particular and, I think, the ambiance of Castle Joyeous in general. In the parade of sins, therefore, Spenser seems to intend bacchic Gluttony rather than cruel Lechery to foreshadow his treatment of luxuria in Book II of *The Faerie Queene* — along with "greedy *Auarice*" (I, iv, 27), the sin who prefigures Mammon.

So, especially in *The Faerie Queene*, Book II, the traditional pact between Gluttony and Lechery seems to be figured forth in an alliance between bacchic and venerean figures. Spenser had warrant for the ways in which he links these figures because Bacchus was associated with Venus as often as Gluttony was with Lechery. Emblem books repeatedly showed Bacchus and Venus together, often in connection with the Fall of Man. Sambucus does so, for instance, in his emblem, "The Triumph of Voluptuousness," and in one of his epigrams, where he says that men fall quickly into sin when Venus and Bacchus work together. Junius also associates

gluttony and Venus in ways that Whitney and perhaps Spenser pick up.
The motto of one emblem tells us that the belly, the bed, and Venus cause
Glory to fly. The picture shows a man eating as he lies in bed with Venus
while Lady Glory runs out the door. Junius interprets his picture by saying that fallen man has chosen to be the servant of Venus and the slave
of gluttony.[6] Whitney in *A Choice of Emblemes* takes over this picture
too, and explicitly identifies Bacchus with gluttony. "Driue VENVS
hence," says Glory; "let BACCHVS further packe, / If not, behowlde I
flie out of thie gate":

> I haue noe likinge of that place,
> Where slothfull men, doe sleepe in beddes of downe:
> And fleshlie luste, doth dwell with fowle excesse.   (P. 42)

Whitney joins gluttony, lust, and sloth under the names of Venus and
Bacchus and opposes all three sins to Glory in a configuration not unlike
that found throughout Books I and II of *The Faerie Queene*. In the Bower
of Bliss, Spenser even makes of "fowle excesse" a woman who offers Guyon
the poisoned wine of Bacchus.

Spenser enlarges upon his identification of Bacchus with the sins of
luxuria and gluttony in the Mordant-Amavia episode that begins the quest
of Temperance. Amavia says that Acrasia uses the poisoned cup of Bacchus to make her lovers "drunken mad" and drive them to their deaths
(II, i, 52, 55). Spenser thinks of the wine of Bacchus allegorically as the
wine of concupiscence and opposes it to the waters of temperance, a virtue which is defined here as abstinence and associated with virginity, as
the metamorphosis of Diana's nymph suggests. Mordant dies when he
drinks from a well, the source of whose waters are the tears of a virgin
nymph who was transformed to stone by Diana, goddess of chastity, when
she chose to die rather than yield to the lustful Dan Faunus, one of the
traditional companions of Bacchus. In constructing this opposition, Spenser develops traditional medieval psychomachia in which only *temper-
antia*, defined as virgin chastity, can conquer *luxuria*, and only the waters
of temperance quench the fires of lust.[7] The opposition of virginity and
temperance to lust which the Amavia-Mordant episode suggests is further developed in Book II by the implacable opposition of the chaste and
presumably virgin Guyon to Acrasia herself—for Guyon, alone among
the knights, does not aspire to marriage. Rather, he bears on his shield
the image of the "heauenly Mayd" who appears in Book II only as
Belphoebe, Diana, the virgin mirror of "rare chastitee" (II, i, 28; III,
proem). But Spenser goes further yet in this episode to suggest what he
will later develop at length in the contrast between the Bower of Bliss

and the Garden of Adonis, that the bacchic wine which signifies the temptations of Acrasia is magically charmed, a deadly "venim," opposed to life-giving waters either "indewd / By great Dame Nature" or the "gift of later grace" (II, ii, 4, 6). The opposition of death-dealing lust to nature's life-giving love is humanized in the opposition of Mordant's death to the woodland birth of the bloody babe (II, i, 53; cf. II, ii, 2, 6), although the death of the child's parents and its own stained hands suggest allegorically that natural love can neither flourish nor be sanctified until after the Bower of Bliss is destroyed.

Something like the figure of the young Bacchus emerges fully rounded in the figure of the Porter at the gate of the Bower of Bliss. He is a "comely personage of stature tall, / and semblaunce pleasing, more than naturall":

> With diuerse flowres he daintily was deckt,
> And strowed round about, and by his side
> A mighty Mazer bowle of wine was set,
> As if it had to him bene sacrifide;
> Wherewith all new-come guests he gratifide. (II, xii, 46, 49)

Because he has apparently disguised himself as the true genius (for the false Genius is dark and ugly), the Porter is strewn with the flowers and wine Conti said were sacrificed to the good Genius.[8] But the real nature of this false Genius is evident in his wanton behavior and lax stance (II, xii, 46). Consequently, Spenser's false Genius is more like Cartari's young Bacchus than Conti's Genius, for Cartari's Bacchus is young, handsome, sleepy, and effeminate, a god, Cartari says, who closely resembles another god of revelry, Comus.[9] As the illustration in *Le Imagini* shows, Comus is a drunken, sleepy, and unsteady god, scarcely able to hold up his Thyrsus-like staff. Lascivious and soft, like the Porter who guards the gate of the Bower in which Acrasia and Verdant lie hidden, Comus also guards the door of "two who enjoy the fruits of love" (p. 415). Thus Cartari's bacchic Comus both resembles and performs the function of the false Genius at the entrance of the Bower. Cartari goes further yet in directions Spenser will take when he emphasizes Bacchus's relations with the libidinous Venus and repeats the story that Priapus was born of the union between them (pp. 442–43). For Cartari relates Priapus with "Lari," who were guardians of the house and sometimes "Demonii d'inferno" (p. 448). He relates all these figures with the true and the false Genii because Genius, he said, like Comus, is another domestic numen and thus another god of hospitality and pleasure (p. 451). It may be, consequently, that Spenser's false Genius not only is disguised as a true Genius but also has taken on the semblances, attitudes, and dress of the young Bacchus, Comus, and the Lari, especially as they are described in Cartari's *Imagini*.

Although Pleasure's Porter is not crowned with the ivy nor draped with the vine leaves and grapes proper to Bacchus, the vine and their enticing grapes adorn the next porch where Excesse reclines, and their temptation is that traditionally assigned to Bacchus:

> So fashioned a Porch with rare deuice,
> Archt ouer head with an embracing vine,
> Whose bounches hanging downe, seemed to entice
> All passers by, to tast their lushious wine,
> And did themselues into their hands incline,
> As freely offering to be gathered.   (II, xii, 54)

The embracing vine and the enticing grapes of Bacchus, like Excesse herself, are given the feminine attributes of Acrasia as Spenser conflates the functions of Bacchus and Venus in a synthesis reminiscent of the traditional pairing of the two gods. In the second porch, furthermore, foul "*Excesse*" replicates the temptation of the Porter and anticipates that of Acrasia as she performs the bacchic function of squeezing grapes into wine:

> In her left hand a Cup of gold she held,
> And with her right the riper fruit did reach,
> Whose sappy liquor, that with fulnesse sweld,
> Into her cup she scruzd, with daintie breach
> Of her fine fingers, without fowle empeach,
> That so faire wine-presse made the wine more sweet. (II, xii, 56)

"Clad in faire weedes, but fowle disordered" (II, xii, 55), Excesse has the slovenly appearance but not the wild activity of the bacchantes who regularly followed Bacchus in emblem books and mythologies and who were often identified with "intemperantia."[10] Thus it appears that Spenser has constructed a set of almost static emblematic tableaux at the entrances to the Bower (partly to indicate the stasis of the garden, perhaps) composed of the false Genius, Excesse, and their overarching porches. In these tableaux, Spenser links the voluptuousness of Bacchus to the eroticism of the bacchantes and points to the presence deeper in the bower of a false and sterile Venus who tempts men to worse ends than Circe ever did. As if to suggest that these Bacchic and Venerean temptations succeed, Guyon finds beyond that second porch an overflowing phallus-like fountain decorated with the ivy sacred to Bacchus and wrought with the shapes of Venus's "naked boyes" (II, xii, 60).

But the Porter in the Bower is not simply a false Genius. He is also, it seems, a false Bacchus, for the fecundity which the Renaissance associated with his grapes and wine is only apparent.[11] Many of Excesse's grapes, for instance, are unnatural artifacts: "some were of burnisht gold, / So made by art, to beautifie the rest" (II, xii, 55). The "trayle of yuie" on the fountain was made "of purest gold . . . the rich metall . . . so coloured, / That wight, who did not well auis'd it vew / Would surely deeme it to be yuie trew" (II, xii, 61). The hidden "art" (II, xii, 58) which wrought these golden grapes, constructed this fountain, and perhaps governs the Bower may well be the same art which wrought the Garden of Proserpine near Mammon's Cave and governs those black and deadly waters in which Tantalus reaches for golden apples placed forever beyond his grasp. The figure of "greedie *Tantalus*" (II, vii, 60) in the Garden of Proserpine, therefore, may represent the source and end of the bacchic gluttony which permeates the Bower. (In fact, Mignault, commenting on Alciati's description of Tantalus as Avarice, associates Tantalus with intemperance and suggests that Tantalus himself signifies the constant and insatiable thirst of voluptuaries which is accompanied by "perturbations, sorrows, and fears."[12] That Tantalus may represent the last end of the gluttonous lust which Bacchus symbolizes in the Bower is fitting because Bacchus is the son of Proserpine in some legends and so a god in hell. Thus the end of excess is eternal want: "The whiles he steru'd with hunger and with drouth / He daily dyed, yet neuer throughly dyen couth" (II, vii, 58).

After the destruction of the Bower and the capture of Acrasia, fully realized, evil-intending bacchic figures are banished from the narrative action of the poem. Bacchus, the wine god, retreats to his traditional Renaissance form as a mythological character in a fabulous world. We find him represented in figures of speech, in stories, on a tapestry in Busirane's castle. Thus, although he still appears in the contexts of drinking and lust, he no longer seems demonic. He is reduced, for instance, to an allegorical figure signifying his wild followers and called "*Bacchante*" in Castle Joyeous, but there, in Britomart's eyes, he is only one of six "shadowes" (III, i, 45; cf. 51). Bacchus is figuratively related to the follies of courtly love in the castle of Malbecco, as Paridell, following Horace and Ovid, makes the "guilty cup" of "*Bacchus* fruit" part of the dangerous game of illicit love (III, ix, 30–31).[13]

When Spenser describes how Busirane capured Amoret, however, he relates Bacchus and his wine to the pleasures of the Bower in more sinister ways. For Busirane seized Amoret after he brought his masque into her "bridale feast, whilest euery man / Surcharg'd with wine, were heedlesse and ill hedded" (IV, i, 3). Busirane's intent to conquer Amoret through rape rather than temptation, as in the Bower of Bliss, is further revealed in the tapestries of "*Cupids* warres" (III, xi, 29) on his castle walls. One of these tapestries, Bacchus's rape of Philyra, specifically recalls the temptations of Excesse in the Bower of Bliss:

> So proou'd it eke that gracious God of wine,
> When for to compasse *Philliras* hard loue,
> He turnd himselfe into a fruitfull vine,
> And into her faire bosome made his grapes decline.
>
> (III, xi, 43; cf. II, xii, 54)

It may be, as the androgynous nature of the vine suggests, that we are meant to realize in retrospect that the false Genius and Excesse are mirror images of the same sins. It may be, too, that by the time we see Britomart reach the Castle we are meant to understand that the bacchic, venereal, and circean temptations which animated the Bower of Bliss have become static, possessing only the apparent life and action that the viewer's imagination gives to visual art. But the movement toward the stasis of visual art was already implicit in the emblematic nature of the parade of sins. It was suggested as well in the Mordant-Amavia episode when Amavia called her plight a pageant and Spenser called it a "spectacle" (II, i, 36, 40; cf. II, i, 39, 44, 57 and II, ii, 1). It was obvious when Spenser told us that the very grapes and ivy in the Bower of Bliss were made of gold. Indeed, even the castle of Busirane and its tapestries may be no more than magical illusions hiding the dungeon beneath. For Busirane, having captured Amoret

> By strong enchauntments and blacke Magicke leare,
> Hath in a dungeon deepe her close embard,
> And many dreadfull feends hath pointed to her gard. (III, xi, 16)

Because Spenser tells us that Busirane constructed his masque and castle by magic, he may intend us to understand that he is describing a series of surface metamorphoses in which the spirit of evil, of the archmagician, perhaps, underlies not only the figures of Archimago and the false Genius but also that of Busirane. The false Genius, in other words, may have assumed the appearance of lassitude, just as he assumed the appearance of the good Genius, vanishing when Guyon destroys the Bower in order to reappear later as Busirane, whose busy activity reminds us of Archimago's and whose form and ends remind us of Lechery's, the figure who rode after Gluttony in the parade of sins. Spenser retains the connections with Bacchus even in Busirane's name, for Busiris was both the place and the cruel king of the site where Osiris, the Egyptian

Bacchus, was buried.[14] It may be, therefore, that when Britomart overcomes the violent lust of Busirane, we are also meant to understand that she has finally overcome the other side of that lust which gave the Bower its being.

With the Bower of Bliss destroyed, Busirane conquered, and his tapestried castle "vanisht vtterly" (III, xii, 42), Spenser apparently felt it possible to introduce into the Temple of Isis a figure from one of the few beneficent portions of the Bacchus myths, the Egyptian Bacchus, Osiris, whom Spenser relates to Hercules and thus to Artegal:

> Such first was *Bacchus*, that with furious might
> All th'East before vntam'd did ouerronne,
> And wrong repressed, and establisht right.   (V, i, 2)

Spenser distances his Egyptian Bacchus from the Roman Bacchus by distinguishing among their attributes. He says, for instance, that the Egyptian Bacchus was a man, not a god.[15] It was the "antique world" that invented the myth of Osiris's godhead: "For that *Osyris*, whilest he liued here, / The iustest man aliue, and truest did appeare" (V, vii, 2). Following Plutarch in *Of Isis and Osiris*, Spenser also forbids the priests of Osiris and presumably Osiris himself to drink wine. They do not "drinke of wine" because it has the power, as bacchic myths emphasize, of driving men to fury and madness:[16]

> Such is the powre of that same fruit, that nought
> The fell contagion may thereof restraine,
> Ne within reasons rule, her madding mood containe.
>   (V, vii, 10–11)

Thus Spenser identifies a mortal Bacchus with a mortal Osiris and both with Artegal — contrary to Plutarch, who sees Osiris as a demon who was later transformed to a god, and the mythographers, most of whom see Osiris as the Egyptian counterpart of Bacchus.[17]

Spenser follows Plutarch and others, however, especially Giraldi and Cartari, when he identifies Osiris with the generative powers of the sun (V, vii, 4; Giraldi, p. 389; Cartari, p. 436) and thus, by implication, with the god, Priapus, who was identified with the lost *membrum virile* of Osiris. Cartari emphasizes, for instance, that Bacchus and Osiris figure identically in the large generation myths: "Priapus was born of Bacchus in order to show the whole seminal virtue that takes its force from the sun, in animals as in plants and other things produced in the earth. This was also understood in the image of Osiris" (Cartari, p. 441). Thus it seems right, as Alastair Fowler suggests, to see in the union of Isis and the crocodile that symbolizes the union of Britomart and Artegal, Britomart's participation in a "cosmogonic myth running through the poem."[18] Spenser's association of Osiris with the flames of passion and generation (V, vii, 14–15) is also related to elements in the Osiris myth, for Osiris as the sun is "flame-like" (Giraldi, p. 390), dressed in "a red cloak which has around it that celestial heat that gives force even to the seeds in the bowels of the earth" (Cartari, p. 441).

But Spenser identifies Osiris, in addition, with a crocodile, contrary to the myths of Osiris wherein the crocodile is Osiris's brother, the ferocious Typhon, who killed Osiris and tore his body in pieces and who was later conquered by Isis and turned into a crocodile (Giraldi, p. 390; Cartari, pp. 437–39).[19] Cartari associates Typhon with forces like the flames of war that Spenser associates with the crocodile (Cartari, p. 438; V, vii, 23). Cartari also identifies Typhon with earthy evils and Osiris with the "virtu" that overcomes them (p. 439). Plutarch interpreted the struggle between Osiris and Typhon in more complex terms yet, suggesting that Osiris is "the mind and reason" in the human soul as well as the force which orders the seasons, temperatures, and rotations of the earth. Typhon, on the other hand, "is the element in the soul which is passionate . . . without reason, and brutish," and in the bodies of man and earth, he is "the element of the corporeal which is subject to death, disease, and confusion" (chapter 49). But Plutarch muddled these antitheses later in his work where the crocodile, though perhaps not Typhon, is "divine reason" and a "likeness of God" (chapter 75) and Osiris is "the primal element which is spiritually intelligible" (chapter 77). Spenser may have felt justified in conflating the lawgiving, generative, and rational attributes of Osiris with the destructive attributes of the Typhon-crocodile because of the ambiguities in Plutarch and the sibling relationship of Osiris and Typhon. If so, Spenser may be suggesting that the perturbations within the crocodile, "that stormy stowre" (V, vii, 15), not only signify the rigorous enforcement of law but also the struggles between reason and passion, spirit and sense. Spenser may also be suggesting that these struggles are pacified and made fruitful when the passion of the Typhon-crocodile is subdued by its rational Osirian self through the agency of Isis—that is, through the love, grace, and mercy figured forth in Isis, in Britomart, and in Gloriana, whose union with Arthur is prefigured by the union of Britomart and Artegal and symbolized in Britomart's vision of the primal union of Isis and Osiris, the moon and the sun.

The last large metamorphosis of Bacchus in *The Faerie Queene*, therefore, occurs in a dream vision which looks backward at statues portraying ancient generation myths and forward to British history. It occurs in a temple that seems to be the antithesis of Busirane's palace, wherein the few remaining destructive impulses of Bacchus are subdued and he, as his statue comes to life, is enabled through love to achieve his generative and lawgiving powers. In terms of the larger scope of the poem, we may be supposed to believe that the demonic and seductive attributes of Bacchus are vitiated when the Bower of Bliss is destroyed, that the murdering lust of Bacchus is conquered when the Castle of Busirane is caused to vanish, and that the beneficent attributes of the Egyptian Bacchus are liberated for consummation and fruition in the Temple of Isis. Because Spenser relates Osiris to generational myths, he may also mean to identify Osiris with Adonis. If so, Osiris would be the rectified version of Bacchus, the False Genius, and Excesse, as the Garden of Adonis is of the Bower of Bliss.

Spenser's visions of the triumph of chastity over lust and the marriages which ensue become progressively more human and earthly as the narrative advances. At moments in their quests, Red Cross and Guyon are both microchristi and their antagonists satanic. The marriage which Red Cross and Una contract binds Christ to his church and reflects the marriage of the lamb. After Books I and II, however, *The Faerie Queene* moves away from the grand conflicts between heaven and hell over the soul of man that Milton will record in *Paradise Lost* to more worldly conflicts and more earthly unions. In Books III and IV, for instance, the marriage of Britomart and Artegal involves the founding of a wartorn dynasty that culminates in the rule of Elizabeth. At the same time, their marriage embodies the fertility of nature which is reflected in the marriage of Florimel and Marinell and which originates in the primal fecundity of the Garden of Adonis.

II

In his *Mask*, Milton largely rejects Spenser's resolution of the struggle between chastity and lust and the marriages that ensue. His rejection explains, perhaps, why he ignores the last three books of *The Faerie Queene* and focuses upon the earlier books. It also may explain why he appears to move his Spenserian figures and plots toward a more spiritualized conclusion in which Spenser's Garden of Adonis is lifted from earth to the skies and made a stage in the soul's further flight. Milton gives Comus many of the characteristics of Spenser's false Genius, as A. Kent Hieatt suggested,[20] together with characteristics like those of Lechery in the parade of sins and powers like those of Busirane over Amoret. But Milton relegates Bacchus himself to a partly original mythopoetic past and places the son of Bacchus in an allegorical forest which seems to be

conceived of as later in time than Spenser's wandering wood partly because it contains persons belonging to the historical present. Unlike Spenser, Milton places his virgin Lady at the center of the action and raises
her virginity to the level of sage and serious doctrine which armors her
person as it did Una's against the onslaughts of "savage fierce, bandit,
or mountaineer" (A Mask, 426) and preserves the freedom of her mind
against the errors of Comus's. Unlike Guyon's and Britomart's chastity,
however, and more like Una's, the Lady's chastity is valuable not only
in itself, for wisdom and intelligence are traditionally the gifts of chastity,[21] but also because it leads to charity, that virtue which unites human
and divine love.

Milton seems to have wanted to improve on Spenser in other ways,
too. He raises what Spenser thought of as emblematic pageants—the
parade of sins, the spectacle of Mordant and Amavia, the masque of
Cupid—into a public function played out before the Earl of Bridgewater.
Thus he moves what Spenser thought of as allegory within allegory out
onto a stage and into the verifiable present. At the same time, Milton
takes what for Spenser was the epic matter of a journey through a dark
wood and places it in a pastoral context. He turns Spenser's epic matter,
in other words, into the conventional pastoral antecedent of what he came
to believe was the only true epic matter, the story of paradise lost.

Milton's presentation of Comus and the invitation to luxuria also differs from Spenser's temptations. Where Spenser develops the scope and
consequences of luxuria associatively through the accretion of figures and
places, Milton precisely distinguishes among related figures, their functions, and their environs. Thus Milton not only distinguishes between Bacchus and Comus; he also indicates their fictive and symbolic relationships to each other, to Circe, and to Venus. It is as though Milton were
intent upon clarifying Spenser's visions of gluttony and lust presented in
the parade of sins, the temptations of Duessa and Phaedria, the Bower
of Bliss, and the Castle of Busirane.

Milton's Comus, furthermore, is unlike those bacchic tempters in
Spenser's Bower of Bliss in that he indulges in neither food nor drink.
In this, he is also unlike earlier descriptions of Bacchus and Comus, who
are usually shown as drunken and half-asleep, the prey of their own desires. Nor does Milton's Comus appear to possess the degenerate elegance
he has in Philostratus or Cartari or later in the French translation of
Philostratus by Blaise de Vigenère. Milton's Comus is also unlike Jonson's. In Pleasure Reconcild to Vertue, which was indebted to Spenser
and read by Milton, Jonson's Comus is an old, fat Bacchus like those in
the emblem tradition. In fact, Busino's eyewitness account of the masque

and Inigo Jones's sketch of Comus reveal nothing like traditional descriptions of Comus. Busino thought he was looking at Bacchus: ". . . come sarebbe à dir' il Dio Bacco Grassissmo. sopra un Carro," and Inigo Jones shows Comus as a Bacchus figure, nude and fat, under a vine arbor, his "Bacchanalian Spear" and bowl carried by attendants.[22]

If Milton's Comus does not succumb to the dangerous self-indulgence associated with Bacchus and Comus, however, he is not immune from temptations of another sort. Like Busirane's desire for Amoret, perhaps, or even the satyrs' worship of Una, Comus is enthralled by the Lady and her song, which tempt him to make her his "queen" (*A Mask*, 265). Unlike Archimago or Busirane, however, as soon as Comus tries to seduce the Lady, he falls prey to his own desires and sets in motion his own degradation. Thus Milton conceives of Comus as a more complex figure than either Bacchus or Comus was traditionally. He also conceives of Comus as a more changing and complex figure than either Spenser's false Genius or Busirane, both of whose attributes within bower and castle remain fixed and whose persons disappear once they are overcome.

In Milton's *Mask* Bacchus is, if not defunct, at least vanished; certainly he is "parted thence" (56). He is remembered, however, as the young Bacchus, "blithe" with youth, his "clust'ring locks" like clustering grapes, his head wreathed with ivy berries (54, 55). Unlike his son, furthermore, Bacchus was free and untrammeled; he coasted the shores as the "winds listed" (49) and was able to leave Circe at will — as could none of the men she seduced. Circe, however, did not seduce Bacchus; it was the now-vanished beauty of Bacchus which she "gazed" upon (54) that tempted the temptress so strongly that before he left her, apparently unchanged by her "charmèd cup" (51), she had by him a son (56).

But this is the last we hear of Circe and her island, too; for both, like Bacchus, have also been banished from our view. Indeed, if Milton is, among other purposes, reinterpreting Spenser's temptations and continuing, even finishing, Spenser's fable, then perhaps the distancing in time and space of Bacchus, Circe, and her sunlit island from Comus's dark woods is not unrelated to the slaying of the dragon in Book I, to Guyon's destruction of the Bower, to Acrasia's capture in a "subtile net" (II, xii, 81), and to the unexplained escape of her bacchic Porter. For it is Busirane, who enters Fairyland after the destruction of the Bower, who most resembles Milton's Comus, and Busirane's palace and the riots tapestried on his walls that most resemble the palace and revels of Comus. Like Busirane, Comus indulges in riot only at night and, like Busirane's, Comus's palace appears magically in a dark and dangerous forest. Neither of these antagonists, furthermore, nor their palaces are felt to be tempt-

ing. On the contrary, they are all obviously perilous and frightening, unlike Circe and Acrasia and their rich, bright, flowering gardens. So, when
the Lady tells us that she mistrusts "tap'stry halls" (*A Mask*, 324), we recall Britomart's wariness in Busirane's castle. We also remember those
tapestries picturing men and women, "kings and kesars," brought into
"thraldome" (III, xi, 29) and destructive lust, the "sweet consuming woe"
(III, xi, 45), turning even gods into beasts. Milton shows us men turned
beasts, of course, in his *Mask*. Spenser showed us a similar revolt in the
second room of Busirane's palace, where we saw both meanings of bru-
tality in the "thousand monstrous formes" which lust there takes (III, xi,
51). Just as the reveling in the mask of Busirane seems to anticipate the
dance of Comus and his rout, so it also suggests the sound the Lady hears
"of riot and ill-managed merriment" (*A Mask*, 172): "a ioyous fellowship
issewd / of Minstrals, making goodly meriment, / With wanton Bardes,
and Rymers impudent" (III, xii, 5). The ends of Comus, finally, are identical with Busirane's: to confound "the feeble senses . . . And the fraile
soule in deepe delight nigh dround" (III, xii, 6).[23] Like Busirane, in other
words, Comus seems to embody an assault upon the senses which is uglier
and later than those old temptations of Circe and the more recent temptations of Acrasia, as the elder brother intimates, too, when he speaks
of the goddess, Diana, as both ancient and fabulous, a fiction recalled
from "Antiquity," "the old schools of Greece" (439).[24]

Although Milton's Circe was not captured as was Acrasia, she was
abandoned, first by Bacchus and then by her son, Comus, when he was
"ripe and frolic of his full-grown age" (59). Thus, before he initiates the
main action of *A Mask*, Milton suggests that many old gods, demigods,
and nymphs have either vanished or been abandoned. In the process,
Milton formulates a theory of mythopoetic history and a new fable which
relate older classical gods to newer Renaissance gods in terms of the cessation of the oracles and the fall of the pagan gods that occurred at the
Incarnation, for the Incarnation altered those old gods almost beyond
recognition into demons driven and under attack. Spenser described a
similar fall when he moved from Book I to Book II of *The Faerie Queene*.
Lucifera, Orgoglio, and the old dragon walk freely on the surface of the
earth until Red Cross slays the dragon. In Book II, however, they appear
near or in hell, underground and imprisoned, in the more circumscribed
guises of Philotime and Mammon. Milton himself described the restriction of Satan and the fall of the gods in his ode, *On the Morning of Christ's
Nativity:* at the moment of the Incarnation, that old Spenserian dragon,
"In straiter limits bound, / Not half so far casts his usurpèd sway" (169–
70). "The parting Genius is with sighing sent . . . The nymphs in twi-

light shade of tangled thickets mourn" (186, 188). "Nor is Osiris seen / In Memphian grove or green . . . Naught but profoundest hell can be his shroud" (213–14; 218). The advent causes old gods and powers, so many of whom resemble beings in *The Faerie Queene*, to "Troop to th'infernal jail" (233). The ode itself appears to describe the event that predates the events in *A Mask*, for the fall of wickedly disposed pagan gods seems to underlie the movement of Comus from his mother's sunlit island to the "drear wood" (*A Mask*, 37) he inhabits at the opening of the drama.[25]

What remains in the new age described in *A Mask*, therefore, is the legacy of bad old gods, a half god, Comus, whose datable history begins late in antiquity, after the Incarnation, in the *Imagines* of Philostratus (ca. 170–245 A.D.) where he is described as a flushed and delicate half-grown youth, "asleep under the influence of drink."[26] But Milton never shows us the young Comus. Instead we see a being who seems even older than he was when he left his mother's island, "ripe and frolic of his full-grown age" (*A Mask*, 59). It is an older Comus, therefore, who functions in the diminished wood of *A Mask* as one of the fallen demons whom Milton identified in his Nativity ode, in *Paradise Lost*, and in *Paradise Regained* with spirits sent from hell — in contrast to the good demon, the attendant Spirit. Like the demons and dragons imprisoned in Mammon's hell, like the fallen gods and new-made shadows in Milton's ode, Comus also seems to be somehow imprisoned, in what the Elder Brother calls a "close dungeon of innumerous boughs" (*A Mask*, 349). He is separated from life in a "dark sequestered nook" (500) and walled in by funereal woods "Immured in cypress shades" (521). Denied the light of day, he performs his magic in the dark of night, "in thick shelter of black shades imbow'red" (62). Even if Comus were to move in the light, Milton may intend us to believe, as does the Elder Brother, that he who "hides a dark soul and foul thoughts / Benighted walks under the mid-day sun; / Himself is his own dungeon" (383–85).

Nonetheless, Milton apparently wants us also to think that the temptations of sunnier pagan gods prefigured the darker temptations of demons like Mammon in *The Faerie Queene*, who practiced near "rifted rocks whose entrance leads to hell" (*A Mask*, 518). Even when Bacchus and Circe flourished, Milton tells us, the "misusèd wine" was "sweet poison" (47), and Circe's charmed cup transformed the men who drank from it into "groveling swine" (53) — although her spells, unlike those of her son, neither altered the mind nor lasted beyond the grave. Comus, however, "Excels his Mother at her mighty art" (63). His orient liquor likewise reminds us more of the eastern potions of Duessa and Acrasia than they do Circe's, for those who taste his cup out of "fond intemperate thirst" (67) lose their likeness to the creator, "unmolding reason's mintage / Charáctered in the face" (529–30). If, however, in the new dispensation described in *A Mask* a lower god has been imprisoned in a "hideous wood" to practice "hellish charms" (520, 613), and if higher gods have been lifted from earth to the stars, men have been raised out of ignorance into knowledge (witness the Elder Brother), have taken on "Th' express resemblance of the gods" (69), and possess the potential to turn their minds "by degrees to the soul's essence" (462).[27] When men fall into the snares of Comus, therefore, Milton makes it clear that they become worse than the beasts in Circe's fold. Their souls become "clotted by contagion" (467), and so "perfect" is their misery, they do not know they lie prone, like the prisoners of Acrasia, rolling "with pleasure in a sensual sty" (73, 77). Thus Milton conflates the sins of gluttony, lust, and sloth in language not unlike Spenser's (cf. II, xii, 1) and suggests that the fall occurs when man forgets "the excellence / Of his creation, when he life began" (II, xii, 87).

Not until Milton allows us to hear Comus himself, however, rather than to hear about him from the attendant Spirit, do we begin to understand the nature of the wizard, his relationship to past tempters, and the force and extent of his temptation. As I suggested earlier, Comus is unlike Spenser's Archimago and false Genius and more like Mammon and Busirane in that Comus is more straitly circumscribed. His appearance as well as his invitation to sin are also uglier and more obviously sinister than those of Jonson's Comus or Spenser's false Genius or even Archimago, whose true aspect we never see. Comus pretends to likeness with the attendant Spirit when he claims that he can "Imitate the starry quire" (112) to which the Spirit truly belongs (3, 80–81). Comus, like Mutabilitie, also claims to be the agent of nature, guiding its months and years, seas and sands. But we know from the beginning of *A Mask* that only the attendant Spirit moves nature and spans the heavens and earth (494–95; 80–81; 87–88), and we soon discover that only Sabrina embodies the sustaining and regenerating power of grace working through nature. Comus, furthermore, soon reveals that he has no claim to heavenly, natural, or mortal being. Instead, as he traveled from Circe's island to his dark wood, he became the priest of "Dark-veiled Cotytto" (129), goddess of the "dragon womb / Of Stygian darkness" (131–32), and thus the enemy of man, nature, and the "enthroned gods" (11) as well.[28]

Just as Una and Guyon, weary travelers both, were the intended "prey" of disguised magicians, so the Lady is Comus's "wished prey," for whom he fashions a "deadly snare" with "hellish charms" (574, 567, 613).

When the Lady first meets Comus and asserts that courtesy is sooner found in "lowly sheds" than in "tap'stry halls / And courts of princes" (323–25) and when the Elder Brother asserts that she, "like a quivered nymph . . . May trace huge forests and unharbored heaths" (422–23), we remember Una's first encounter with Archimago (I, i, 29–35) as well as Belphoebe's encounter with Braggadocchio (II, iii, 21–42). Once captured, however, the Lady's steadfast refusal to accede to Comus's assaults recalls Amoret's equally steadfast refusal to accede to Busirane's. The Lady's imprisonment also resembles Amoret's in that each is held in what seems a palace, but is really an illusion created by magic arts. Because Comus, when he makes the Lady a prisoner in his palace, is more like Busirane than Archimago or the false Genius, Milton may be suggesting that the Lady's pilgrimage has already encompassed the trials of Una and Belphoebe, who escaped the assaults of lust, and the trials of Guyon, who resisted its temptation. He may also be suggesting that the Lady will achieve Amoret's status as "th'ensample of true loue alone" (III, vi, 52). That Milton's Lady is meant both to embody and surpass the achievements of Spenser's early heroines and his chaste knight may be one reason why Milton calls her simply "Lady," for such anonymity implies that she allegorically represents not truth, or temperance, or chastity, or even goodly womanhood, but all of these as they are realized in the growth of the virtuous soul — which the Spirit also implies at the masque's end when he calls Virtue "she" (1019). That the Lady is also Lady Alice Egerton and thus, to some extent, playing herself is another indication how far Milton has taken his best teacher, Spenser, whose knights and ladies are always limited by their allegorical significations. Thus Milton not only raises the Lady and her brothers higher on what appears to be a Neoplatonic scale of being, but also endows his human characters with a degree of actuality that Spenser largely denies to his figures and which Milton denies to Comus himself. This is because Comus remains in *A Mask* a fabulous being whose fictive nature is emphasized by his lack of connections to classical mythology; for Comus's imaginary genealogy has no literary or historical basis, as Milton says when he points out its doubly fictive nature early in the poem (43–45). (The relatively more fictitious and shadowy being of Comus may have been further emphasized when *A Mask* was performed at Ludlow if Comus, unlike the Lady, her brothers, or the attendant Spirit, was played by a professional actor — by someone, in other words, who was not acting out a part commensurate with his true self.)

Should the lady fall, therefore, Milton makes it clear that she would not only fall into damnation but also that she would fall into the more static realms of fiction and relative nonbeing to which Comus belongs —

fiction that is less "free" or "real" than the Lady was when *A Mask* was presented. Because the Lady is not simply Comus's "wished prey" but also his wished-for "queen," she is potentially a new Venus, potentially more enchanting and ravishing than his mother, Circe (265, 245), potentially more devastating than either. It is fitting, therefore, that Comus presents the actual temptation to gluttony and lust in an emblematic dumb show wherein we see a *"stately palace, set out with all manner of deliciousness: soft music, tables spread with all dainties"* (*A Mask*, p. 130). The dumb show is a fitting vehicle for Comus because it is a regressive art form, reminiscent of the dumb shows of the false Genius and Excesse, antecedent to and more limited than the masque form.[29] It is also fitting because it is an art form which appeals only to the five senses, like Comus's temptation itself, not to the reasoning mind whose instrument is speech. The Lady, however, *"puts by"* (*A Mask*, p. 130) the glass which Comus offers her, rejecting the temptation on its own terms before Comus begins to argue for it. Thus Balachandra Rajan's point that the Lady is rejecting Comus rather than arguing with him is important, I think, because it suggests she knows that his arguments are spurious and that he is debasing the high purpose of language (756–59), as she later says when she calls his arguments "false rules pranked in reason's garb" (759).[30]

Milton, however, surely does not expect us to believe that the Lady will fall. Unlike Spenser, who rarely reveals the full wickedness of his antagonists at the outset, Milton tells us at the beginning of the masque what Comus is. When the Lady sees the banquet of sense, she too learns what Comus is. But she knows even before she sees the banquet that Comus is a fraud: he did not lead her to a plain shepherd's hut as he promised, as Archimago in a similar situation led Una; he offers a cup she knows is poisoned, having seen "These ugly-headed monsters" (695), as Guyon knew the cup offered by the false Genius was poisoned, having seen Mordant dead and Amavia die; and he imprisons her body, as Busirane did Amoret's. In her acquisition of knowledge, then, the Lady is unlike Una, who could not see beneath Archimago's disguise, and more like Guyon as he proceeds through the cave of Mammon and the "bower of earthly bliss," as Milton said, in order that he might see and know and yet abstain. As the Lady listens to the speeches of Comus, therefore, we know that she will find in them only a further revelation of vice.

Nowhere does Milton suggest that the arguments of Comus are the product of reason which strives for truth. On the contrary, Comus presents his arguments on behalf of gluttony and lust in such thoroughly conventionalized ways that their rejection by the reader, too, who has heard these arguments set forth with greater skill by artists better endowed than

Comus, seems certain. Samuel Johnson's complaint that the speeches in *A Mask* resemble "rather declamations deliberately composed and formally repeated, on a moral question" such that the "auditor therefore listens as to a lecture, without passion, without anxiety,"[31] is, I think, precisely the effect Milton wished to create — unlike the deliberately sensuous descriptions of the Bower of Bliss, wherein Spenser tempts his readers and Guyon both. From the deliberate use of easily recognizable literary echoes, it seems evident that Milton expects informed readers of the longer version of the masque, even more than he did the masque's first audience, to reject the arguments of Comus as quickly as the Lady does and to see in them a formally presented synthesis of many such speeches delivered with more heat to readers more engaged.

In fact, the attendant Spirit tells us at the beginning of *A Mask* to listen for echoes of former poets and to consider the truths such echoes contain because those poets, he says (like the Lady herself, perhaps, who also composes songs), were taught "by th' heav'nly Muse" what they "Storied of old in high immortal verse" (515–16; 230–43) — tales that were not "vain or fabulous" (513). Thus the literary echoes which pervade the speeches of Comus are direct and obvious, not oblique and glancing as they were in Spenser's descriptions of Mammon's cave and the Bower of Bliss, for instance, or as they will be in Satan's temptation of Eve. When Comus urges the Lady to enjoy "Refreshment after toil, ease after pain" (687), Milton may well expect us to remember that Despaire, who spoke lines very like these, wished to drive Red Cross to suicide (I, ix, 40). When Comus describes nature's plenitude in the distorted terms of gluttonous indulgence and lavish waste, "Covering the earth with odors, fruits, and flocks, / Thronging the seas with spawn innumerable" (712–14), Milton may have wished his readers to remember Boethius on the proper use of nature's goods and Guyon's like response to Mammon (II, vii, 15–17); to remember the intent behind Volpone's similarly phrased invitation to Celia; and to realize, because Milton wrote for literate Christians, that the bounties of nature were not created to "sate the curious taste" but to feed the hungry, reward the good, and glorify God — as the Lady tells us, too. Comus's variations on the *carpe diem* theme, "If you let slip time, like a neglected rose / It withers on the stalk with languished head" (743–44), is certainly meant to recall a throng of Renaissance antecedents and their suspect contexts — the bird's song in Armida's garden, the rose song in Acrasia's Bower, Theseus in *A Midsummer Night's Dream*, threatening death or the convent — which all involve temptations ending in loss or death.

But the Lady is more than a singer; she is also a virtuous and chaste virgin—like Diana (442), not the absent Venus whom Comus claims is his ally but who appears in *A Mask* only in its last vision, sad beside a sleeping Adonis. Because the Lady not only is virtuous in herself but also seems to be an allegorical representation of the virtuous soul, the Lady recognizes evil more quickly than the chaste but unchanging and susceptible Guyon did and understands that Comus describes not natural good but rather "lewdly pampered luxury" and "swinish gluttony" (770, 776). Thus she refuses Comus and condemns gluttony in Christian terms that go back to the early Middle Ages:

> swinish gluttony
> Ne'er looks to Heav'n amidst his gorgeous feast,
> But with besotted base ingratitude
> Crams, and blasphemes his Feeder.   (776–79)

If the Lady is not tempted to taste of Comus's "treasonous offer" (702), however, then the "trial" (329, 970) she undergoes involves the purifying of virtue described in the *Areopagitica* and goes beyond Guyon's ability to see, know, and yet abstain because it moves her nearer to perfection: "that which purifies us is trial, and trial is by what is contrary." The Elder Brother's Neoplatonic vision of human perfectability, the result of philosophical knowledge perhaps gained through the teachings of the shepherd Thyrsis, describes an orderly process whereby converse with "heav'nly habitants" turns "The unpolluted temple of the mind . . . by degrees to the soul's essence, / Till all be made immortal" (459–63).[32] When the Lady first hears the sounds of Comus's riot, she mistakes it for human "riot and ill-managed merriment" (172). The fantasies which throng into the Lady's memory upon hearing these sounds, however, force her spirits upward, not downward, and occasion a new and "solemn vision" (457) of the angel forms of Faith, Hope, and Chastity (213–15), although she may need to wait until after she receives the gift of grace from Sabrina to embrace Charity. This vision strengthens her conviction of heaven's protection and is confirmed by a providential gleam that lightens her darkness, newly enlivens her spirits (228), and prompts her to song. Thus, even before the Lady meets Comus, the sounds of his riot have the effect of bringing her closer to her sources of being, increasing her faith, and furnishing her with a new perception in song of the harmonious relationship of earth and heaven. She is consequently more easily enabled to reject the perverse and illogical arguments of Comus. So, although Comus could deceive her at first by disguising himself as a shepherd, he cannot later, she says, trap her "With lickerish baits fit to ensnare a brute" (700). As she rejects Comus's arguments, furthermore, even though her senses are bound, her spirits are lifted higher yet, becoming "rapt" with a "sacred vehemence" (794–95) which could shatter his "magic structures" (798) and which forces him to acknowledge a "cold shudd'ring" set off by "some superior power" (801–02).

As the Lady's triumph over Comus moves her closer to her own perfection, it brings him closer to his ultimate fall, even though he escapes immediate punishment with some measure of his power intact — he could still work an "other new device" (941). That the Lady's senses have been freed, however, and Comus driven deeper into the woods implies that his powers have diminished. Sabrina's presence and song, moreover, have brightened the night, anticipated dawn (956), and invested the previously darkened world with color, starlight, and beauty. The brothers and the Lady are now more fully human because they are defined at last by their historical selves as well as by their acquired virtues (of knowledge in the case of the brothers and goodness in the case of the Lady). The attendant Spirit's last prophetic vision shows them a glimpse of a further, more beautiful world that man could achieve were he to become more spiritualized yet. Indeed, the epilogue to the printed version of *A Mask* promises man a paradise within which is "Higher" than Jove's court (1021). It is a paradise illumined by perpetual day and defined by the soul's celestial marriage, wherein chastity is fructified by love. (Depending upon how we are to interpret Adonis's "Waxing well," such a paradise may not prohibit earthly marriage and human fruit.) Given the Spirit's last pronouncements about the nature of the triumph "*O'er sensual folly and intemperance*" (975) — lust and gluttony in their largest terms — it may be that Milton also expects us to consider and apply to Comus himself the Neoplatonic view of the fall of the soul described by the Elder Brother: the "lewd and lavish act of sin" (465) which "Imbodies and imbrutes" the soul "till she quite lose / The divine property of her first being" (465–69). For the Elder Brother envisions the final defeat of gluttony, of evil, in ways which make the sin its own punishment:

> But evil on itself shall back recoil,
> And mix no more with goodness, when at last,
> Gathered like scum, and settled to itself,
> It shall be in eternal restless change
> Self-fed and self-consumed.   (593–97)

The Elder Brother's vision not only seems to prophesy the ultimate downfall of Comus and his rout. It also seems to anticipate Milton's vision of Sin and Death in *Paradise Lost*, where Milton moves beyond the mythopoetic and allegorical confines of *A Mask*. Milton's *Mask* certainly describes the triumph of virtue over vice. But it does not describe, as does *Paradise Lost*, what Milton believed were the truths of Christian history. (Indeed, the allegorical myths which shape so much of *The Faerie Queene* and *A Mask* become merely illustrative similes in *Paradise Lost*.) Not until the composition of *Paradise Lost*, therefore, does Milton lay bare the true nature of sin and death and reveal gluttony in its true form, stripped of the bacchic attractions with which Comus was rhetorically able to invest it. Satan tells Sin and Death, for instance, about a new world created by God where their gluttony can be indulged, where they "shall be fed and filled / Immeasurably; all things" their "prey" (II, 843–44). After man falls, however, the fallen angels are further reduced to a fate like but worse than that suffered by Tantalus in Spenser's Garden of Proserpine. Transformed into serpents, they are "parched with scalding thirst and hunger fierce," "plagued / And worn with famine" (X, 556, 572–73). "All-conquering Death" starves even as he feeds on "herbs, and fruits, and flow'rs" and man, his "last and sweetest prey" (X, 591, 603, 609). At this point in the narrative, God prophesies the prisoning of evil in far more explicit terms than those which Milton allowed the Elder Brother to use and at which the containment of Comus only hints. At the same time he prophesies the final end of the gluttony that has come to characterize evil: the forces of evil are "dogs of hell," drawn thither "to lick up the draff and filth":

> Which man's polluting sin with taint hath shed
> On what was pure, till crammed and gorged, nigh burst
> With sucked and glutted offal . . .
> Both *Sin*, and *Death*, and yawning grave at last
> Through Chaos hurled, obstruct the mouth of hell
> For ever, and seal up his ravenous jaws.   (X, 616, 630–37)

The gradual identification of Bacchus with the sin of gluttony and lust reveals that Milton, spurred on, I think, by Spenser's powerful amalgamations, allows gluttony in particular to take over the figures that represent it. The myths which were understood by Spenser as emblematic and allegorical, and by Milton at first as symbolically true and historically useful, disappear in his blazing vision of the war between God and Satan. Thus it is Sin and Death, not Circe and Bacchus, whom Satan encounters and Satan, not Tantalus, who is sealed in the jaws of hell. What begins before Spenser as a moral emblem of greed becomes in *Paradise Lost* part of the apocalypse. In this last powerful vision, Bacchus and all the classical myths, perhaps, as well as their Renaissance formulations, pale into shadows and vanish. It may be, therefore, that Milton, who seems to have set out consciously to extend the first three books of *The Faerie Queene* in the writing of his *Mask*, concludes by repudiating the means if not the ends of his best teacher along with *A Mask* that may have been so carefully wrought to crown Spenser's labors. For the sense of moral and artistic achievement as well as the vision of the fulfillment of "Pure and vnspotted" love (III, vi, 3) at *A Mask*'s end are qualified, if not thwarted, by Satan's temptation in the only real garden and by the vision of Adam and Eve driven out of that newly fallen garden into a wilderness larger than the forest in which Comus dwelt, to take up, "with wand'ring steps and slow," "their solitary way." But Adam and Eve are also promised that their way can lead them to a "paradise within" and their punishment, death, to the "gate of life" through the redemptive acts of the "true vine," Christ, "temperance invincible," who will bring man the sacramental cup all others parody.[33]

University of Illinois at Urbana-Champaign

NOTES

1. "The Parson's Tale," 836; "The Pardoner's Tale," 484, 481–82, in *The Complete Poetry and Prose of Geoffrey Chaucer*, ed. John H. Fisher (New York, 1977). A. C. Hamilton, in his edition of *The Faerie Queene* (London, 1980), quotes the Parson's line in his note to I, iv, 24, p. 69. *The Faerie Queene* is quoted throughout from this edition.

2. See Adolf Katzenellenbogen, *Allegories of the Virtues and Vices in Medieval Art* (1939; rpt. New York, 1964), p. 11; Morton W. Bloomfield, *The Seven Deadly Sins* (1952; rpt. Lansing, 1967), pp. 127, 230; and Rosemond Tuve, *Allegorical Imagery* (Princeton, 1966), pp. 104, 210–11, Appendix. *Comus, A Mask Presented at Ludlow Castle*, 740, 776, in *The Complete Poetical Works of John Milton*, ed. Douglas Bush (Boston, 1965). This edition is cited throughout as *A Mask*.

3. There may be a larger relationship between the emblem tradition and *The Faerie Queene*. The ordering of Andrea Alciati's emblems in his *Diverse Imprese* (Lione, 1549), for instance, like the ordering of the books of *The Faerie Queene*, seems to be indebted to medieval descriptions of the virtues and vices. Just as Spenser begins *The Faerie Queene* with the Book of Holiness, Alciati begins his *Imprese* with the image of God or true religion (p. 5). Alciati's third emblem is Feigned Religion ("Finta Religione"), wherein the scarlet whore rides her many-headed beast (p. 7). His fifth emblem shows man as a pilgrim on the strait way (p. 9). Only after Alciati constructs emblems which describe the virtues and vices does he, like Spenser later, turn to moral and social concerns.

4. For the association between Bacchus and ivy, see Giovanni Boccaccio, *Genealogie Deorum Gentilium*, ed. Vincenzo Romano (Bari, 1951), vol. I, p. 263; Natale Conti, "De Baccho," in *Mythologiae* (Venice, 1568), V, xiii, fol. 149. In his *Imprese*, p. 64, Alciati's emblem "Gola," the gullet or Gluttony, describes the medieval clothed Gluttony, not Bacchus. In Alciati's emblem, "On the statue of Bacchus," p. 26, although Bacchus is a fat youth, surrounded by vines, grapes, and his cup, he is not related to gluttony.

5. Geoffrey Whitney, *A Choice of Emblemes* (Leyden, 1586), p. 187. All subsequent references to Whitney are cited in the text by page number. Spenser may have known other identifications of Bacchus with Gluttony: Christine de Pisan, *The Epistle of Othea to Hector or the Boke of Knyghthode* (ca. 1406), trans. Stephen Scrope (from the French, ca. 1450), ed. George F. Warner (London, 1904), pp. 34–35, said: "Be the god Bachus we may vndirstond the synne off glotenye." Stephen Bateman (Batman), in *A Christall Glasse of Christian Reformation* (1569), Sig. Fii, includes a woodcut showing Bacchus on a bear preceded by two male figures signifying "excesse."

6. Johannes Sambucus, "Voluptatis triumphus" in *Emblemata* (Antwerp, 1566), pp. 148–49, and "Amicitia" in "Epigrammata," p. 269. Hadrianus Junius, *Emblemata* (Antwerp, 1565), emblema LII, p. 58: "Venter, pluma, Venus laudem fugienda sequenti." Guillaume de La Perrière, in *Le Theatre Des Bons Engins* (Lyon, 1583), embleme II, says "Que Vin & Femme, attrappent le plus sage," and shows a naked Venus and a vineclad Bacchus throwing a net over a fallen Minerva. Unless otherwise noted, all translations are mine.

7. In the Middle Ages, chastity, most often represented as virginity, opposed and conquered lust in the battle between the virtues and vices. See, for instance, Katzenellenbogen, Appendix, p. 82 n. 2; p. 83 n. 1. He also quotes Julianus Pomerius, p. 55, who said of water that "Ignem libidinosae voluptatis extinguit." This idea was commonplace in the emblem books. Alciati, for instance, in the subscription to Emblem XXIIII, "Prudentes vino abstinent," *Emblemata*, p. 112, says "*virgo fugit Bromium.*" (Mignault notes, in *Omnia Andreae Alciati Emblemata* (Antwerp, 1581) p. 114, that Bromius is another name for Bacchus.) See Tuve, *Allegorical Imagery*, pp. 184 and 368 n. 23 as well as her Appendix, "The Virtues and Vices." For a different view of these passages in *The Faerie Queene* see Carol V. Kaske, "The Bacchus Who Wouldn't Wash: *Faerie Queene* II.i–ii," *Renaissance Quarterly*, XXIX (1976), 195–209.

8. "De Genio," in *Mythologiae*, IV, iii, fol. 92^v. See also Lilio Gregorio Giraldi, "Genivs," in *De Deis Gentium* (Basel, 1548), p. 599.

9. Vincenzo Cartari, *Le Imagini de i Dei de gli Antichi* (Venice, 1580), pp. 414–15. All mythographers described the young, handsome Bacchus. See Boccaccio, Vol. I, V, xxv, p. 263: "Tu puer eternus et formosissimus." Also, see p. 268. See also Conti, V, xiii, fol. 148; *Fulgentius the Mythographer*, trans. Leslie George Whitbread (Columbus, 1971), p. 77; Ovid, *Metamorphoses*, Book IV, 11–30, trans. Frank J. Miller, 2nd ed. (1921; rpt. Cambridge, Mass., 1946), vol. I, pp. 178–81. Among the mythographers, however, only Cartari relates Comus, Priapus, the Lari, Genius, and Osiris with Bacchus.

10. Conti, fol. 149. See also Cartari, pp. 423, 426.

11. That Bacchus is a god of generation was commonplace. Giraldi, p. 389 and Cartari, p. 436, associated Bacchus with the sun and its generative powers. See also Conti, "De Baccho," V, xiii, fol. 156. All associated Bacchus with both the phallus and Priapus and thus with human generation. See Conti, V, xiii, fol. 153: "Alii phallum ideo consecratum Dionysio putarunt, quia sit autor creditus generationis." See also Cartari, pp. 418–19, 436–42, and Giraldi, pp. 390–91.

12. *Emblemata*, emblema LXXXIIII, pp. 311–12. John Holloway connects Tantalus with Gluttony in "The Seven Deadly Sins in *The Faerie Queene*, Book II," *RES*, no. 3 (1952), 13–18. But see also Robert C. Fox, "Temperance and the Seven Deadly Sins in *The Faerie Queene*, Book II," *RES*, no. 12 (1961) 1–6.

13. See A. C. Hamilton's note to III, ix, 30–31, p. 388, and James Nohrnberg, *The Analogy of The Faerie Queene* (Princeton, 1976), pp. 602–03.

14. See Thomas P. Roche, Jr., *The Kindly Flame* (Princeton, 1964), pp. 81–82.

15. Spenser also said in "The Teares of the Muses" that Bacchus was only a man, but Calliope claims euhemeristically that she deified him: *"Bacchus* and *Hercules* I raised to heauen, / And *Charlemaine*, amongst the Starris seauen" (460–62). *The Minor Poems, Part Two*, in *The Works of Edmund Spenser, A Variorum Edition*, ed. Charles G. Osgood, et al. 11 vols. (Baltimore, 1947), vol. VIII, p. 75.

16. *Fulgentius the Mythographer*, p. 77; Boccaccio, vol. I, p. 266; Giraldi, p. 374; Conti, V, xiii, fol. 151.

17. Plutarch, *De Iside et Osiride*, ed. and trans. J. Gwyn Griffiths (Cambridge, 1970), chapters 25, 27; Giraldi, p. 389; Conti, V, xiii, fol. 150; Cartari, p. 435. A. Kent Hieatt, in *Chaucer, Spenser, Milton: Mythopoetic Continuities and Transformations* (Montreal, 1975), p. 141, emphasizes the identification of Bacchus and Osiris. See also Nohrnberg, p. 374.

18. Alastair Fowler, *Spenser and the Numbers of Time* (New York, 1964), p. 213.

19. A. Kent Hieatt, *Chaucer, Spenser, Milton*, pp. 138–45, reproduces Cartari's illustration of Typhon, summarizes the Typhon-Osiris story, and discusses it in the light of the union of Britomart and Artegal in the Temple of Isis.

20. Ibid., pp. 157–60, although he does not link Cartari's images of Bacchus and Comus to Spenser's false Genius.

21. Tuve, Appendix, 6, 7; p. 101.

22. *Ben Jonson*, ed. C. H. Herford, Percy and Evelyn Simpson (1950; rpt. Oxford, 1961), vol. X, pp. 582, 585. Stephen Orgel in *The Jonsonian Masque* (Cambridge, Mass., 1965), pp. 153–57, notes the difference between Cartari's and Philostratus's descriptions of Comus and that of Jonson.

23. Orgel, p. 155, quotes Blaise de Vigenère's French adaptation of Philostratus (1614), which seems relevant to Milton's *Mask:* "Tout ainsi fait Comus à celui là qu'il aime: / Car il se perd en fin dedans les voluptez." A. Kent Hieatt, p. 191, notes a similar effect between what "Amavia says of her husband's situation on Acrasia's island" and the servants of Milton's Comus *(A Mask*, 73–74). See also *A Mask*, 256–61. For the many other literary antecedents of Comus's palace see *A Variorum Commentary on The Poems of John Milton*, ed. A. S. P. Woodhouse and Douglas Bush (New York, 1972), vol. II, part 3, pp. 755–73 and notes to the relevant passages, especially those on pp. 880–81, 939–40.

24. Spenser distances his figures by placing them in "the antique world" (V, proem, 1), which is in Book I the world of the Captivity, although Book I also prefigures the world after the Incarnation. Later books bring the narrative allegorically closer to Spenser's present world, but the narrative does not enter it directly. Milton, however, seems to place his figures in the world after the Incarnation and concludes his narrative in the present.

25. For specific antecedents of Milton's description of the fall of the pagan gods in *On the Morning of Christ's Nativity*, see notes to lines 168–228 in *A Variorum Commentary on the Poems of John Milton*, vol. II, part 1, pp. 94–106. On the movement of the old dragon and Lucifera down to the underworld where Mammon and Philotime are housed, see my article, "From Errour to Acrasia," *The Huntington Library Quarterly*, XLI, no. 3 (1978), 190–92. The meaning of the fallen gods is illuminated by *Paradise Lost* I, 476–82, and their fall reiterated in *Paradise Regained* 455–64. Balachandra Rajan, *The Lofty Rhyme* (Florida, 1970), pp. 20–22, discusses the relationship between the fallen gods in the ode and those in *Paradise Lost*.

26. Philostratus, *Imagines*, trans. Arthur Fairbanks (Cambridge, Mass., 1931; rpt. 1960), p. 9. For a synopsis of discussions about the antecedents of Milton's Comus, see *A Variorium Commentary on the Poems of John Milton*, vol. II, part 3, pp. 768–73, 775–76, notes to lines 50–56, p. 864; lines 56–57, pp. 865–66; and John Arthos, *On A Mask*

Presented at Ludlow-Castle (Ann Arbor, 1954), p. 42. Armand Himy, "Bacchus et Comus" in *Etudes Anglaises*, XXVII, no. 4 (1974), 436–49, looks at Bacchus's classical sources. He does not believe that Comus is demonic: "Comus est esprit de la terre ou des bois" (443). Alice-Lyle Scoufos in "The Mysteries in Milton's *Masque*," *Milton Studies*, VI, ed. James D. Simmonds (Pittsburgh, 1975), pp. 128–29, considers Comus in the light of the antichrist tradition. Karl P. Wentersdorf in "The 'Rout of Monsters' in *Comus*," *MQ*, XII, no. 4 (1978), 119–25, discusses classical and Renaissance antecedents of Comus's followers.

    27. For various interpretations of the gods in the attendant Spirit's opening lines, see *A Variorum Commentary on The Poems of John Milton*, vol. II, part 3, pp. 854–62. On the elevation of the gods, compare Spenser's description of "*Ioues* faire Palace, fixt in heauens hight" VII, vi, 15; also VII, vi, 19).

    28. Angus Fletcher, *The Transcendental Masque* (Ithaca, 1971), p. 165, says that "Comus will become the enemy of humanizing change . . . as Mutabilitie . . . would, by her triumph, have destroyed her own principle of being." Balachandra Rajan in *The Lofty Rhyme*, p. 39, says that "grace and nature ultimately act in unison."

    29. See Peter M. Daly, *Literature in the Light of the Emblem* (Toronto, 1979), pp. 149–53, 162–67.

    30. Rajan, p. 36.

    31. Samuel Johnson, *Lives*, quoted in *A Variorum Commentary on The Poems of John Milton*, vol. II, part 3, p. 785. For synopses of some of the literary echoes in Comus's speech, see pp. 940–49.

    32. Lawes insists upon identifying his actual role as teacher in the Egerton household with his double, even triple, role within *A Mask* as shepherd, musician, and demon when, in the epistle to "*John, Lord Viscount Brackley*" preceding *A Mask*, he refers to himself as "*your* attendant Thyrsis" (my italics), p. 113. In *Il Penseroso*, Milton urges similar correspondences between the growth of the ability to hear "the Muses in a ring / Aye round about Jove's altar sing" and the ascent to Platonic knowledge of "The immortal mind that hath forsook / Her mansion in this fleshly nook" (48–49; 89–92). See Notes to *Il Penseroso*, in *A Variorum Commentary of The Poems of John Milton*, vol. 2, part 1, pp. 317–19, 324–26. See Franklin R. Baruch on the relationship between actual and masquing roles in "Milton's *Comus*: Skill, Virtue, and Henry Lawes," *Milton Studies*, ed. James D. Simmonds (Pittsburgh, 1973), p. 290. On the relationships among music, philosophy, and the attendant Spirit in *A Mask* see Louis L. Martz, *Poet of Exile: A Study of Milton's Poetry* (New Haven, 1980), p. 6.

    33. *Paradise Lost* XII, 571–87; John xv, 1; *Paradise Regained* II, 408, 378–86. Contrast *Paradise Regained* II, 350–53.

DEFERENCE AND SILENCE:
MILTON'S NATIVITY ODE

Gregory F. Goekjian

*O*DE ON *the Morning of Christ's Nativity* is awkward for critics. It is usually considered Milton's first great poem, because it shares with his later masterpieces many of the features that make them great: it treats a Christian subject through both classical and Christian images; it makes the powerful "noise" Eliot has taught us to expect from Milton; it is in English. Yet it is often judged rough, abrupt, and irregular, and, perhaps most damagingly, it presents a fleshless Incarnation where readers would be more comfortable with the potential human warmth of the Nativity. Even though Stanley Fish has taught us that reader comfort is rarely a concern of Milton's, we have not yet learned to read Milton with even theoretical equanimity.[1] All of the poems have their problems: *Paradise Lost* is plagued by a God who is cold, indifferent, and obviously inhuman; *Paradise Regained* is made plotless and slow-moving by a passive Christ; *Samson Agonistes* is an exercise in painful repetition. But the Nativity ode is in some ways even more difficult, because it at once combines these problems and links them less firmly to a scriptural text than do the later works. Critics seem to think this poem should be more naive and simpler than the later poems, truer to their own trinitarian religious beliefs or to their unitary critical preconceptions.

Considerable critical effort has been spent in trying to naturalize, or, perhaps, to domesticate this poem, to find order in its apparent disorder, to Christianize its pagan imagery, and to make sense of its shifts in tense and time, but it remains a poem of extremes, and it is difficult to tell from moment to moment where Milton stands in relation to his subject or, in fact, where we do.[2] Yet this problem is certainly ours and not Milton's. In reading the Nativity ode our desire, like the desire expressed in the ode itself, is for a secure authority that will allow us to read or to write in confidence. But for all of the apparent confidence in Milton's work, authority is always a problem, for Milton's choice of a scriptural model for his Christian poems always leaves the authority of the poet in doubt. In the Nativity ode, Milton asks a question that will enter all of his poems: how does the human, and especially the po-

etic, logos function within the context of the logos of God? This question, I think, never reaches a firm answer, and, indeed, in the later works
the resolution is precisely that there can be no firm conclusions after the
Fall, but it is just this problem that leads critics as diverse as T. S. Eliot,
Christopher Ricks, and J. B. Broadbent to find Milton's poetry less satis-
factory, more "external" than the work of other great poets.[3]

Although Milton can claim in his *Apology* that there is a "plain authority of Scripture," for the poet authority is never so clear. In the late
poems, the masks of drama and epic, like the political and social mi-
lieu of the prose tracts, provide conventional models for the "great argument" that is Milton's goal, but in the early Christian lyrics Milton's
self-consciousness about his authorial role is apparent. The tenuousness
of the boundary between heavenly authority and human is, of course,
a problem faced not only by poets but by all thinkers of the seventeenth
century, but Milton's struggle to resolve the problem is always evident
in his poems.[4] In fact, I believe that the struggle is characteristic of all
of Milton's religious poetry.

Renaissance awareness of the problem of the author in a Christian
universe is amply recorded in Sir Philip Sidney's *Apology for Poetry*,
wherein Sidney's distinction among three kinds of poets is a direct attempt to find a place for poetic authority. Poets are divine, philosophical, or "right," and their authority is limited according to subject. The
divine poet is to imitate the "inconceivable excellencies of God," but the
only examples Sidney can find are scriptural, or those like "Orpheus, Am-
phion, Homer in his *Hymns*," who imitate God, but in "full wrong divinity."[5] Next come the philosophical poets whose work is only disputably
poetic, because it is "wrapped within the fold of its own subject." Both
of these types are limited by the subject under study — God or man. Only
the "right" poet, bounded solely by the "zodiac of his own wit," is free
of the constraints of subject and even truth, for he "nothing affirms" and
therefore can never lie.

Sidney's poetic authority gives up truth as subject, substituting for
it the affirmation of "nothing." Neither the divine nor the philosophical
poet is really an author, since what the divine poet imitates is "inconceivable," and the philosophical poet's work is already wrapped and folded
before he treats it. Both may be true, but their truth is limited before
they are made poetic. The "right" poet chooses affirmation over truth,
thereby altering the subject to bring it into line with the possibilities of
human authority.

Yet none of these categories will serve Milton, for though his subject
is true in both the divine and human senses, the poem must still be au-

thored, and for Milton the Incarnation becomes something of an analogue to what the "divine" poet does; for though the Christian poet's word must be God's word, his words must also be his own, and Milton's struggle with this problem, manifested in the Nativity ode in abrupt changes in subject and direction, accounts for both the poem's strength and for the uneasiness of its critics.

II

Recent critics of the ode have suggested that its structure may be more deliberate and subtle than was previously believed.[6] If the poem halts and turns abruptly, the sudden changes in direction and focus may well reflect a deliberate self-subversion on the part of the poet, who strategically halts each movement he creates, intending the poem's structure to be analogous to its subject. A particularly important example of this process is the beginning of stanza xvi where, following four stanzas of speculation on the music of the spheres to follow the Last Judgment, the poem suddenly stops: "But wisest Fate says no, / This must not yet be so."[7] Nearly all of the ode's critics find a significant break in structure here, a major shift in direction and a movement away from continuity.[8] Yet this is not a unique or even particularly surprising moment in the poem; rather, it is the culmination and solidification of a series of such moments that mark the structure throughout. In his study of "Milton's Light-Harnessed Ode," Paul Fry summarizes the effect of the structural pattern in terms of imagery:

In each new figural shift, the expansive freedom of light and "unexpressive" harmony is replaced by enclosure in some wished-for or involuntarily inherited prisonhouse. That is, the ode keeps describing the disappearance of full presence into embodiment. This is hardly surprising on the anniversary of the Incarnation, but the steady repetition of that sacred figural descent at every level of experience is almost compulsive.[9]

But the figures Milton introduces are never simply enclosed, and if the poet is compulsive, he is compelled by the need to assert God's authority through his own. At every turn expectations created by the poem are diminished and cast out, until all that is left is the simple presence of Christ attended by the "Bright-harness'd Angels" of his future and our present. Displacement and cancellation are the order of Milton's day. At the outset of "The Hymn," Nature's fear and guilt are obviated by Peace. The "amaze" of the stars is obliterated and dismissed by "their Lord," and "The Sun himself withheld his wonted speed" in deference to Christ, the "greater Sun" (i–vii). The chatter of the shepherds is stilled and replaced by heavenly music, but such music, like the speculation about a return to the golden age it leads to, "must not yet be so." The oracles and false gods of paganism are invoked only to be exposed and cast out.

The self-negation of this structure, in its constant repetition, may well reflect quite simply a distinct sense of hierarchy and order, including the inadequacy of man in contrast to God's power. The elements of nature and the inventions of man are invoked only to be overruled. If the human artifact that is the poem seems inadequate to the occasion, that fact itself affirms God's order, for even man's most valuable measure of the universe, time, proves insufficient over and over again. In the process of creation and dismissal, Milton contrasts the permanence of the mystery of the Incarnation and Nativity to the flux of man and nature which surrounds it. Repeatedly, Milton brings the "inconceivable" of the divine into contact with the conceived limits of human philosophy, but that contact is always brief and tenuous, for to unite the two would be to exert an authority beyond that granted to the Christian poet.[10]

Milton's deference to truth becomes obvious, I think, in his attitude toward truth's poetic substitute — not falsehood, but convention. Convention is a mediating device in the ode, but it is also used to extend the poet's power without coming into conflict with truth. In other words, Milton's extending of convention becomes the mark of a poetic authority that can potentially contain truth. The process is evident, I think, in Milton's treatment of the "Heav'nly Muse," conventional enough in religious poems, but pushed to an extreme here. When he addresses the muse, Milton does so only in terms of assertive rhetorical questions and poetic commands:

> Hast thou no verse, no hymn, or solemn strain,
> To welcome him to this his new abode,
> Now while the Heav'n by the Sun's team untrod,
>   Hath took no print of the approaching light,
> And all the spangled host keep watch in squadrons bright?
>
> See how from far upon the Eastern road
> The Star-led Wizards haste with odors sweet:
> O run, prevent them with thy humble ode,
> And lay it lowly at his blessed feet;
> Have thou the honor first, thy lord to greet.   (17–26)

In his use of the muse, Milton asserts his authority even while denying it. As Fry has noted, there is a hectoring tone to Milton's invocation, in sharp contrast to the brief, simple, "voiceless" presentation of the Nativity scene to follow.[11] Milton's conscious use of the muse as convention, as poetic fiction under his direction, allows him to exert control over the poem without infringing on its truth. In a sense, the muse becomes the kind of "true ornament" (unlike rhyme in *Paradise Lost*, which is "no true ornament") that justifies the voice of the poet in a universe of divine making. The muse is itself a metaphor for authority, but it is a metaphor that is under the control of the poet who uses it.

Less obvious than Milton's manipulation of the muse is his use of a plural speaker: "we" at the outset refers to Christian mankind, but the attribution of the "humble ode" to the muse in the last stanza of the proem complicates the issue. When the voice of the muse is joined "unto the Angel Choir" (27), the reference of "we" in "The Hymn" seems to be set: it refers to muse and choir together. But as "The Hymn" progresses, it becomes increasingly clear that the plural subject has returned to collective humanity: "Ring out ye Crystal spheres, / Once bless our human ears" (125–26). By the end of the poem a reference to "our tedious Song" (239) seems to include poet as well as muse and angel choir. Given these changes, one finds that the reference is always somewhat ambiguous, even though it seems so carefully determined at the beginning of the poem. Through use of a plural speaking subject, Milton subverts any possibility of distinction between the angelic, divine voice and his own, even while he seems to make this distinction clear.

Milton's treatment of time in the ode has led to the most interesting critical discussions of the poem as well as to the greatest discomfort of its readers. The ode's time does not progress with the linear predictability of human history, but through shifts in tense seems to include present, past, and future in an irregular pattern, and sometimes simultaneously. The first line of the poem refers to *this* month and *this* morn, indicating both calendrical time (this *is* the month Christ *was* born) and the moment of the poem's composition. By the end of the poem, the ambiguity is stretched to include the historical moment of Christ's birth as well: "But see! the Virgin blest, / Hath laid her Babe to rest. / Time is our tedious Song should here have ending" (237–39).

Lowry Nelson, Jr., in an argument for the poem's baroque roots, sees in the mix of tenses a meaningful confusion of the reader's time sense which is necessary to the creation of a "momentaneous present," accounting for the poem's immediate treatment of a past event.[12] Nelson implies that the reader is brought to see what the poet sees because of the temporal confusion. If we accept Nelson's reading, we accept a paradox (which is really Nelson's sense of the baroque): the treatment of time creates the impression of immediacy through overt mediation, making time meaningful in divine terms because we experience its meaninglessness in

the human terms of the poem. Edward W. Tayler's argument for a typological reading of the poem creates a solid theoretical basis for the temporal developments suggested by Nelson. In fact, Tayler finds that "all
the elements of the poem — tenses, imagery, structure — seem calculated
to effect one end: defining the eternal significance of an occurrence in
time, measuring its meaning in respect to the past and future of scriptural history, seeing the event as a 'shadowy Type' to be fulfilled according to the decree of Eternal Providence."[13] Tayler's discussion of the poem
is particularly provocative because it implies a real difference between
typological reading and conscious typological writing — the use of typology
as a device for the expression of a historical truth. In Milton's case, as
Tayler notes, typological writing is not used consistently: "Milton ap-
proached the theological events of the Circumcision and Nativity by placing them in Time and relating them to Eternity. Instead of following this
method in *The Passion* Milton attempts a variety of other techniques, none
of which was to emerge as an important element of his mature style"
(p. 33).

As Tayler suggests, the conscious conflation or confusion of present,
past, and future may well be an element of Miltonic style rather than
the result of a working historical theory or a system of belief. Yet clearly,
especially in the early poems, Milton's use of time indicates a critical experimentation, and that experimentation suggests a struggle with his scriptural text. Typology, after all, is a critical system and not a creative one,
and even as Milton uses it his eye seems fixed more closely on the text
from which he works than on the one he produces. The indeterminacy
of Milton's treatment of time in the Nativity ode is just what allows
"This . . . month and this . . . happy morn" to participate in the context of the Scripture from which it is born. Writing typologically is for
Milton a means to embrace Scripture while escaping its bonds.

The same, in fact, may be said for the ode's treatment of place. It
begins in a heavenly atmosphere, moves to a conventionally wintry scene
representing the birthplace of Christ — a scene more English, certainly,
than Middle Eastern — examines the various locations of the false gods
and oracles, and returns to the manger scene at the end. Throughout the
poem, visual perspective shifts as radically as time, vacillating between
the universality of "Light unsufferable" in stanza ii and the specific con-
cretion of the shepherds "in a rustic row" in stanza viii. The poem's place
will not be fixed any more firmly than its time, yet its still "center" is
surely the manger scene with which it ends. But even this point is complicated by the odd juncture of time and space in the last stanza: "Time
is our tedious Song should here have ending" (239). Milton asserts the

poet's prerogative — to stop — even while he focuses the reader's thoughts on the brief scriptural account from which the poem emerged. It is not only time for the song to end: we are told that "Time" is "here," in the text, and the text is what makes time perceivable at all.

In the Nativity ode the conventions of poetry are extended considerably, and I suggest that this is because Milton is searching for a reasonable ground for his poetic authority. The conventions I have discussed — muse, speaker, and spatio-temporal limits — all share the problems of discontinuity, undecidability, and inconclusiveness. Usually such qualities would simply indicate an ill-executed or, perhaps, too ambitious poem ("beyond the years he had when he wrote it"). But here Milton is careful to point out the "problems," and in fact does not seem to see them as problems at all. Rather, they are the poem's structure, proclaiming conventionality while demonstrating the necessity of aconventionality. Even Milton's choice of a form, the Pindaric ode, echoes this process. The "controlled asymmetry" of Pindar's verse, with its leaps in time and space, shares a good deal with Milton's "humble ode," and Milton's use of the muse seems as well to owe something to Pindar's treatment.[14] But I suspect that the greatest attraction of the ode form was, for Milton, its lack of firm definition. The ode's complexity, wherein apparent disorder is the instrument of order's creation, is a perfect vehicle for the paradox of the Incarnation.

III

The four-stanza proem opens the play with muse, speaker, and perspective at once. The first two stanzas describe *this* (month and morn) and *that* (glorious form, light unsufferable, blaze of majesty), moving from time to space through apparently parallel deictics. Both are left nonspecific, signifying ambiguously the here and now as well as the then and there. The universal "Our" and "us" of stanzas i and ii are complicated by the discovery of direct address to the muse in stanza iii, allowing further uncertainties about the previous stanzas. In stanza iii, the pronouns *this* and *that*, which have carried so much of the weight of the introductory setting, come together in the emphatic "this" of "this his new abode" (18), putting place into question as well as time. The point is not that a poem must always have a specifiable perspective, but that this poem does not have one and points out that fact so clearly. And it is in this context of uncertainty that the poem's controlling project is announced: "Say, Heav'nly Muse, shall not thy sacred vein / Afford a present to the Infant God?" (15–16).

The muse is asked to "afford a present" in a characteristically double-edged way, for in one sense the reference is simply to a Christmas present. Implicitly the present is gold, the most precious of the traditional gifts, and Milton underscores this by linking the gift to the "sacred vein" of poetry as well as by stressing the gift's competition with the light of the sun. The gold of the sun, like that of the "Star-led Wizards," must be prevented (anticipated), and in fact the wizards in the poem bear only "odors sweet" (23). Yet this present, the gold whose age "Time will run back and fetch" later in the poem, is left uncounted, for there is a more important present: the verbal present of the ode which Christ's infancy, his speechlessness, prevents. The "sacred vein" of the muse both contains the present and is contained by it, and what is to be afforded — brought toward completion — is God's word itself through the poem's presentation of Christ's Incarnation.

That the present Milton has in mind includes verbal presence seems inescapable: again and again Milton stresses Christ's infancy, and it is precisely the voicelessness of his authority that makes poetic authority possible here. Milton's gift is to make present to mankind the mystery of the silent glory of the newborn Christ. Yet even as he seems to make this claim, Milton backs away from it in the assertion that the gift is *to* Christ and not *of* Him. In the proem, each assertion of authority is balanced by a counterassertion, and at the proem's end Milton takes yet a further step back from the claim of "invention," stressing once again not only the voice of the muse, but its enclosure in the collectivity of the angel choir of God.

In the confusion of counterclaims, Milton effectively reserves for himself the privileges of the inventor as well as the protections of the imitator. He successfully claims the conflicting rights of all of Sidney's poets — divine, philosophical, and "right" — at once, and he does so through the vehicle of rhetoric. The muse, after all, is a rhetorical device, and Milton's address is composed of rhetorical questions, all of which lead to the undecidability of the text's authority. For Milton's muse is more than an authoritative convention, a mediator for the poet's thoughts. "Hast thou no verse?" is never a simple question in a poem, and in this one it is precisely the question of authority the poem opens in the context of Christ's infant silence. The question Milton asks is both rhetorical and grammatical, a version of the problem Paul de Man explores in "Semiology and Rhetoric" as he discusses Yeats's *Among School Children*. The questions Yeats poses at the end of that poem, culminating in "How can we know the dancer from the dance?" are, for de Man, "in direct confrontation,"

for the one reading is precisely the error denounced by the other and has to be undone by it. Nor can we in any way make a valid decision as to which of the readings can be given priority over the other; neither can exist in the other's absence. There can be no dance without a dancer, no sign without a referent. On the other hand, the authority of the meaning engendered by the grammatical structure is fully obscured by the duplicity of the figure that cries out for the differentiation that it conceals.[15]

Milton's "Hast thou no Hymn?" appeals precisely to the conflict between human rhetoric (the hymn *is* the Nativity ode) and the grammar of Truth, the preexisting text of the Nativity and the Incarnation. The conflict de Man points out is, of course, the stuff of poetry, but for Milton the conflict represents a more difficult question than the ontological one in de Man's argument: God's grammar is always complicated by the rhetoric of the poet, and the authority of the poetic, fallen word is what makes possible an understanding of the word of God. Yet as poetic authority makes that word available, it obscures and falsifies it, imitating its presence as a mimetic construct. Even the mediation of the muse, that classical link (and barrier) between truth and inspiration, is not enough for Milton, for the Christian poet must question the signifying muse just as he questions the signified poem. The "authority of meaning" is never, for Milton, a simple authority, and the ode will never try to claim it.

Many critics have, of course, confronted this problem, and their solutions to it are often, simply, their readings of the poem. Perhaps the most successful have been the readings fostered by Rosemond Tuve's observation that "this poem's subject is the Incarnation, not the Nativity; that is to say, Christ's Nativity is presented as an event only insofar as that fact enters into its presentation as mystery."[16] Tuve's privileging of mystery over event here is precisely the recognition of the conflict between authorities, and the deference to the unknowable authority of God, but it is clear that for Milton the event, as all that we can know, is important too. In fact, the event is the poem's only source. Without the question of authority, I think, the Nativity ode makes little sense, for it is a question that appears not only in Milton's "technique" or his "style," but also in the poem's eventual subject.

The four-stanza proem is not so much an introduction to "The Hymn" as it is a delineation and exorcism of barriers to its production. Much like the openings of *L'Allegro* and *Il Penseroso*, it casts off oppositions inherent in convention and perspective, and it admits the oppositions of authority. This is a move necessary to Milton, for what he will do with the poem is as unconventional as it is common: the ode will "prevent" the imprint of nature's light by "presenting" the mystery of divine light through speech, the word made flesh, in the medium of poetry.

The stanza of the hymn is very complex, much more so than a

"humble Ode" would seem to require. It matches rhyme to measure for six lines (rhymes bind three-foot to three-foot and five-foot to five-foot lines), and the last rhyme pairs a tetrameter to a hexameter. This last, "irregular" pair is what gives the stanza it strangeness and its force, for the pairing of tetrameter and hexameter equals rhythmically the preceding pentameter couplets, and the hexameter itself parallels the rhythm of the trimeter couplets:

> It was the Winter wild
> While the Heav'n-born child,
>   All meanly wrapt in the rude manger lies;
> Nature in awe to him
> Had doff't her gaudy trim,
>   With her great Master so to sympathize:
> It was no season then for her
> To wanton with the Sun, her lusty Paramour.   (31–36)

The alliteration, assonance and consonance of this first stanza, coupled with the rhythmic play already mentioned, offer an impressively showy technical display, especially considering what the stanza says, for what the full-dress form expresses is the mean wrappings in the rude manger and the stripping of Nature's gaud.[17] Sound is no echo to the sense here until we discover that the contradiction between form and content is a striking echo of the paradox it prepares for: the glory of the Incarnation in the simplicity of the Nativity.

"The Hymn" fulfills the promise of the proem. The manipulation of time, place, and generic conventions begins immediately, and the direct expression (though plural) of a "present" event becomes a narrative apparently fixed in history. The history suggested is human, not divine, for not only are we presented with the familiar wintry scene, but even nature and the sun are personified, a humanization emphasized by the fleshly suggestion of "gaudy trim," "wanton," and particularly "Paramour." This is a long way from the heavenly, fleshless setting of the proem, and the leap seems to aim toward event rather than mystery, yet as we proceed beyond the first stanza of "The Hymn," we discover that all of the particularity of human and natural event is presented negatively. The poem's eventual content, the Nativity, is static, reflecting the straightforward brevity of its sources in Scripture. Nature's "great Master" is Milton's, and He has already dictated the event. What Milton can do is make the paradoxical mystery of the event evident and present in the poem, but he must constrain himself to human agency in order to do so without appearing to challenge the authority of God.

The first seventeen stanzas of the poem follow, in different ways, the course set in motion by the first stanza. An impressive play of sound is used to set forth a rather conventional array of events, even though their subject is not sense, but absence. In the first seven stanzas sound, like the light that surrounds it, is created only to be dismissed. The "speeches fair" of Nature, with which she "woos the gentle Air," are struck silent by a wave of the myrtle wand of Peace. Nature is "Confounded" by "her Maker's eyes" in her attempt to cover "her foul deformities," and Peace, who brings silence, is herself characterized by silence: "The Trumpet spake not." The winds are stilled, the ocean "hath quite forgot to rave," and "The Stars . . . stand fixt,"

> Bending one way their precious influence,
> And will not take their flight,
> For all the morning light,
> Or *Lucifer* that often warned them thence;
> But in their glimmering Orbs did glow,
> Until their Lord himself bespake, and bid them go.   (71–76)

Stillness is the order of God, beyond the motion of nature's space and time as understood by man. It is immune to external influence, for whether Lucifer is a further personification of nature or Satan himself, he is powerless to give orders in God's universe. Only the speech of "their Lord himself," present in the poem as a speechless infant, will control the motion of the stars, of time and space. This extended, static moment is not only the moment of the Nativity, but that of the poem itself, the moment that "prevents" the sun. The mere human experience of the universe, of nature, of peace, and of the poem is put in its proper place, controlled by the "unsufferable" authority of God. The images of sight and sound, so various and differentiated, are unified in silent deference.

Following stanza vii, human interpretation of the universe is again presented, but this time it begins not with personification, but with persons. The chatter of the shepherds (87), the only distinctly mortal figures in the poem, is presented as "simple," "silly," and "busy," terms which might well represent all human discourse. The chatter is silenced by the musical discourse of the angels, "Harping in loud and solemn choir, / With unexpressive notes to Heav'n's new-born Heir" (115–16). Unlike the speech of the shepherds, whose discourse is characteristically human ("Perhaps their loves, or else their sheep"), the song of the angels is "unexpressive," inexpressible by man, but also uninterpretable. Whereas human beings must differentiate, the music of heaven is undifferentiated, whole, and all-encompassing. Yet it is at just this point that the poem's discourse, the man-made artifact, builds to its own verbal crescendo:

> Ring out ye Crystal spheres,
> Once bless our human ears,
>   (If ye have power to touch our senses so)
> And let your silver chime
> Move in melodious time;
>   And let the Bass of Heav'n's deep Organ blow,
> And with your ninefold harmony
> Make up full consort to th'Angelic symphony.   (125–32)

Here Milton has not only invoked the music of the spheres, but he has reproduced it as well. This is a risky move for the poet, for he has himself "invented" "Such Music (as 'tis said) / Before was never made, / But when of old the sons of morning sung" (118–20). Music, that of the poem and that which the poem represents, is potentially dangerous, "Dead things with inbreath'd sense able to pierce."[18] Milton's mimesis of the divine music here is accompanied by a stream of parenthetical qualifications and specifications, preserving a clear division between the human and the divine even in their conjunction. The message is clear enough: human authority is limited.

And it is at just this moment that Milton chooses to point out the danger of human interpretation and the ease with which the human mind can conceive of overstepping its bounds:

> For if such holy Song
> Enwrap our fancy long,
>   Time will run back and fetch the age of gold,
> And speckl'd vanity
> Will sicken soon and die,
>   And leprous sin will melt from earthly mold,
> And Hell itself will pass away,
> And leave her dolorous mansions to the peering day.   (133–40)

A speculative solution, an end to the sins of the world, is just the kind of error implied in human thought throughout the poem. The simplicity of the Nativity leads the human mind to jump to an oversimple interpretation of its cause. "Time will run back" is simply a reshuffling of human history, not a recognition of the power of the divine order. The poem's soaring movement suddenly stops: "But wisest Fate says no, / This must not yet be so, / The Babe lies yet in smiling Infancy" (150–52). Milton recalls his own speculation, a speculation made collectively human through the plural subject of "our fancy." Time will not "run back" until

Christ glorifies "himself and us" (154) and the Last Judgment has been pronounced (xvii). Yet the speculation of the poet includes more than a vain desire for heaven on earth. The poet's own invention, the poem itself, expressing as it does the "unexpressive notes" of the angelic choir, must be included in what "must not yet be so." In a way made understandable by the proem, "This" has reference beyond its immediate implications. "Wisest Fate says no" to more than the reversal of human history and the return of the Golden Age. The opening of heaven is linked in contingency to all that Milton has invented in the poem: the descent of truth and justice, the passing of hell, and the music of the spheres. Human fancy, enwrapped by the "holy Song" Milton has reproduced, is easily misled, and the decree of fate calls into question and finally suggests that we dismiss all that the poet has invented.

The entire Nativity ode has prepared us for this moment. In Milton, human authority is always that which is not. Fate's decree against the return of the Golden Age is based on the fact that such a reversal of human history is simply ahistorical: human experience cannot be changed until Christ has suffered and the Last Judgment come. The decree against Milton's song is equally logical: the voice which can truly sing the mystery "lies yet in smiling Infancy." Even when enwrapped in holy song, human fancy is no match for Christ's infancy. Milton's effacement of his own voice in favor of the speechless infant is a reification of the voice of God. Like human time, human utterance defers to the divine in the process of vocalization. Just as the chatter of the shepherds is overpowered by the "unexpressive notes" of the angels, the poet's voice must defer to the voice of higher authority, no matter how silent it may be.

And silence is precisely the subject of the poem's final section. The cessation of the oracles is, after all, what the poem has presented all along. Here Milton ceases his play with time, perspective, and speaker in a forthright description of the silence of false authority: "The Oracles are dumb, / No voice or hideous hum / Runs through the arched roof in words deceiving" (173–75). Voices of weeping and sighing accompany the departure of the genius (xx); moan and plaint, "a drear and dying sound / Affrights the *Flamens* . . . while each particular power forgoes his wonted seat" (xxi). We discover absence in the making, but the construction again allows Milton the creation of poetry as powerful in its dissonance as was the music of the spheres in its harmony:

> *Peor* and *Baalim*
> Forsake their Temples dim,
>   With that twice battered god of Palestine,

And mooned *Ashtaroth*
Heav'n's Queen and Mother both,
　　Now sits not girt with Tapers' holy shine,
The Lybic *Hammon* shrinks his horn,
In vain the *Tyrian* maids their wounded *Thammuz* mourn.

And sullen *Moloch* fled,
Hath left in shadows dread
　　His burning Idol all of blackest hue;
In vain with Cymbals' ring
They call the grisly king,
　　In dismal dance about the furnace blue;
The brutish gods of *Nile* as fast,
Isis and *Orus* and the Dog *Anubis* haste.

Nor is *Osiris* seen
In *Memphian* Grove or Green,
　　Trampling the unshow'r'd Grass with lowings loud:
Nor can he be at rest
Within his sacred chest,
　　Naught but profoundest Hell can be his shroud:
In vain with Timbrel'd Anthems dark
The sable-stoled Sorcerers bear his worshipt Ark.　　　　(197–220)

"In vain," "In vain," "In vain," Milton tells us, is all of this sound and fury. All is presented in negative: it is what is not. The false gods and oracles are the creations and vocal agents of human misinterpretation in its most powerful state, and they too are stunned to sudden silence by the silent Babe: "Our Babe, to show his Godhead true, / Can in his swaddling bands control the damned crew" (258–59).

　　As the voices of the oracles are silenced, so too is the voice of the poet. In the critically infamous stanza xxiii, with its image of the chin-pillowing sun, Milton returns to nature in a domestication of the effect of Christ's silent power. From the harsh cacophony of the pagan rout, the poem drops in pitch to a quiet statement of fact, in a simile that diminishes not Christ's unquestionable control over pagan error, but only the difficulty it presents for human understanding:

So when the Sun in bed,
Curtain'd with cloudy red,
　　Pillows his chin upon an Orient wave,
The flocking shadows pale
Troop to th'infernal jail;
　　Each fetter'd Ghost slips to his several grave,
And the yellow-skirted *Fays*
Fly after the Night-steeds, leaving their Moon-loved maze. (229–36)

Christ's control over the universe is shown to be as natural and inevitable as the coming of day, and his overthrow of the false gods is, for Him, no more surprising than a fairy tale. The image of the sun in bed is shocking, I think, not because of *what* it is (the same sun, after all, is Nature's wanton paramour in "The Hymn's" first stanza), but because of *where* it is in the poem. The image, collapsing as it does its grandiose analogical counterpart, creates an astonishing anticlimax. Even given the emblematic significance many critics have argued,[19] the simile just doesn't seem adequate, and the sudden shift from the dusk of paganism to the rosy dawn of Christianity is petty. But this is just the point. In the simile, Milton surrenders any pretensions to interpretive authority he might have retained. By suggesting that the power of God is the natural order, he suggests as well that all human speculation about that order, including his poem, is always bound by the limits of human thought, and destined to be expressed within the inadequate bounds of human expression.

With a final abrupt shift, the poem ends in the manger where it began, and all is silence. "But see! " introduces the last stanza, suggesting again the superfluity of the preceding poem in the simple presence of the sleeping, speechless infant. "Time is our tedious song should here have ending" (239) because we have not arrived at an end, but at a beginning.

Milton's diminishment of his poem is perhaps not so much self-effacement as it is the establishment of a conscious distance from his subject, an act of deference to divine authority. If we feel cheated, especially in moments when what we have been given is taken away, the feeling is a product of our own critical presumption, a security assumed by the critic because of his own sense of distance from the work. And this presumption may explain a good deal of the dissatisfaction expressed by some of the ode's best critics.

"The Ode does not admit 'The uncontrollable mystery on the bestial floor,'" says J. B. Broadbent, certainly the poem's most trenchant critic, "partly because Milton associated the animal with sin, and mystery with chaos; but also because he was a magus determined to control the mystery."[20] This judgment ignores the entire development of the poem even as it describes the poem's matter accurately. Milton does not in fact explore the mystery; rather, he provides a time and a place for the mystery to occur *in the present*. Milton's gift, like that of the poem's missing magus, is one of present anticipation and attendance, not of past action. To present the mystery directly would be to interpret it, and that is exactly what Milton wants to avoid.

It seems reasonable to circumscribe Milton's motives, as well as our own, with the same circle the poem presents, and in this sense Milton creates a topos for his subject, a local habitation for the mystery of the

Incarnation, but he will not claim personal authority for the mystery. In the act of writing Milton authorizes himself, but in the act of efface-ment he recognizes that human poetry can only make a place for the ap-pearance of the silent logos.

"His poems feel like acts," complains Broadbent. Precisely. And the Nativity ode is an act of faith.

Portland State University

NOTES

1. Fish, especially in *Surprised by Sin: The Reader in "Paradise Lost"* (New York, 1967), has made it clear that Milton rarely gives us what we expect, and that, in fact, our misplaced expectations often become central to our understanding of the poems.

2. Arthur Barker's "The Pattern of the Nativity Ode," *UTQ*, X (1940–41), 167–81, presents the most widely accepted structural analysis of the poem. Rosemond Tuve's *Images and Themes in Five Poems by Milton* (Cambridge, Mass., 1957), pp. 37–72, is the most useful general study of imagery. Lowry Nelson, Jr.'s *Baroque Lyric Poetry* (New Haven, 1961), pp. 64–76, discusses Milton's treatment of time in the poem objectively and in great detail.

3. Milton's "bad influence" on English poetry is primarily the result of his blind-ness, particularly damaging since his "sensuousness, such as it was, had been withered early by book-learning" in Eliot's quirky history, "Milton I," in *On Poetry and Poets* (New York, 1957), pp. 156–64. "External is Ricks's term in "Sound and Sense in *Paradise Lost*," in *Essays by Divers Hands* (London, 1977), XXXIX, pp. 92–111. Ricks tries to excuse Mil-ton's distance from the reader through a discussion of Milton's personal sense of exclusion from the world. Broadbent sees Milton as power hungry and therefore above his audience in "The Nativity Ode," in *The Living Milton*, ed. Frank Kermode (London, 1960), pp. 12–31.

4. Although the relationship between poetic and religious authority is not often treated, an excellent discussion of the problem of religious and political authority in the period is Gerald R. Cragg's *Freedom and Authority: A Study of English Thought in the Early Seventeenth Century* (Philadelphia, 1975), especially "The Puritans: The Authority of the Word," pp. 127–58.

5. Sidney, *An Apology for Poetry*, in *Critical Theory Since Plato*, ed. Hazard Adams (New York, 1971), p. 158.

6. The most radical new reading of the poem is Paul H. Fry's "Milton's Light-Harnessed Ode," in *The Poet's Calling in the English Ode* (New Haven, 1980), pp. 37–48. Edward W. Tayler's typological reading in *Milton's Poetry: Its Development in Time* (Pitts-burgh, 1979) also suggests new ways of looking at the poem's structure. Both will be dis-cussed below.

7. *Ode on the Morning of Christ's Nativity*, 150–51, in *John Milton: Complete Poems and Major Prose*, ed. Merritt Y. Hughes (New York, 1957). Quotations from Mil-ton's poems throughout are from this edition.

8. Both Barker's tripartite structure and the two part structure of C. Brooks and

J. E. Hardy, *Poems of Mr. John Milton* (New York, 1951), consider this point in the poem to be a major break.

9. Fry's reading makes the poem a Miltonic search for vocation: "I hope to have shown from my own point of view why it is important for Milton to insist with dispropor-tionate emphasis that 'The Oracles are dumm' (173): in that case only one vocal oracle would remain, his own" (p. 45). Although I find much of what Fry does in the poem, his reading of the ode, like Stanley Fish's Milton readings, makes Milton much more self-centered than is warranted, for, in fact, Milton is careful to undercut every potentially oracular statement he makes.

10. In Milton's less successful early experiments with the problems posed by authori-ty for a Christian poet, *On the Death of a Fair Infant, Dying of a Cough* and *The Passion*, the pitfalls of an overextension of authority become obvious. In the *Fair Infant* the poet's self-interest is obtrusive, and his subject is always clearly an excuse for the poem he would make of it. The admitted failure of *The Passion* springs from the poet's inability to get beyond speculation about his poem to the subject it would treat.

11. Fry, "Milton's Light-Harnessed Ode," p. 44.

12. Nelson, *Baroque Lyric Poetry*, pp. 47–49.

13. Tayler, *Milton's Poetry*, pp. 38–39.

14. "Controlled asymmetry" is Gilbert Highet's phrase, *The Classical Tradition: Greek and Roman Influences on Western Literature* (New York, 1964), p. 238. C. M. Bowra's discussion of Pindar's theory of poetry, especially as it deals with the muse, suggests many parallels between Milton's ode and the odes of Pindar: *Pindar* (Oxford, 1964), pp. 1–41. In "Milton's Nativity Poem and the Decorum of Genre," *Milton Studies*, VII, ed. James D. Simmonds (Pittsburgh, 1975), pp. 165–88, Philip Rollinson argues that the poem's proper genre is the literary hymn and not the ode, and he finds many adoptions of the hymn's conventions and *topoi* in Milton's poem. Yet whether or not the poem has a "proper" genre, what is clear is that Milton here makes his own poem in spite of definable generic restric-tions as often as he does in accord with them.

15. Paul de Man, "Semiology and Rhetoric," *Diacritics*, III, no. 3 (1979), 30.

16. Tuve, *Images and Themes*, p. 37.

17. The medial caesura of the last line underscores the double rhythmic game the stanza plays.

18. *At a Solemn Music*, 4. A view of the power of music which Milton might have shared may be found in *The Letters of Marcilio Ficino*, trans. The Language Department of the London School of Economics (London, 1975), vol. I, 45–46: "But the soul receives the sweetest harmonies and numbers through the ears, and by these echoes is reminded and aroused to the divine music which may be heard by the more subtle and penetrating sense of mind. . . . Some, who imitate the divine and heavenly harmony with deeper and sounder judgment, render a sense of its inner reason and knowledge into verse, feet, and numbers. It is these who, inspired by the divine spirit, give forth with full voice the most solemn and glorious song."

19. E.g., Tuve, *Elizabethan and Metaphysical Imagery* (Chicago, 1947), p. 315.

20. Broadbent, "The Nativity Ode," p. 31.

APOCRYPHAL NARRATION: MILTON, RAPHAEL, AND THE BOOK OF TOBIT

Mark A. Wollaeger

WONDERING WHETHER Milton "would ruin" the "sacred Truths" of Scripture, Andrew Marvell may have been the first to sense a hidden narrative in *Paradise Lost:* "(So *Sampson* grop'd the Temple's Posts in spite)," he added in a wary parenthetical analogy, "The World o'erwhelming to revenge his sight."[1] Questioning the propriety of Milton's secular representation of sacred truths, Marvell raised an important issue of authority in *Paradise Lost.* But Milton, highly conscious of the danger of profanation, was aware also of a third term not present in Marvell's dedicatory poem: the Apocrypha, which he regarded as "closest to the scriptures in authority," though not the word of God.[2] Since Adam and Eve's divine intermediary, Raphael, appears only in the Apocrypha, the problem of narrative authority in *Paradise Lost* can be focused in Raphael's role as (literally) the central narrator of the epic. The rationalism of Raphael's conversations with Adam and Eve is characteristic of apocryphal texts, and this Hellenistic strain should be understood in relation to suggestions that in *Paradise Lost* Milton was attracted to the telling of a different story. One version of this story, which has a happier ending for Adam, Eve, and the poet himself, is drawn from the Book of Tobit, an apocryphal book of the Bible that Milton chose as a model for what may be considered a counternarrative. Through Raphael, I will argue, Milton's counternarrative asserts a critical distance from the story of the Fall.[3]

Any story, particularly one as complex as the Fall, is likely to generate more stories. Narrativity, Frank Kermode has observed, "always entails a measure of opacity," and interpretation seeks to make opacities transparent by assimilating concealed meanings into the manifest sense that obscures them.[4] That *Paradise Lost* can be understod as an interpretation of the Bible in the form of poetic narrative has long been recognized. And like any narrative, interpretive or otherwise, even as it clarifies, *Paradise Lost* also creates new opacities, or what Kermode calls "narrative secrets."[5] I am concerned with secrets that derive from Milton's interpretation of the Book of Tobit, and an inquiry into its hidden presence as a counternarrative in *Paradise Lost* will require a historical understanding of the significance of Milton's allusions to the Apocrypha.

The term *apocrypha* derives from the Greek *apokryphos*, meaning "hidden, spurious (books)," and the critical canon seems to have developed in accordance with this etymology. The Holy Scriptures, Milton writes in *Christian Doctrine*, are divinely inspired and express the word of God, but the apocryphal books "have nothing like the same authority as the canonical, and are not admitted as evidence in deciding points of faith" (*YP* VI, p. 574). As Virginia Mollenkott rightly observes, Milton considered the Apocrypha, together with other noncanonical texts, to be human writings whose authority must be earned "by means of [their] own reasonableness and power."[6] Yet despite this explicit formulation of the relative authority of the Apocrypha versus the Canon, critics have generally overlooked the peculiar significance of apocryphal writings when interpreting Milton's poetry.[7]

The apocryphal books were bound together with the Canon in Milton's bibles,[8] and though he referred to all of them throughout his career, the Book of Tobit, given its patent structural importance to *Paradise Lost*, has been particularly slighted in discussions of Milton's biblical sources. Raphael's narration of the War in Heaven and the Creation occurs within the context of the relationship between the angel, Adam, Eve, and God; and Milton based his depiction of this relationship, which occupies the central third of the poem, on that between Raphael, Tobias, Sara, and God in the Book of Tobit. Though Milton's direct allusions to Tobit have received critical attention, commentary has been lacking in two respects: the parallels between Tobit and *Paradise Lost* are more sustained and extend further than the annotated allusions initially suggest, and these correspondences have not been interpreted within the essential context of their implication in Milton's hierarchy of biblical authority.[9] Exploiting the crucial distinction in *Christian Doctrine*, I will show how Milton invokes the Book of Tobit as a human perspective on the Fall without, as Marvell feared, ruining the sacred truths of Scripture.

The story of Tobias and the angel was very popular in the Renaissance. Florentine painters of the quattrocento turned out many paintings on the subject, as did early engravers.[10] Most scholars agree that the primary doctrinal aim of the Book of Tobit is "to reassert the validity of faith at a time when God had apparently abandoned his people."[11] After Tobit and Sara, who suffer under false reproaches, pray for relief, God sends down Raphael ("the medicine of God") to reward the pious, and justice finally reigns. This powerful vindication of the ways of God to man tempts one to correlate the strong appeal of the Book of Tobit with the political upheaval and rapid secularization of fifteenth-century Italy; but no theory, to my knowledge, has adequately explained the unusual popularity of the Tobit theme in the visual arts of this period. The sociological argument would, of course, carry even more weight in relation to seventeenth-century England, where, as the widespread contemporary metaphor put it, the world was turned upside down.[12] But an intertextual analysis of Tobit and *Paradise Lost*, together with a look at Milton's biography, reveals more precisely the complex nature of the appeal the story held for Milton.

Milton draws on the Book of Tobit through direct and indirect allusions, implicit parallels, and verbal echoes. The first of the direct allusions comes as a simile describing Satan's initial approach to Paradise:

> So entertain'd those odorous sweets the Fiend
> Who came thir bane, though with them better pleas'd
> Than *Asmodeus* with the fishy fume,
> That drove him, though enamor'd, from the Spouse
> Of *Tobit's* Son, and with a vengeance sent
> From *Media* post to *Egypt*, there fast bound.   (IV, 166–71)

The second prefaces God's charge to Raphael, as they gaze down on Adam and Eve's gardening, to speak with "the human pair" "half this day as friend with friend" (V, 227, 229):

> Them thus imploy'd beheld
> With pity Heav'n's high King, and to him call'd
> *Raphael*, the sociable Spirit, that deign'd
> To travel with *Tobias*, and secur'd
> His marriage with the seven-times-wedded Maid.   (V, 219–23)

Thomas Greene and Virginia Mollenkott have written the best general descriptions of these allusions to date. In addition to emphasizing the "sociability of Raphael," writes Greene, the parallel reminds us that

the purpose of Raphael's visit is to warn Adam against Satan, and we remember that in the Tobias story Raphael succeeds in bilking Satan. . . . Asmodeus or Satan has sexual designs upon Sara, the spouse of Tobias, just as Satan designs to seduce Eve. Raphael appears in Tobit as the protector of marriage . . . the role which he is about to play here. . . . Raphael's solicitude in Tobit for the uniquely human institution also graces the domestic scenes in Adam's bower. But this spouse he cannot protect.[13]

Adam and Even deserve God's pity, Greene remarks, "because they exemplify marriage threatened by the devil" (p. 396). The sexual threat posed by Asmodeus becomes more insistent with Milton's allusion to Belial in *Paradise Regained*, the "dissolutest" and "sensuallest" of all the fallen angels, "and after *Asmodai* / The fleshliest Incubus" (*PR* II, 150–52). Thus in the third allusion, according to Mollenkott, where Raphael recounts his defeat of Asmodeus in the War in Heaven (VI, 362–68), Milton "completes the symbolism. . . . Raphael the healer, the obedient messenger of God, is pitted against Asmodeus, the destroyer and the lustful, so that Raphael's personal triumph over Asmodeus . . . symbolizes the ultimate triumph of right reason over passion, and of the forces of creation over those of destruction" (p. 29). These allusions establish the basic correspondences Milton exploits, and the useful commentaries excerpted above neatly describe the narrative of marital protection Milton invokes from Tobit. But the symbolism is far from complete.

An odd grammatical feature of the third allusion points toward the kind of complication that Greene and Mollenkott overlook. Describing his victory over Asmodeus, Raphael refers to himself as "*Raphaël*," who vanquished "his vaunting foe, / Though huge, and in a Rock of Diamond Arm'd" (VI, 363–65). Raphael oscillates between first and third person narration throughout his account of the War in Heaven (see, for example, VI, 68, 200, 571), and so renders himself simultaneously the speaker and object of the narrative. Splitting himself, Raphael reminds us of his alternative role, the far more successful one of the Book of Tobit, which in the above allusion is praised, as it were, by a narrative alter ego. A closer look at the other allusions will open up a discussion of an analogous dialogue of narratives at work throughout *Paradise Lost*.

The simile describing Satan's approach to Paradise is an example of Milton's technique of prolepsis: on the brink of Satan's greatest triumph Milton foreshadows his ultimate defeat. But the simile also points to the impending failure of Raphael's descent, not simply through the negative parallel with his success in Tobit, but through the suggestion of premature apocalypse in the binding of Satan-Asmodeus. At the approach of Satan in the Heavenly War, Michael indulges a similar wish, "hoping here to end / Intestine War in Heav'n, the Arch-foe subdu'd / Or Captive dragged in Chains" (VI, 258–60). Like Abdiel in VI, 186, Michael seems to mistake Satan for the more easily thwarted and bound demon of the Book of Tobit, and, in his Miltonic impatience to skip over any "middle flight," he tries prematurely to play the role of the Angel of Revelation. Since it is Raphael who, within the simile, threatens to bind Asmodeus, and since Raphael was often interpreted as a type of the Angel of Revelation, he too is implicated in this impatience.[14] But God does not send down Raphael to counsel Adam and Eve about the end of history—his mission is rather to advise them about avoiding the fall *into* human history. The middle flight that seems to drop out is the crucial period in which Adam and Even must encounter and resist temptation. Only a satanic middle remains, "the sensuous delay, the slackening course," of the Satan-sailor figures who are arrested in mid-voyage by "*Sabean* Odors from the spicy shore."[15]

What Milton tends to elide, then, in the first allusion to the Book of Tobit, is Raphael's warning about the approach of Satan that the simile describes. In Book IV Milton would have liked to supply that warning, whose absence is felt in the books to come:

> O for that warning voice, which he who saw
> Th' *Apocalypse*, heard cry in Heav'n aloud,
> Then when the Dragon, put to second rout,
> Came furious down to be reveng'd on men,
> *Woe to the inhabitants on Earth!* that now,
> While time was, our first Parents had been warn'd
> The coming of thir secret foe, and scap'd
> Haply so scap'd his mortal snare.   (IV, 1–8)

The repetition in the last lines underscores the intensity of the emotion here; Milton's narrator hovers over Adam and Eve like a stricken father. When the warning does come, as we shall see, its inadequacy contrasts sharply with the clarity of Raphael's instructions in Tobit, a narrative in which the characters do, happily, escape.

The parallel between the double figure of Raphael and Satan-Asmodeus becomes more complicated when we recognize that verbal echoes link Raphael's descent to earth with Satan's entry into Paradise in Book IV and with the flight of the inspired poet in Books I, III, and VII.[16] Milton's decision to draw parallels between figures as divergent as Raphael, Satan, and the poet suggests that this technique constitutes one of his methods of establishing a principle of difference. Christopher Ricks has shown such a principle to be at work in some of Milton's similes, as when Satan, "Stupidly good" for a moment (IX, 465), is compared to a pent-up city dweller who is relieved to enjoy a pastoral respite from urban blight.[17] Accordingly, when Milton compares the flights of Raphael and Satan, he implicitly emphasizes the disparity of motive between the angelic and demonic visitors.

But when Satan and Raphael both become involved in the flights of the narrator, the issue gets trickier, for it is the narrator whom we habitually trust to alert us to the differences between associated figures. Thus, when the reader becomes taken with the beauty of Satan's

weekend escape to the country, the narrator steps in with the kind of rep-
rimand so admired by Stanley Fish: "But the hot Hell that always in him
burns . . . soon ended his delight" (IX, 467–68). As long as Milton preserves the connection between Raphael and his own invocations while
at the same time suppressing the similarities between Raphael and Satan,
there is little danger that the parallels will collapse into each other and
destroy the moral hierarchy he wishes to maintain. But while the possible merging of parody and its object might be considered a threat, it
is nevertheless a threat Milton deliberately courts. As Satan informs the
unfallen angels, "Not to know mee argues yourselves unknown" (IV, 830).

Milton maintains a similar counterpoint of contraries on the level
of the main narrative through implicit parallels and echoes of the Book
of Tobit. Some are important simply because they show that Milton had
Tobit in mind more often than his direct allusions would indicate.[18] But
when Adam and Eve pray before indulging "the Rites / Mysterious of
connubial Love" (IV, 742–43), the parallel with the prayer of Sara and
Tobias on their wedding night is telling. Reflecting on "this delicious
place / For us too large," Adam and Eve address their God:

> But thou hast promis'd from us two a Race
> To fill the Earth, who shall with us extol
> Thy goodness infinite, both when we wake,
> And when we seek, as now, thy gift of sleep.
>
> (IV, 729–30, 733–35)

Adam and Eve's children do join in their praise of God, and, in so doing,
Sara and Tobias hark back to the parents of humanity:

> Thou madest Adam, and gavest him Eve his wife for a helper and a stay: of
> them came the seed of men: thou didst say, It is not good that the man should
> be alone; let us make him a helper unto him. And now, O Lord, I take not this
> my sister for lust, but in truth: command that I may find mercy and grow old
> with her. And she said with him, Amen. And they slept both that night. (Tob.
> viii, 6–9)

The parallel here is implicated in an extensive network of temporal ironies
that are characteristically Miltonic, for just as Genesis loses its claim to
priority in the epic sequence of Milton's poem, so Milton is able to "hark
back" to a prior text that describes the children of his own characters.
Paradise Lost thus appears to father the Book of Tobit.

Sustaining the parallel, after Adam and Eve pray Milton takes up
Tobias's distinction between lust and innocent sexuality, elaborating and
defending it in the panegyric to "wedded Love":

> By thee adulterous lust was driv'n from men
> Among the bestial herds to range, by thee
> Founded in Reason, Loyal, Just, and Pure,
> Relations dear, and all the Charities
> Of Father, Son, and Brother first were known.
>
>   (IV, 750, 753–57)

Here is the symbolism emphasized by Mollenkott: right reason triumphing over lust. But the darker side of the parallel contrasts the happy, untroubled sleep of Sara and Tobias, who wake to the first day of a fourteen-day wedding feast, with the "unquiet rest" of Eve (V, 11). By carrying out Raphael's instructions about burning the heart and liver of the fish they have caught, Tobias succeeds in freeing Sara from the demon lover who has slain her seven previous husbands on their wedding night. Raphael then pursues Asmodeus and binds him. But when Milton's Ithuriel and Zephon search the Garden, they discover Satan,

> Squat like a Toad, close at the ear of *Eve;*
> Assaying by his Devilish art to reach
> The Organs of her Fancy, and with them forge
> Illusions as he list.   (IV, 800–03)

Given the shared distinction between lust and wedded love, we can read Milton's scene as a rewriting of Asmodeus's sexual possession of Sara in Tobit.[19] Though Milton leaves the degree of Satan's success ambiguous — the angelic guards apprehend Satan in the act of "assaying" — Adam will later accuse Eve of being wedded to the serpent. The prayer scene in *Paradise Lost* is thus an ironic counterpoint to that in Tobit, where the answer to the newlyweds' plea is immediately realized in the effective presence of the fishy fume.

With an indirect allusion in Book V Milton again turns to the Book of Tobit, and so gives us an opportunity to confront, at long last, the issue of Raphael's authority as a narrator. When Raphael first arrives and consents to eat with Adam and Eve, Milton boldly states his position on the controversy surrounding the materiality of angels:

> So down they sat,
> And to thir viands fell, nor seemingly
> The Angel, nor in mist, the common gloss
> Of Theologians, but with keen dispatch
> Of real hunger, and concoctive heat
> To transubstantiate.   (V, 433–38)

The gloss Milton so scornfully dismisses was usually Tobit xiii, 19–20: "All these days did I appear unto you," says Raphael, "and I did neither

eat nor drink, but ye saw a vision." Against this apocryphal authority
Milton opposes Genesis xviii, 5–8, where Abraham and Sarah prepare
a feast for the visiting angels, and xix, 3, where two angels feast with
Lot, and "they did eat." Milton echoes these canonical authorities twice
before negating Raphael's statement in Tobit (V, 299–31, 359–60). As
James Sims has written, in this instance "it is clear that Milton rejected
the authority of the Apocryphal story."[20] If, in accordance with his
apocryphal status, Raphael too speaks only with the dubious authority
of a theologian, we may wonder why Milton chose to have God send down
Raphael, as opposed to a more authoritative figure, to warn Adam "to
beware" (V, 237).

At this juncture, two likely objections to my line of argument must
be met. The problem could be dismissed by arguing that Milton's hierarchy of biblical authority does not pertain to Raphael, since *Paradise
Lost* does not, unlike *Christian Doctrine*, directly attempt to adjudicate
doctrinal issues.[21] But any critical assumption that separates Milton the
prose writer from Milton the poet seems to me mistaken, particularly
since excellent arguments have been advanced for taking seriously Milton's aspiration to locate himself within a long line of Christian prophets.[22] If Milton truly wished to "justify the ways of God to man," then
to reduce his poetry to what I. A. Richards termed "pseudo-statements"
would directly contradict the poet's understanding of his life's work. Another objection might argue that the narrative of marital protection in
Tobit so perfectly fits Milton's immediate needs that its origin in the
Apocrypha probably never entered into his compositional plan. Granted,
the Tobit story seems tailor-made as a model of angelic descent, but if
Milton had wished to devise a divinely sanctioned narrator, Michael —
the guardian angel of the Jews in Daniel — could have done double duty
as a pre- and post-lapsarian advisor. Or Gabriel, who appears in the
Canon but is sketched only vaguely, could have taken on a role expanded
beyond his hopeless vigilance outside the gates of Paradise.[23]

But my argument does not depend on Milton's having selected Raphael *because* of his origin in the Apocrypha, nor on the availability of
canonical alternatives. It is my contention that Milton recognized that
Raphael's apocryphal status could be exploited, that a virtue could be
made of what may well at first have seemed only a convenience.[24]

When Milton dismisses "the common gloss / Of Theologians," he
does not subordinate the authority of the Apocrypha to that of the Canon
merely to set up the joke that there was "No fear lest Dinner cool" (V,
396). Asserting that angels "profited by earthly food," Milton links the
lesser authority of the Apocrypha with "a basic resemblance of man to
angel in the whole of their beings."[25] The resemblance is articulated most

directly in the theory of a continuous scale of being that Raphael expounds for Adam:

> Wonder not then, what God for you saw good
> If I refuse not, but convert, as you,
> To proper substance; time may come when men
> With Angels may participate, and find
> No inconvenient Diet, not too light Fare:
> And from these corporal nutriments perhaps
> Your bodies may at last turn all to spirit,
> Improv'd by tract of time, and wing'd ascend
> Ethereal, as wee, or may at choice
> Here or in Heav'nly Paradises dwell;
> If ye be found obedient, and retain
> Unalterably firm his love entire
> Whose progeny you are. Meanwhile enjoy
> Your fill what happiness this happy state
> Can comprehend, incapable of more.   (V, 491–505)

Though Raphael speaks in an authoritative tone, the substance of his speech denies the existence of any firm hierarchical advantage; in time Adam and Raphael may always sup at the same table. In fact, when Raphael first arrives, it is Adam who seems in the superior position. He walks forth to meet Raphael:

> without more train
> Accompanied than with his own complete
> Perfections; in himself was all his state,
> More solemn than the tedious pomp that waits
> On Princes.   (V, 351–55)

Raphael is subtly assimilated to "the tedious pomp" in a muted version of Gabriel's strangely satanic description of angelic adoration. *Before* rebelling, alleges Gabriel, Satan "Once fawn'd, and cring'd, and servilely ador'd / Heavn's' awful Monarch" (IV, 959–60). (The rest of the angels, presumably, were engaged in a less obsequious style of worship.) Subtending this initial juxtaposition of Raphael and Adam may be a thought later voiced by Satan as he contemplates Earth's potential superiority to heaven: "For what God after better worse would build?" (IX, 102). Without demonizing Raphael, we can say that his role as Adam's tutor does not automatically grant him an unequivocally superior position, and this ambiguity carries over into his authority as a narrator.

The humanization of Raphael takes place on several levels in his narration to Adam and Eve. In Books V through VIII Milton frequently reminds us of Raphael's potential fallibility, even as he slowly develops a parallel between Raphael's storytelling and his own. Raphael's authority as a narrator is thus linked to Milton's. Immediately after arriving, Raphael informs Adam that "these mid-hours, till Ev'ning rise / I have at will" (V, 376–77). Asserting his free will, Raphael introduces the possibility that he may stray from his commission. That possibility becomes a fear when Adam desires to hear more about the War in Heaven: "how last unfold," Raphael wonders, "the secrets of another World, perhaps / Not lawful to reveal?" (V, 568–70). As we realize that Raphael is unsure of the limits of his mandate, an echo of Milton's own anxiety reverberates in the background: "May I express thee unblam'd?" (III, 3). Milton senses the danger of transgression most acutely when approaching the Creation, where the sacred story in Genesis is far fuller than any other biblical source for the poem: "Above the flight of *Pegasean* wing" he means to soar, and hopes to be with "like safety guided down," "Lest from this flying Steed unrein'd, (as once / *Bellerophon*, though from a lower Clime) / Dismounted, on th' *Aleian* Field I fall / Erroneous there to wander and forlorn" (VII, 4, 15–20). Milton also fears a worse punishment — *sparagmos*, or a ritual tearing asunder — and calls for protection to Urania:

> drive far off the barbarous dissonance
> Of *Bacchus* and his Revellers, the Race
> Of that wild Rout that tore the *Thracian* Bard
> In *Rhodope*, where Woods and Rocks had Ears
> To rapture, till the savage clamor drown'd
> Both Harp and Voice; nor could the Muse defend
> Her Son. So fail not thou, who thee implores;
> For thou art Heav'nly, shee an empty dream.   (VII, 32–39)

As a Christian Orpheus, Milton must oppose his music to Bacchus's, and if he is to survive, he must predominate. Having requested that Urania "fit audience find, though few" (VII, 31), Milton imagines the "wild rout" of bacchantes to be his unfit audience, and their "savage clamor" threatens his poem as much as himself.[26] Raphael's momentary expression of doubt is thus amplified and sustained in the mythological subtext of Milton's invocation.

For Milton, "with dangers compast round," forbidden knowledge threatens to bring on the hostility of an evil audience, or, as with the blinding of Tiresias, divine retribution. In Tobit, however, the doctrine of forbidden knowledge has no place, nor is it consonant with the spirit of the Apocrypha as a whole. The Raphael of the Book of Tobit seems to speak directly to the fears of his Miltonic counterpart: "It is good to keep close the secret of a king, but to reveal gloriously the works of God" (Tob. xii, 7). Milton's Raphael feels less confident about revealing the works of God, and when Adam asks about the mystery of celestial motions, he is "doubt-fully answer'd" (Arg. VIII). Yet Raphael remains ambiguous on this issue: he counsels Adam that "Heav'n is for thee too high / To know what passes there; be lowly wise" (VIII, 172–73) only *after* his series of rather coy hypotheses about the possible organization of the universe has implicitly encouraged Adam to dream of other worlds. Where the Raphael of Tobit declares unequivocally, "Surely I will keep close nothing from you" (xii, 11), Milton's Raphael attempts to circumscribe curiosity even as he stimu-lates it. Such contrasts tend to substantiate Mollenkott's claim that the "Apocrypha's emphasis on the worthy life as the life of virtue based upon reason, including of course the knowledge of God, is more insistent than that of the Old Testament Canon and differs widely from the apparent suspicion of intellect in the New Testament." Milton carefully distin-guished between Hellenic and Hebraic values — knowledge and wisdom as opposed to virtue, reason, and faith — but he believed that these values must be integrated, as in the Apocrypha, in order for one to achieve true wisdom.[27] The Raphael of Tobit and the Raphael of *Paradise Lost* give different emphases to these constellations of value, the former embrac-ing man's quest for knowledge, the latter counseling an ambiguously qualified acceptance of lowly wisdom.

When Raphael reflects on the act of narrating the stuff of lowly wis-dom, he frequently pauses to ponder the potential inadequacy of his trans-lation of divine truth into human language:

> how shall I relate
> To human sense th' invisible exploits
> Of warring Spirits.   (V, 564–66)
> . . . .
> The Palace of great *Lucifer*, (so call
> That Structure in the Dialect of men
> Interpreted).   (V, 760–62)
> . . . .
>   for who, though with the tongue
> Of Angels, can relate, or to what things
> Liken on Earth conspicuous, that may lift
> Human imagination to such a highth
> Of Godlike Power.   (VI, 297–301)

In the first invocation Milton requests to be raised to just such a height: "What in me is dark / Illumine, what is low raise and support" (I, 23–24; see also III, 19–21, VII, 3–4, IX, 41–46). Raphael, in narrating the War in Heaven, clearly becomes a figure for the traditional epic poet; but the shared fear of transgression, coupled with an anxiety about the ability to transgress without stumbling, suggests a more specific connection with an epistemological and theological complication peculiar to Milton's epic ambitions.

The complication is one of accommodation, the theory of biblical exegesis that states that the limitations of human language prevent a precise expression of divine truth, which therefore must be translated into figurative approximations available in "the Dialect of men."[28] Raphael voices the doctrine in Book V: "for thy good / This is dispens't, and what surmounts the reach / Of human sense, I shall delineate so, / By lik'ning spiritual to corporal forms" (570–73). William Kerrigan has argued that Milton's task is analogous to that of Raphael, the "Divine Interpreter" (VII, 72). Milton, according to Kerrigan, believed himself to be a true prophet whose poetic project was to record accommodated Revelation for his fallen readers: "the Muse accommodates divine truth for the narrator, who transcribes this accommodation for the reader. Both the poet and the reader are spectators at the heavenly court" (p. 160). William Madsen, on the other hand, has rejected the analogy by deriding the very claim to inspiration that Kerrigan accepts: "unless we are willing to grant that John Milton was literally inspired, there seems to be no meaningful way to relate this fictional claim to the language of *Paradise Lost*" (pp. 73–74). Here we apparently reach an impasse: how do we evaluate Milton's claim that the language of *Paradise Lost* is already accommodated? Clearly there is no point in arguing whether or not Milton was "literally" inspired, but it is important to see, as Madsen does not, that the claim *is* analogous to Raphael's: each "poet" offers his audience divine truths rendered comprehensible to humankind. Yet even as Raphael asserts the doctrine he puts it in doubt: "what if Earth / Be but the shadow of Heav'n, and things therein / Each to other like, more than on Earth is thought?" (V, 574–76). The debate about the status of Milton's text is thus already inscribed within it, for Raphael's crucial equivocation raises the question of whether accommodation is necessary at all. I will return to this issue, but it should be clear already that the categories of sacred and secular texts are not adequate to the complexities of Milton's narrative.

Though the narrative perspectives of Raphael and Milton can be considered analogous, Raphael's equivocation points to an important difference between them: Milton assumes a higher authority than the angel. When Raphael remarks of the War in Heaven that "in other parts like deeds deserv'd / Memorial" (VI, 354–55), Stanley Fish notes that he is "the victim of a gentle irony, since in context Michael's 'deed' is faintly ridiculous."[29] But Raphael is not merely the victim *of* irony; here and elsewhere he is victimized *by* Milton's irony (and not always gently). Raphael's shadow in the Book of Tobit, whose guidance has a strikingly firm authority, is the source for Milton's most severe irony. After the fish almost swallows young Tobias, Raphael tells him how to capture it, and then gives detailed instructions regarding the use of its heart, liver, and gall (Tob. vi, 2–5). Returning together to Tobit after the marriage, Raphael reminds Tobias about the next step in God's therapy: the gall will remove the "white film" from Tobit's eyes (Tob. v, 8). In contrast, when Adam asks Milton's Raphael, "But say, / What meant that caution join'd, *if ye be found / Obedient?* (V, 512–14), the angel for once does not answer in terms of eating, but instead explains the doctrine of free will. No doubt free will is more important to Milton than the relative specificity of Raphael's warning, but one wonders why Raphael never tells Adam "What nearer might concern him" (VII, 62); namely, that Satan was there the previous night, that he was discovered whispering into Eve's ear! Surely such a warning would fulfill more fairly what Greene has described as the petty legalism of God's mandate to Raphael:

> tell him withal
> His danger, and from whom, what enemy
> Late fall'n himself from Heaven, is plotting now
> The fall of others from like state of bliss;
> By violence, no, for that shall be withstood,
> But by deceit and lies; this let him know,
> Lest wilfully transgressing he pretend
> Surprisal, unadmonisht, unforewarn'd.   (V, 238–45)

Had they been able to, Adam and Eve would have been better off exchanging Milton's "affable angel" for Tobit's guardian angel.

Raphael is subjected to Milton's irony in part because the subplot of the edification of the angels requires gaps in their understanding. Just as Adam is curious about Raphael's sex life, so Raphael is eager to hear the story of Adam's creation:

> Nor less think wee in Heav'n of thee on Earth
> Than of our fellow servant, and inquire
> Gladly into the ways of God with Man:
> For God we see hath honor'd thee, and set
> On Man his Equal Love: say therefore on;
> For I that Day was absent.   (VIII, 224–29)

Raphael was dutifully guarding the gate of Hell, just as Gabriel would later guard the gates of Paradise, both tasks designed by God "to enure / Our prompt obedience" (VIII, 239–40). Thus Milton's ambivalent sense of superiority to Adam (though he feels humbled by Adam's unfallen purity, Milton also feels elevated by his more comprehensive sense of human history), carries over to Raphael too.[30] The poet presides over the education of man and angel alike.

The authority Milton exercises as a teacher also derives from his sense of a prophetic mission. Many critics of *Paradise Lost* have attended to the single voice of a fallen epic narrator.[31] But Kerrigan, to whose thesis we turn again, distinguishes two voices, a "privileged mortal" (the poet) and a "divine educator." When the poet asks, "say first what cause / Mov'd our Grand Parents," the spirit addressed responds: "Th' infernal Serpent; hee it was" (I, 28–30, 34). In Book II, when the divine educator repeats the words of the human invocation in Book I — "all our woe" (I, 3, II, 872) — the voices merge, thus giving "prophetic authority to the verse of the poem" (Kerrigan, pp. 140–41).

Accepting Milton's claim to inspiration permits Kerrigan to distinguish between the narrative necessity of a secular text and the unconstraining foreknowledge of vatic discourse.[32] Narrative sequence will not have consequences, the aspiring prophet implies,[33]

> If answerable style I can obtain
> Of my Celestial Patroness, who deigns
> Her nightly visitation unimplor'd,
> And dictates to me slumb'ring, or inspires
> Easy my unpremeditated Verse.   (IX, 20–24)

Removed from the realm of human motivation, the epic story will be understood as innocently transcribing in a temporal mode the free actions of Adam and Eve as they exist in the timeless foreknowledge of God. If, however, inspiration fails, Adam and Eve become mere characters in a poem, subject as all fictional characters are to the whims of their creator. Deprived of free will, they would have good reason to agree with Empson that their God (Milton) is unmercifully coercive, a possibility Milton's God attempts to counter directly by asserting that there exists "no Decree of mine / Concurring to necessitate his Fall" (X, 43–44).

But if *Paradise Lost* aspires to the status of Scripture, must we therefore read it as if it were a sacred text? John Guillory has pointed out that the problem is as elusive as intentionality itself.[34] Though critics readily admit that authorial intentions are not, in theory, wholly recoverable, every act of interpretation implicitly lays claim to having found its way "inside" a text, where intentions, in our common figure, await attention. "The method of accommodation," in Guillory's words, "translates intentionality into theological language by transferring intention itself to the mind of divinity" (p. 161). The critical debate then advances through the displacement of hypotheses: where Kerrigan accepts the idea of divine intentions, critics like Madsen reject them by substituting "a host of specifically personal intentions, ranging from the desire for literary fame to the possibility of reaction to the failure of the English Revolution" (p. 156). Though a reconciliation of the conflicting hypotheses can be effected by positing "unconscious" intentions, all strategies force us to experience "something of the futility of guessing" (p. 155).

Here my own line of educated speculation draws again on the authority of the Apocrypha, in order to keep the poem open both to the divine intentions represented in the invocations and to the personal dimension of Milton's historical situation. Without accepting the rigid dichotomies criticism has established — sacred/secular, fallen/unfallen — I choose to credit Milton's inspirationalist claim. But we can still grant Milton the ultimate intention of authoring his poem (as certainly it would seem perverse to do otherwise) without negating the claim to inspiration made by the invocations and so transforming God into what Kenneth Burke would call a "God-term": the neglected category of apocryphal texts operates as a third term between the poetic and the sacred.[35] Guillory has argued that the end of inspiration coincides with the origin of imagination,[36] and Satan has frequently been championed as a figure of the human poet, one whose inspiration has failed. But Raphael, speaking doubtfully (and equivocally) to Adam and Eve, can be considered a human artist too, creating something like an apocryphal text.[37] The ambiguity of his explanation of accommodation locates the language of his "translation" in the gray area between the sacred and the secular that is mapped by the authors of the Apocrypha. Guillory notes that when Raphael wavers in his confidence, he "casts himself momentarily in the role of imagination. . . . But the moment passes" (p. 160). I am arguing, in contrast, that the wavering of authority is *sustained* in Milton's presentation of Raphael's narration. By inscribing within his Testament a poem spoken by a poet of the Apocrypha, Milton qualifies the authority of the angel God sends down to render man inexcusable. Unsure of the proper tack to take as he attempts to bring on "such discourse . . . As may advise him of his happy state," Milton's Raphael explores the problematic relationship between secular and divine texts, and raises the dark possibility that Adam and Eve are constrained by a narrative determinism intrinsic to secular texts.[38]

But Milton retreats from the blasphemy of reducing God to the status of a divine editor who governs the production of secular texts. Reminding us in the invocation to Book VII that Raphael's narration is itself narrated, Milton implicitly defines Raphael's poetry as an imaginative fiction residing uneasily within the discourse of inspiration. Most important, Raphael does not narrate the Fall itself: circumscribing the humanity of Raphael's angelic voice, the vatic voice of the inspired narrator claims to protect the freedom of Adam and Eve.

Raphael's voice is muted, not negated, however, and it lingers in the hieratic space of Milton's epic, whispering Tobit's story of human wish fulfillment. But the Tobit subtext does not only project in human terms a more blissful version of the plight of Adam and Eve. It tells also the story of the redemption of its narrator in terms that redirect us from the body of poetry to that of the poet. (The two are conflated, we recall, in the invocation to Book VII.) Milton turned to the Book of Tobit for a key detail in describing the advent of Adam's visionary experience in Book XI: "*Michael* from *Adam's* eyes the Film remov'd / Which that false Fruit that promis'd clearer sight / Had bred" (412–14). Though blindness is often cured in the Bible, only in Tobit is a film removed from the eyes. Milton's enemies charged that he was struck blind as retribution for having defended the execution of Charles I,[39] and in his *Second Defense* Milton protested against the accusation, perhaps too much, claiming that he was destined to lose his eyesight in pursuing his lofty duty as a pamphleteer for the Commonwealth. Though critical commentary has focused exclusively on Tobias and Sara, Milton clearly identified the story of Tobias's father as a version of his own. Tobit, who narrates his own tale of a virtuous life in exile, also goes blind after fulfilling his duty to his countrymen. Suffering too greatly from false reproaches, Tobit prays for death: "command my spirit to be taken from me, that I may be released, and become earth" (Tob. iii, 6). "How gladly would I meet / Mortality my sentence, and be Earth / Insensible," says Adam (X, 775–77). Milton — embittered by the failure of the Revolution, "fall'n on evil days," and enraged by the false reproaches of Salmasius — had a host of personal reasons to feel a deep empathy with Tobit. Through God, the Son cures the father in the Book of Tobit. In the *Second Defense* Milton claims that, like Tiresias, he was compensated for his blindness with "an inner and far more enduring light" (*YP* IV, p. 590). Might he not have hoped that, like Tobit, his long suffering would end in revisiting not only the "Eternal Coeternal Beam" but the actual light of the sun?

Milton's exploitation of the Apocrypha, then, operates on several levels. Instead of communicating directly with God, as Adam does when first created, Adam and Eve must receive their education through the fallible, quasi-human mediation of Raphael. Milton thus allows the possibility that they might not have been as free as God repeatedly claims they are: to the extent that Raphael is a figure for the human poet who is guided, like the authors of the Apocrypha, by his own reason, Adam and Eve are bound by the narrative necessity of his secular poem. Though the aspirations to canonicity of the surrounding text work to unravel such necessity, it remains nevertheless as a shadowy alternative within the light-centered world of *Paradise Lost*.

Milton's attraction to the Book of Tobit also reflects the appeal of the Apocrypha's more liberal, rationalist acceptance of the Hellenic valorization of knowledge as virtue. As Tillyard once put it, "we feel that Milton, stranded in his own Paradise, would very soon have eaten the apple on his own responsibility and immediately justified the act in a polemical pamphlet."[40] If so, Raphael's niggling about proper spheres of knowledge may well have grated on him. As a counternarrative of divine justice, the Book of Tobit enters the poem as a human voice that is firm in its proclamation of salvation: "It is good . . . to reveal gloriously the works of God," says Raphael's apocryphal double, because God has nothing to hide. The voice cries out for a more protective deity, one who will alleviate the earthly suffering of the falsely reproached, and remove from men's eyes, once and for all, what Milton in *Of Reformation* (*YP* I, p. 566) calls the "film of *ignorance*."

Yale University

NOTES

I would like to thank here several people who offered helpful criticism of earlier drafts of my manuscript: Lars Engle, Geraldine Friedman, and John Guillory. I am especially grateful for the generous advice and editorial acumen of Margaret Ferguson, who first suggested I revise this essay for publication.

1. "On Paradise Lost," 7–10. These lines and all quotations from Milton's poetry are from *Complete Poems and Major Prose*, ed. Merritt Y. Hughes (Indianapolis, 1957), and hereafter will be cited in the text. Marvell's poem was added to the second edition of *Paradise Lost* (1674).

2. *Christian Doctrine*, in *Complete Prose Works of John Milton*, ed. Don M. Wolfe et al. (New Haven, 1953–82), vol. VI, p. 306; all quotations from Milton's prose are from this edition, hereafter cited as *YP*.

3. I am preceded in the detection of a hidden narrative in *Paradise Lost* by Geoffrey H. Hartman, "Milton's Counterplot," in *Beyond Formalism: Literary Essays 1958–1970* (New Haven, 1970), who argues that Milton's similes project an observer *ab extra* whose perspective of "divine imperturbability" presides over the turmoil of the Fall. What Hartman calls a "plot," however, is strictly speaking not a narrative, since it refers to an atemporal perspective that transcends the sequential actions of Satan's plot: it is a "feeling (if *feeling* is the proper word) for imperturbable providence [that] radiates from many levels of the text" (p. 115). The counternarrative I describe operates through allusion (that is, not only through allusive similes) and refers to an identifiable sequence of events in a specific subtext.

4. Frank Kermode, *The Genesis of Secrecy: On the Interpretation of Narrative* (Cambridge, 1979), p. 25; see also the rest of chapter two, "Hoti's Business: Why Are Narratives Obscure?" This paragraph and my thinking generally about narrative are indebted to Kermode's work on the subject.

5. Kermode, *The Genesis of Secrecy*, pp. x–xi. See also "Secrets and Narrative Se-

quence," in Kermode's *The Art of Telling: Essays on Fiction* (Cambridge, 1983); originally published in *Critical Inquiry*, VII (1980), 83–101.

6. Virginia Mollenkott, "The Pervasive Influence of the Apocrypha in Milton's Thought and Art," in *Milton and the Art of Sacred Song*, ed. J. Max Patrick and Roger H. Sundell (Madison, 1979), p. 33; quotations hereafter cited in the text by page number only. In descending order of authority the other non-canonical texts are "the Pseudepigrapha and the older midrashim" and "the later Jewish legends and commentaries, such as the cabalistic *Zohar* or the *Pseudo-Josephus*" (p. 26). My essay is indebted to Mollenkott's thorough scholarship, but our use of these sources differs greatly. For a history of the Apocrypha, including textual history of individual books, see Robert Pfeiffer, "Literature and Religion of the Apocrypha," in *The Interpreter's Bible*, ed. George A. Buttrick et al. (New York, 1952–57), vol. I, 391–402.

7. The most extensive published study is *Milton and the Art of Sacred Song*, especially the essays by Mollenkott and James H. Sims. *A Milton Encyclopedia*, ed. William Hunter et al. (Lewisburg, Pa., 1978) cites many parallels but does not discuss them. Sims's *The Bible in Milton's Epics* (Gainesville, 1962) distinguishes between the authority of the Apocrypha and the Canon in one crucial instance (see my note 20), but does not sustain the inquiry. His tables of biblical allusions are very useful but fail to note two important echoes of Tobit in *Paradise Lost*, Books X–XI. For a more comprehensive list of allusions to the Apocrypha in Milton, see Mollenkott's "Milton and the Apocrypha," (Ph.D. diss. New York University 1964). Michael Lieb's *Poetics of the Holy: A Reading of "Paradise Lost"* (Chapel Hill, 1981) singles out the Apocrypha (without mentioning Tobit) but does not consider Milton's discussion of the Apocrypha in *Christian Doctrine*.

8. Madeline S. Miller and J. Lane Miller, *Harper's Bible Dictionary* (New York, 1973), p. 25. Only since 1827 has the Apocrypha been systematically excluded from English bibles.

9. Milton alludes directly to Tobit three times in *Paradise Lost* (IV, 166–71, V, 221–23, VI, 362–68) and once in *Paradise Regained* (II, 150–52). The most detailed analyses of these allusions are in Mollenkott's essay and Thomas Greene's *The Descent From Heaven: A Study in Epic Continuity* (New Haven, 1963).

10. E. H. Gombrich, *Symbolic Images: Studies in the Art of the Renaissance* (London, 1972), devotes an entire chapter to Tobias and Raphael. Pictorial representations of the Book of Tobit in the Renaissance center on Tobias and Raphael to the exclusion of Sara and Tobit.

11. Demetrius R. Dumm, "Tobit, Judith, Esther," in *The Jerome Biblical Commentary*, ed. Raymond Brown et al. (Englewood Cliffs, 1968), vol. I, p. 620. For general commentary on the Book of Tobit, see also George Nickelsburg, *Jewish Literature Between the Bible and Mishnah: A Historical and Literary Introduction* (Philadelphia, 1981).

12. Gombrich provides a bibliography and a mercantile theory focusing on the theme of debt collection; see also Christopher Hill, *The World Turned Upside Down: Radical Issues During the English Revolution* (New Haven, 1963), pp. 13–19.

13. Greene, *The Descent From Heaven*, pp. 396–97.

14. Gombrich, *Symbolic Images*, p. 28.

15. Arnold Stein, *Answerable Style: Essays on "Paradise Lost"* (Minneapolis, 1953), p. 59.

16. For different treatments of these structural parallels, see Isabel MacCaffrey, *"Paradise Lost" as "Myth"* (Cambridge, 1959), pp. 62–63, and William Riggs, *The Christian Poet in Paradise Lost* (Berkeley: University of California Press, 1972), pp. 105–09.

17. Christopher Ricks, *Milton's Grand Style* (London, 1963), pp. 127–32.

18. The "Kingly Palace Gate" of Heaven, for example, "With Frontispiece of Dia-

mond and Gold / Imbellisht; thick with sparkling orient Gems" (III, 505–07), draws its ornamentation as much from the Book of Tobit (xiii, 16) as from the usual gloss, Revelation, chapter xxi. References to the angelic messengers in *Paradise Lost* III, 65ff and Tob. xii, 15 also demonstrate that Milton often turned to Tobit and other apocryphal books for descriptive detail where it was lacking in the Canon; see Mollenkott, p. 28. All quotations from the Book of Tobit are from *The Apocrypha* (Cambridge, 1896), hereafter cited in the text.

19. "Organs," Fowler notes, is "punning between 'instruments' and a sense nearer to the modern ('functionally adapted parts of the body')" in *The Poems of John Milton*, ed. John Carey and Alastair Fowler (London, 1968), p. 661.

20. Sims, *The Bible in Milton's Epics*, p. 28.

21. See, for example, Balachandra Rajan, *"Paradise Lost" and the Seventeenth Century Reader* (1947; rpt. Ann Arbor, 1967), pp. 22–38. Mollenkott, "The Pervasive Influence," concisely formulates the usual assumption: "In poetry . . . [Milton] was not arguing but rather creating imaginative experience for his readers" (p. 28). But I see no reason why "argument" and "imaginative experience" must be mutually exclusive.

22. See William Kerrigan, *The Prophetic Milton* (Charlottesville, 1974) and Joseph Anthony Wittreich, Jr., *Visionary Poetics: Milton's Tradition and his Legacy* (San Marino, 1979). Quotations from Kerrigan hereafter will be cited in the text by page number only.

23. In the Cambridge manuscript none of the four drafts of a projected tragedy on the theme of *Paradise Lost* refers to Raphael. The first draft includes Michael; neither the second nor third names any unfallen angel; and in the fourth it is Gabriel who descends to earth to describe Paradise. See *The Works of John Milton*, ed. F. A. Patterson et al. (New York, 1931–38), vol. XVIII, pp. 228–31.

24. Margaret Ferguson has suggested to me that Raphael Hythloday in Thomas More's *Utopia* may also have influenced Milton's decision to develop Raphael for his own version of paradise.

25. Robert West, *Milton and the Angels* (Athens, Ga., 1955), pp. 167–68. West argues that Milton followed the angelologist Robert Fludd on this point. On the question of angelic sex, according to West, "Milton here enters into questions debated among angelologists and almost unanimously decided against his view" (p. 106; see also pp. 114–15). Milton even diverges from Mark xii, 25: "When they shall rise from the dead, they neither marry nor are given in marriage, But are as the Angels which are in Heaven" (p. 122). Milton's heterodoxy here, along with his decision to make Raphael blush, further corroborates Sims's assertion, in *The Bible in Milton's Epics*, p. 28, that Milton wished "to establish the basic similarity of men, angels, and all created things."

26. See Kerrigan, *The Prophetic Milton*, pp. 133–34.

27. Mollenkott, "The Pervasive Influence," pp. 34, 35–36.

28. For a basic exposition of the doctrine see Roland Frye, *God, Man, and Satan* (Princeton, 1960), pp. 9–17; for theological sources see C. A. Patrides, *Milton and the Christian Tradition* (Oxford, 1966), pp. 7–14; for the critique of accommodated language I argue against see William Madsen, *From Shadowy Types to Truth: Studies in Milton's Symbolism* (New Haven, 1968), pp. 54–84. Quotations from Madsen hereafter will be cited in the text by page number only. For an analysis of Milton's "poetics of accommodation" as it relates to Raphael's representation as a phoenix, see Geoffrey H. Hartman, "Adam on the Grass with Balsamum," in *Beyond Formalism*, and references there.

29. Stanely Fish, *Surprised by Sin: The Reader in "Paradise Lost"* (Berkeley, University of California Press, 1971), p. 179.

30. Cf. William Empson, *Some Versions of Pastoral* (1950; rpt. New York, 1968), p. 189.

31. For example, Anne Ferry, *Milton's Epic Voice: The Narrator in "Paradise Lost"* (Cambridge, 1963), p. 49, et passim.

32. Kerrigan, *The Prophetic Milton*, p. 146–59. What follows is indebted to Kerrigan's fine discussion of freedom and the poet's characters.

33. I thank Elizabeth Leavell for the pun. Cf. Michael Seidel, *Satiric Inheritance: Rabelais to Sterne* (Princeton, 1979), p. 35: "when Milton writes that in justifying God to men he 'may assert Eternal Providence' (I, 25), he says, in effect, that he will put into sequence or narrate (assert = *adserere* = connect) events seen before (*pro-videre*) and known outside of time (*e-ternal*)."

34. John Guillory, *Poetic Authority: Spenser, Milton, and Literary History* (New York, 1983), pp. 151–61; quotations from Guillory hereafter will be cited in the text by page number only.

35. For Kenneth Burke's discussion of rhetorical names for God, see *A Rhetoric of Motives* (1950; rpt. Berkeley: University of California Press, 1969), pp. 298–301.

36. See the first chapter of Guillory, *Poetic Authority*. Cf. Kermode, *The Genesis of Secrecy*, pp. 81–83, who argues that midrash — a species of apocryphal text — should be identified with fiction.

37. Barbara Lewalski, "The Genres of *Paradise Lost:* Literary Genre as a Means of Accommodation," in *Milton Studies*, XVII, ed. Richard S. Ide and Joseph Wittreich (Pittsburgh, 1983), has refined the sense in which Raphael's narration can be called poetic by demonstrating that "the subordinate narrators Milton creates in *Paradise Lost* are imagined as poets inventing literary forms . . . as a means to accommodate particular subjects to a specific audience, Adam and Eve" (p. 98). Lewalski then suggests that this poetic procedure accurately reflects Milton's own, and that generic choice is consequently more important than prophetic authority or affective entrapment as a means of moral instruction. But Lewalski's impressive exposition of the generic "inventions" of Raphael and Michael does not take into account the issue of sacred, apocryphal, and poetic texts, where genre and prophetic authority merge. The genres Raphael invents are imagined as inscribed in a particular kind of text, and that text is apocryphal.

38. Cf. William Empson's paraphrase in *Milton's God* (London, 1965), p. 147, of one of his Chinese postgraduates: "Adam and Eve would never have fallen unless God had sent Raphael to talk to them, supposedly to strengthen their resistance to temptation." Though extreme to the point of parody, the remark nonetheless penetrates to an issue that more resolutely Christian eyes have been conditioned to overlook. The most sustained apology for Raphael I have come across is Philip J. Gallagher, "The Role of Raphael in *Samson Agonistes*," in *Milton Studies*, XVIII, ed. James D. Simmonds (Pittsburgh, 1983), who attempts to forestall all claims that Raphael is *not* an embodiment of "prevenient grace sent by the deity to initiate the regeneration of fallen man before he has fallen" (p. 256). Gallagher essentially adopts the perspective of Milton's God, arguing that "far from requiring, as the condition of sufficiency, the insights about Satan he acquires from Raphael, Adam need not even know of the Devil's existence" (p. 265). But Milton includes a more compassionate human perspective on such doctrinal severity by invoking the Book of Tobit, which he would have regarded as a more authoritative subtext than the Greek parallels adduced by Gallagher.

39. William Riley Parker, *Milton: A Biography* (Oxford, 1968), pp. 430, 562, 569.

40. E. M. W. Tillyard, *Milton* (London, 1930), p. 282. William Empson gleefully paraphrases the remark in *Some Versions of Pastoral*, though he later notes in *Milton's God* (p. 172), that E. M. W. Tillyard implicitly retracts the statement in *Studies in Milton* (London, 1960), pp. 67–70.

"THOUGH OF THIR NAMES":
THE DEVILS IN *PARADISE LOST*

John Leonard

E VERY STUDENT of *Paradise Lost* knows that the names by which
the fallen angels are introduced in the catalogue of Book I and distinguished in the council of Book II are names of devils or pagan gods.
But the importance of this is easily obscured due to the difficulty of speaking about a character from a novel, poem, or play without naming him.
Thus we all call Satan "Satan," Beelzebub "Beelzebub," and Belial "Belial"
as if these were their names as Adam is "Adam." Yet, when speaking
to each other, Satan and the other rebels never use the names which Milton has given them. In the lines with which he introduces the catalogue,
Milton makes clear that the names he is to use are not the names the
angels had borne in Heaven:

> Then were they known to men by various Names,
> And various Idols through the Heathen World.
> Say, Muse, thir Names then known. (I, 374–76)[1]

Richard Bentley altered the second "then" to "when" so as to emphasize
the fact that the fallen angels' new names are subsequent to the Fall of
Man.[2] Zachary Pearce thus defended the sense of the passage as it stands:
"the sense is, Muse say or declare the Names by which they were then
known when 'wandring' over the Earth they got them new names."[3]
Bentley's emendation may be dismissed, but the meaning he has noticed
and emphasized is valid: Milton's repeated "then" warns us off assigning
the devils their names now as they bestir themselves at Satan's call.

The poet states explicitly that the rebels have lost their original names
and not yet acquired new ones:

> of thir Names in heav'nly Records now
> Be no memorial, blotted out and ras'd
> By thir Rebellion, from the Books of Life.
> Nor had they yet among the Sons of *Eve*
> Got them new Names, till wandring ore the Earth
> Through Gods high sufferance for the tryal of man,
> By falsities and lyes the greatest part
> Of Mankind they corrupted. (I, 361–68)

"Got them new Names" looks forward to the motive later attributed to the builders of Babel — that they should "get themselves a name, least far disperst / In foraign Lands thir memorie be lost" (XII, 45–46). The getting of names is quite different from the receiving of one's right name from God or (as transpires with the beasts) from God through Adam, His image on earth. The word "got" contrasts with the cognate "begot," used in the naming of the Son as "Messiah" in Book V. The Son does not get himself his new name, but receives it as a gift befitting his nature.

Even before the catalogue, the devils' names sit uneasily upon them. Satan's "bold Compeer" is not simply "Beelzebub," but "One next himself in power, and next in crime, / Long after known in *Palestine*, and nam'd / *Beelzebub*" (I, 79–81). For ease of narration Milton must make use of a name, but his equivocating syntax draws back from surrendering it to the angel as he welters by Satan's side. The poet names him "Beelzebub" but refers the name to a time "long after" his fall from Heaven. Throughout the catalogue of devils' names, the names are prophecies of future degeneration imposed upon the angels as sentences of doom:

> Next came one
> Who mourn'd in earnest, when the Captive Ark
> Maim'd his brute Image, head and hands lopt off
> In his own Temple, on the grunsel edge,
> Where he fell flat, and sham'd his Worshipers:
> *Dagon* his Name, Sea Monster, upward Man
> And downward Fish: yet had his Temple high
> Rear'd in *Azotus*.   (I, 457–64)

Like Beelzebub, Dagon is first ushered into the poem as "one." But his name is not tacked on; he is thrown down into it. Alastair Fowler tells us that "dag" is Hebrew for "fish" and that, on the authority of this etymology, John Selden and others had represented the Dagon of 1 Samuel as half fish.[4] The image of a human form brought low by the brute which defiles it captures perfectly the predicament of the fallen angels. Not yet wholly brutalized, they still strive upward but are claimed by the names of shame the poet imposes on them. The "fall'n cherube" of I, 157 would be dismayed to learn that he will one day be "Beelzebub," literally "Lord of Flies" in Hebrew.

I shall argue that Satan's followers (but not Satan himself) are without names throughout the action of *Paradise Lost*. Not yet possessed of the names by which the poet distinguishes them, they have lost the names they had borne in Heaven. The evidence for this is not the absence of unfallen names among the rebels — that is only to be expected, for Milton has no way of knowing what their heavenly names were. Every name of an angel, fallen or unfallen, has been taken either from the Bible or from the Apocrypha: like other poets of his time who wrote of angels, Milton is unwilling to mar the seriousness and truth of his subject by inventing names.[5] But the absence of the devils' names from their own speeches sets Milton's poem apart from the works of other seventeenth-century poets. In the *Lucifer* of Joost van Vondel, for example, Apollyon, Belial, and Beelzebub (to name only some of the rebels in that play) bear and speak these names both before and after their rebellion and fall. The one exception to this general pattern is Lucifer himself, an angel for whom Scripture (according to patristic tradition) has provided an unfallen name.[6] Lucifer changes name to become "Sathan" in Vondel's play. We find the same pattern of name-bearing and speaking in Dryden's *State of Innocence*. Dryden changed the name of Milton's Satan to Lucifer and made the fallen angels address each other by devils' names. This goes part of the way to accounting for why Dryden's work is so weak compared with its epic model. When Lucifer cries "ho, Asmadai awake!" the proper name concedes that the angels have lost Heaven to become devils; but Satan's magnificent line, "Awake, arise, or be for ever fall'n" (I, 330) addresses his host as an army of angels. The two playwrights have no choice but to place devils' names in the mouths of their rebellious angels, for the stage demands that those who speak on it are swiftly and clearly identified to the audience. But Milton's epic form gives him more freedom. He is able to build in a contrast between his own ready naming of the rebels and their eschewing of names.

In each of their speeches in Books I and II the fallen angels either address each other by grand titles or else find some other circumlocution. Grand titles and forms of address are an epic topos, but in other epics and elsewhere in *Paradise Lost* these embellish names—they do not replace them. Thus in the *Iliad* Agamemnon will say: "O Nestor, son of Neleus, great glory of the Achaeans" (XIV, 41), but he does not omit the name. On the contrary, he states it as a principle that warriors should always be addressed by their family names: "call every man by the name of his descent, his father's name, his name of dignity" (X, 67–68). In the first two Books of *Paradise Lost*, more than anywhere else in epic poetry, the reader depends upon the poet-narrator for his knowledge of who is speaking to whom. Consider Satan's first words in the poem:

> If thou beest he; But O how fall'n! how chang'd
> From him, who in the happy Realms of Light
> Cloth'd with transcendent brightness didst out-shine
> Myriads though bright.   (I, 84–87)

The "If" is not idle: we have been told that this angel is to be known as "Beelzebub"—but there is nothing in Satan's words to match this name with the pronoun to which he keeps returning. Critics usually identify this "neerest Mate" with the "Companion dear" Satan first seduces to his side in Book V: but there is nothing in *Paradise Lost* to make the identification certain. Before his fall Satan's deputy is not "Beelzebub" and it is to Milton's credit that he does not use this name of him in Book V.

In the council in Hell the rebels do not address each other as individuals—something which speakers in Homer's and Virgil's councils always do—nor do they refer back to the previous speaker, save in the most cursory way. Thus Belial answers Moloch:

> I should be much for open Warr, O Peers,
> As not behind in hate; if what was urg'd
> Main reason to perswade immediate Warr,
> Did not disswade me most.   (II, 119–22)

Belial's passive "what was urg'd" helps not only to shift the mood from urgency to pacification, it also avoids any reference to the previous speaker's name. There is no such anonymity in the rejoinder with which Satan puts Belial down in the council in Book II of *Paradise Regained*. When Belial recommends women as the way to Jesus' undoing, Satan's reply is brisk and to the point: "To whom quick answer Satan thus return'd: / *Belial*, in much uneven scale thou weightst / All others by thyself" (II, 172–74). By the time of Christ's Incarnation the devils have got them new names which facilitate a more contemptuous dismissal of each other than had been possible in the old debate.

The only speaker in *Paradise Lost* (other than the poet) to refer to any of Satan's followers by name is Raphael. This he does in relating the war in Heaven. We hear, for example, of Gabriel's rout of "Moloc" (VI, 357). Adramelec, Asmadai, Ariel, Arioc, and Ramiel all meet similar defeat. These are all devils' names (or names so interpreted in Milton's lifetime) taken from the Bible and Apocrypha. Their presence here does seem to contradict the earlier statement that the devils had not yet "got them new names." I say "seem to" because the contradiction may be resolved if we suppose Raphael to be speaking names he knows the fallen angels will later acquire. This Michael certainly does of the lands Abraham's heirs are to receive in gift: "From *Hamath* Northward to the Desert South / (Things by thir names I call, though yet unnam'd)" (XII, 139–40). There is no such parenthesis in Raphael's lines, but a few lines after mentioning "Arioc" and the rest he says the fallen angels are "by doome / Canceld from Heav'n and sacred memorie, / Nameless in dark oblivion let them dwell" (VI, 378–80). There are two ways of interpreting "Nameless," one more obvious than the other, but less consistent with the rest of the poem. The obvious meaning is that the devils' names Raphael has just spoken should remain unspoken. This is what Raphael means five lines later when he says, "Eternal silence be thir doome" (VI, 385). This "doome" sounds different from the "doome" which had canceled the angels from "sacred memorie" seven lines earlier. Both uses of the word have the sense "judgement" (*OED*, 6), but the second introduces an element of uncertainty with the sense "lot" (*OED*, 4). Whereas the first "doome" is fixed and inescapable, the second is invoked by Raphael. The distinction may be illustrated by a hypothetical modern parallel: were the Master of a College to announce at High Table, "I will not permit the name 'Jacques Derrida' within these walls — never let me hear that name again!" for all his forbidding, Professor Derrida would still bear his name. But the names which have been banished from "sacred memorie" are not just unmentioned, they are "Canceld." These words look back to the statement in Book I that the fallen angels' original names have "no memorial" and are "blotted out and ras'd / By thir Rebellion, from the Books of Life" (I, 360–61). The "memorial" denied the fallen angels is not a fabricated monument of the kind raised by the builders of Babel "least . . . thir memorie be lost," it is the "sacred memorie" of God: His living attention focused in love upon His creature. When this love is withdrawn the creature is "Nameless" not just in the sense that his name is unspoken; he forfeits the name which was given him at his Creation, for he has vitiated the nature which that name rightly befits. Raphael's "Nameless in dark oblivion let them dwell" (VI, 380), applies to the rebels' fallen and unfallen names, but it applies in different ways to each. Applied to the fallen names, his "let" is an imprecation, but applied to the unfallen, there is no doubt as to its fulfillment.

In the exordium to Book III the thoroughness of "blotted out and ras'd" finds matter for comparison and contrast in the limited erasure suffered by the blind bard. He is not struck off the "Books of Life" but for the "Book of knowledg fair" he is

> Presented with a Universal blanc
> Of Natures works to mee expungd and ras'd
> And wisdome at one entrance quite shut out.   (III, 48–50)

The qualifying "to mee" and "At one entrance" acknowledge, even as he laments, that the Book of Nature has itself suffered no deletion by his private loss. There is also the possibility of compensation, for while the "Universal blanc" with which he is confronted is a "void" (*OED*, 6b), it is also a blank page permitting a new entry: the poet may see things "invisible to mortal sight." Bentley dismissed the expression "blanc of . . . works" as "unphilosophical" on the grounds that "one may as well say a blank paper of Words" (p. 79). Even Patrick Hume, whose *Annotations on Paradise Lost* (1695) are far less presumptuous than Bentley's emendations, ventures the following suggestion: "I cannot persuade myself but it should have been a Universal blot, and that it is a mistake of the Printer."[7] Hume's "Blot," though an impoverishment, fortifies the link with the Book I lines. The poet's "blanc" Book of knowledge is capable of both admitting and yielding new knowledge, but the blotted pages of the Books of Life will never readmit the rebel angels.

God's canceling the rebel angels from memory may be compared with a modern work, *The Unnamable* by Samuel Beckett. Described as a "novel" by its publishers, this unnamable work consists of a monologue delivered by a voice whose consciousness and identity are repeatedly challenged and often usurped by a succession of voices to which it gives various names. Unlike Adam, the speaking voice of *The Unnamable* does not receive language as a gift from a superior being, but has language imposed upon it. The voice denies that it belongs to any of the names which claim it (Murphy, Watt, Mercier), but whether it denies them or forgets them, it cannot prevent them from appropriating it. The very dismissing of the names gives them new life to continue the voice: "There's no getting rid of them without naming them and their contraptions, that's the thing to keep in mind. I might as well tell another of Mahood's stories."[8] Mahood and the rest are never "Canceld" from the speaker's consciousness for it draws upon them for its continued, burdensome existence.

Both *Paradise Lost* and *The Unnamable* explore conditions of namelessness, but Milton's poem never calls pronouns into question. The loss of their unfallen names and the suspension of their fallen ones do not call into question the rebel angels' existence or responsibility. Milton could never concur with these words from *The Unnamable:* "all here is sin, you don't know why, you don't know whose, you don't know against whom, someone says you, it's the fault of the pronouns, there is no name for me, no pronoun for me" (p. 122). Milton's pronouns are never at a loss to express where sin lies, even when proper names founder:

> The hasty multitude
> Admiring enter'd and the work some praise
> And some the Architect: his hand was known
> In Heav'n by many a Towred structure high,
> Where Scepter'd Angels held thir residence,

And sat as Princes, whom the supreme King
Exalted to such power, and gave to rule,
Each in his Hierarchie, the Orders bright.
Nor was his name unheard or unador'd
In ancient *Greece;* and in *Ausonian* land
Men call'd him *Mulciber;* and how he fell
From Heav'n, they fabl'd, thrown by angry *Jove*
Sheer o're the Chrystal Battlements, from Morn
To Noon he fell, from Noon to dewy Eve,
A summers day; and with the setting Sun
Dropt from the Zenith like a falling Star,
On *Lemnos* th'*Aegaean* Ile: thus they relate,
Erring; for he with this rebellious rout
Fell long before; nor aught avail'd him now
To have built in Heav'n high Towrs; nor did he scape
By all his Engins, but was headlong sent
With his industrious crew to build in hell.   (I, 730–51)

One is immediately struck by the pattern of alliteration on the letter "h" in these lines. Christopher Ricks has drawn attention to the juxtaposition of "Heav'n" with "high": "To say that Heaven is high would be to risk cliché; but to suggest it while saying something else is another matter."⁹ Words like "Heav'n" and "high" link with "hasty," "hand," "Hierarchie," "headlong," and the repeated "he/him/his" to make "hell" the only name adequate to clothe the bare pronoun this nameless angel has become. This "Architect" is not "Mulciber"; that is a name he is later to acquire in the fallen world. Because "Mulciber" is the only name here given, it is treacherously easy to read it back into the preceding lines where no name appears. The words "Nor was his name unheard" glance back to the lines before to give the false signal that a name had been spoken, but the poet had said only that "his hand was known / In Heav'n by many a Towred structure high." Presumably his name was known in Heaven too, but no mention is made of that original name which is conspicuous only by its absence. Even the "name" referred to in line 738 is not "Mulciber," for it is in "ancient Greece" that this unspoken "name" is said to have been adored. As so often, Bentley's eccentricity is regular then most, when most irregular it seems. He recognizes the unease with which "Mulciber" fits this architect and with brilliant stupidity changes the lines to suit his own principles:

This is carelessly expressd. Why does he not tell his Name in Greece, as well as his Latin Name. And Mulciber was not so common a Name as Vulcan. It may be alter'd and pointed thus:

unheard or unador'd:
In Greece Hephaestos, in th'Ausonian Land
Men call'd him Vulcan: and how once he fell
From Heaven They fabl'd.   (P. 33)

By pinning the angel down in this way, Bentley forfeits the namelessness
which lies at the heart of Milton's lines. Milton's use of the less common
name "Mulciber" confesses (as Bentley's "Hephaestos" and "Vulcan" do
not) the inadequacy of classical names to fallen angels. The poet makes
mention of the architect's name in "ancient Greece," but he does not speak
it: "Hephaestos" is no nearer the original heavenly name than "Mulciber" is, and the withholding of the Greek name here indicates that even
the most ancient of pagan names are conjured up out of nowhere. Well
might the "hasty multitude" haste over their praises or even direct them
to "the work" instead of "the Architect"; to dwell on them too long would
expose the namelessness of the builder, a namelessness they share.

II

The one exception is Satan. He is first introduced in the poem as "th'
Arch-Enemy / And thence in Heav'n call'd Satan" (I, 81–82). Most editors
take the cue from this line to note that "Satan" is Hebrew for "enemy."[10]
The conditioning words "in Heav'n" have been ignored, but they are no
less significant than the gloss they accompany, for the name "Satan" is
scrupulously avoided in Hell, where God, not Satan, is "our great Enemie"
(II, 137). Unlike his followers, Satan has got himself a new name by the
time of his fall from Heaven, but none of his followers ever uses it, nor
does it pass his own lips until he meets Sin and Death for a second time:

Fair Daughter, and thou Son and Grandchild both,
High proof ye now have giv'n to be the Race
Of *Satan* (for I glorie in the name,
Antagonist of Heav'ns Almightie King).   (X, 384–87)

I hope to show that this parenthesis is not just a casual glossing of his name
but an unprecedented concession by Satan and a major development in
his life in the poem.
I shall argue that there are two major changes in Satan's relations
to his names. The first, which occurs in the rebellion in Heaven, is the
loss of his unfallen name and the appearance of the new name "Satan."
The second is his acceptance of this name. The name "Lucifer" occurs
only thrice in *Paradise Lost*, but it is suggested at many places where the
name is not spoken. When Raphael describes the violation of sleep which
precedes Lucifer's open revolt, his name is not spoken, but it is spoken of:

                              but not so wak'd
              Satan, so call him now, his former name
              Is heard no more in Heav'n.   (V, 657–59)

The early Christian fathers, Origen and Tertullian, had attributed the
name "Lucifer" to Satan on the authority of Isaiah, 12: "How art thou
fallen from heaven, O Lucifer, son of the morning!" Calvin had denied
that Satan was being alluded to in this verse, but the tradition had stuck
too fast to be removed.[11] When in *Paradise Lost* we hear of the rebel angel's "great . . . name" which leads his followers astray, it is his "former
name," not "Satan," which is referred to:

                              all obey'd
              The wonted signal, and superior voice
              Of thir great Potentate; for great indeed
              His name, and high was his degree in Heav'n,
              His count'nance, as the Morning Starr that guides
              The starrie flock, allur'd them, and with lyes
              Drew after him the third part of Heav'ns Host.   (V, 704–10)

The proximity of "name" to "Morning Starr" quietly suggests the name
Raphael withholds, for even without reference to Satan, "Lucifer" is a
name for the planet Venus, the morning star (*OED*, 1).

    Bentley changed "Morning Starr" to "Evening Star" on the grounds
that Satan leads from the front:

Morning Star and Evening Star is one and the same star: yet what may be said
of it in the one respect, may not be said of it in the other. As Morning Star, it
does not guide the starry flock, for it goes off the hindmost; as Evening star, it
guides them and comes foremost . . . He must therefore have design'd it here
EVENING STAR.   (P. 172)

Pearce defended "Morning Star" as appropriate to the name "Lucifer"
and dismissed Bentley's objection on the grounds that shepherds lead from
the rear of their flocks. But, as Sir William Empson has pointed out in
Some Versions of Pastoral: "the words are 'drew after him,' and the in-
version acts as part of the conflict of feeling; he leads them only towards
night."[12] In Milton's lines the morning star acts like the evening star: Empson concludes from this that Milton is himself confused about the pertinence of the morning star as a symbol for Satan. Referring to *Paradise
Regained*, where Jesus is called "our Morning Star" (I, 294), Empson
writes: "he becomes Our Morning Star, who is Lucifer, who is Satan:
the doubt about the symbolism fits Milton's secret parallel between the
two" (p. 182). Empson writes as if the names "Lucifer" and "Satan" are

interchangeable, but in doing so he ignores Raphael's "so call him now."
The names are not interchangeable but have changed once and for all
time. Fowler, nevertheless, goes too far in distinguishing Satan from
Lucifer when he says that "the bright face of 'Lucifer, son of the morning' is . . . a mendacious impersonation."[13] Satan's created nature as Lucifer is wholly good, but in withdrawing from God's throne he vitiates this
nature and forfeits the name which goes with it.

Before withdrawing, Satan sends word through the host that:

> now ere Night,
> Now ere dim Night had disincumberd Heav'n
> The great Hierarchal Standard was to move.   (V, 699–701)

There is a beautiful balance of feeling in "disincumberd," which by its
proximity to "starrie flock" (V, 709) lends to Satan's removal the suggestion of a dutiful compliance with the harmony of the universe. It is just
possible for the order to remove to be interpreted by his followers as the
preparation for a special compliment to the Son, a compliment which
befits Satan's created nature as Lucifer:

> The Stars with deep amaze
> Stand fixt in stedfast gaze,
>   Bending one way their pretious influence,
> And will not take their flight,
> For all the morning light,
>   Or *Lucifer* that often warn'd them thence;
> But in their glimmering Orbs did glow,
> Untill their Lord himself bespake, and bid them go.
>   *Nativity Ode*, vi, 41–48

Here, in the Nativity ode, the eagerness of the star Lucifer to depart from
Jesus' sight is wholly innocent and contrasts with the "sullen" flight (xxiii,
205) of the devils Peor, Dagon, Ashtoreth, and Moloc. Withdrawal in
order to furnish greater brilliance and splendor is part of the nature of
Lucifer, both angel and star. In the Nativity ode the star Lucifer is more
faithful than its fellows because it is willing to remove from its Creator.
In their hymn in *Paradise Lost*, Adam and Eve address this star as follows:

> Fairest of starrs, last in the train of Night,
> If better thou belong not to the dawn,
> Sure pledge of day, that crown'st the smiling Morn
> With thy bright Circle.   (V, 166–69)

The star is a "pledge of day," a brilliant light which must yield place to
the far more brilliant sun. Lucifer the angel must yield precedence to

the Son of God, the rising Messiah, but, unlike his stellar namesake, he resists the natural order, withdrawing like the devils of the Nativity ode, in sullen hatred but without their fear. Lucifer's natural office is to usher in the new dawn of the Messiah, but he races to Night, drawing his followers after him by bad example.

Milton acknowledges the existence of a "former name" which contrasts with Satan's new identity as God's enemy, but Raphael's "as the Morning Starr" does not bestow the name "Lucifer" on Satan. More than scholarly caution is at work here. By replacing the name with a simile, Raphael enables the stellar purity of Satan's original nature to slip free from the rebellious context into which he would force it: some thirty lines after the reference to his "great . . . name" we hear that

> *Satan* with his Powers
> Far was advanc't on winged speed, an Host
> Innumerable as the Starrs of Night,
> Or Starrs of Morning, Dew-drops, which the Sun
> Impearls on every leaf and every flouer. (V, 743–47)

When we first read "Starrs of Morning" it seems as if this is an expansion on the "Starrs of Night" simile: Satan and his host are as numberless as the stars in the night or early morning sky. The latter half of the simile is especially appropriate, for as "Lucifer" Satan can stake a direct claim to the morning star which bears his name. The momentary exultation in "Starrs of Morning" then gives way to surprise as the meaning falls away to "Dew-drops": Satan has only a slippery hold upon the morning star. But there is no violence in this falling off. The rebels' splendor is called into question, but not their beauty. The impearling of dew on leaves and flowers is reminiscent of the Garden of Eden where the sun spreads "His orient Beams, on herb, tree, fruit, and flour / Glistring with dew" (IV, 644–45). A few lines later the reader experiences another unsettling moment as he encounters the first of the poem's three instances of "Lucifer":

> At length into the limits of the North
> They came, and *Satan* to his Royal seat
> High on a Hill, far blazing, as a Mount
> Rais'd on a Mount, with Pyramids and Towrs
> From Diamond Quarries hewn, and Rocks of Gold,
> The Palace of Great *Lucifer*, (so call
> That Structure in the Dialect of men
> Interpreted). (V, 755–62)

The sudden appearance of "Lucifer" throws back on "Satan" a doubt which had been absent as he moved through the towers reflective of his splendor. As we pause at the comma after "Lucifer," however, this doubt does not yet call his splendors into question: Satan might step from the one name into the other as easily as he settles into his throne. The bracketed "(so call . . .)" at the end of line 760 seems, for a moment, to herald a renaming of the angel and a revelation of his full glory which will justify his claim on the "Morning Starr" in the earlier lines. But instead of the expected "so call / That angel" we find "so call / That Structure." Raphael's words do not cordon "Lucifer" off from Satan but they do constitute a surprise, a surprise which is greater for the positioning of "(so call" at the end of the line. The word "Structure" is especially sinister, for it had been by "many a Towred structure high" (I, 733), that the hand of the nameless architect not yet called "Mulciber" had been said to be known in Heaven. Satan's structure is greater than these for it is known by a name, not just a "hand," but Raphael does not concede that "Lucifer" is Satan's name. The architect of Book I had learned that his structures could avail him nothing when faced with the fall from Heaven to Hell. Now as Satan returns proudly to his own seat, the echo of line 733 suggests that he, like the nameless architect, is to be a structuralist of a different kind, stripped of the name he claims as his proper sign and hurled into exile.

The second appearance of the name "Lucifer" in *Paradise Lost* is in Book VII, but I quote it here because it looks directly back to the first. Before commencing his account of creation, Raphael says:

> Know then, that after *Lucifer* from Heav'n
> (So call him, brighter once amidst the Host
> Of Angels, then that Starr the Starrs among)
> Fell with his flaming Legions through the Deep
> Into his place . . .   (VII, 131–35)

Here the bracketed words "so call him" do attribute the name "Lucifer" to Satan, but, as before, he is put in his place by a sudden surprise. Raphael's words are a concession and show regret and even love for the being Satan once was, but they lend "Lucifer" as a metaphor, they do not relinquish it as a proper name. We now know why Satan's palace had been called "The Palace of great Lucifer" with the added qualification that this is its name "in the Dialect of men": before anything else, "Lucifer" is the name of the morning star. Milton's eighteenth-century editors noted that the drawing of a distinction between the language of men and that of angels was modeled upon Homer's naming things twice: once in the language of men and again in that of the gods. Thus Richardson writes of "in the Dialect of men": "In imitation of Homer who frequently makes things call'd Differently in the Dialect of Men from what they were by the Gods supposing These to call them by their more Ancient, and obsolete, and those by their modern and Common Names."[14] Newton explains that "the most probable" reason for Homer's naming things twice is "that he attributes those names which are in use only among the learned to the Gods, and those which are in vulgar use to men. However that be, this manner of speaking certainly gives a dignity to the poem, and looks as if the poets had conversed with the Gods themselves."[15] The last point is especially pertinent to Milton's poem, for Raphael is indeed in conversation with Adam as he distinguishes the "Dialect of men" from that of the angels. But neither Richardson nor Newton makes mention of the fact that Milton distinguishes human from angelic language on a principle quite different from that which they accredit to Homer. The name "Lucifer" is the more "Ancient and obsolete" of Satan's two names, yet it is this name which is allocated to the "Dialect of men." Among men it belongs properly to the morning star, a luminary far below the unfallen Satan, but by claiming the name for human language Milton asserts the dignity of prelapsarian human speech. The Adamic language is not a "vulgar use" but is given directly from God to man.[16]

I have so far attended to moments where Satan's names are spoken or at least alluded to. I have argued that Milton is subtle rather than confused in the way he uses the names "Lucifer" and "Satan." He does not equate them as Empson does, but plays them off against each other. Satan's disgrace of his created nature is also suggested by partial resemblances between his appearance and his heavenly surroundings. These resemblances do not depend upon a memory of his change of name, but they are enriched if that change is remembered. Book VI opens with a beautiful description of morning spreading over the plains of Heaven:

> and now went forth the Morn
> Such as in highest Heav'n, array'd in Gold
> Empyreal, from before her vanish't Night,
> Shot through with orient Beams.   (VI, 12–15)

These lines are a topos, but they also contain particular features which are picked up by the description of Satan's host sixty-four lines later:

> Farr in th' Horizon to the North appeer'd
> From skirt to skirt a fierie Region, stretcht
> In battailous aspect, and neerer view
> Bristl'd with upright Beams innumerable
> Of rigid Spears.   (VI, 79–83)

The arising in arms of Lucifer son of the morning is a perversion of true morning, where "Beams" are shafts of light, not spears. Morning in Heaven arises from the Mount of God, not regularly from the east, but, to human ears, the appearance of a "fierie Region" on the northern horizon is a distortion of Nature. Where morning is "array'd in Gold," Satan appears sitting in his "Sun-bright Chariot" "armd in Adamant and Gold" (VI, 110). The appearance of Satan's army with "furious expedition" (VI, 86) in the light of morning displays both his native splendor and his violation of the smiling innocence of the morn.

When Michael encounters Satan in the first day's battle he challenges him thus:

> Author of evil, unknown till thy revolt,
> Unnam'd in Heav'n, now plenteous, as thou seest
> These Acts of hateful strife.   (VI, 262–64)

The prime subject of "unknown" and "unnam'd" is "evil." This is clear from "plenteous," which contrasts the present abundance of evil with its previous nonexistence. But until "plenteous," "Author" is at least as ready a subject for "unknown" and "unnam'd" as evil is, and even after "plenteous," Milton's syntax does not exclude these two words from pertinence to Satan. "Unnam'd" is especially appropriate to him, for Michael does not address his enemy by name. He is not telling Satan that he has always been a nobody, for as "Satan," Lucifer was indeed unnamed until his revolt. "Satan" has come into being with the new name "evil." Michael's words express both the absurdity and tragedy of Satan's revolt: the absurdity of Satan is that he was unnamed until that revolt, but the tragedy of Lucifer is that he lost himself because of it.

When Satan starts into his own shape before Ithuriel and Zephon in Book IV, they at first fail to recognize him:

> Which of those rebell Spirits adjudg'd to Hell
> Com'st thou, escap'd thy prison, and transform'd,
> Why satst thou like an enemie in waite
> Here watching at the head of these that sleep?   (IV, 824–27)

This is a demand for a name, but Satan's magnificent counterquestion scorns his interrogators with an unspoken identity:

> Know ye not then, said *Satan*, fill'd with scorn.
> Know ye not mee? ye knew me once no mate
> For you, there sitting where ye durst not soare;
> Not to know mee argues your selves unknown,
> The lowest of your throng; or if ye know,

> Why ask ye, and superfluous begin
> Your message, like to end as much in vain?   (IV, 828-34)

For Satan the question is "superfluous" because the answer is obvious: he is "Lucifer." If this is realized, the poet's "said *Satan*," dropped quietly between the fallen angel's two "know ye not"s, assumes ironic significance. Like Coriolanus as he unmuffles before Aufidius in Antium, Satan hopes to be recognized from his visible presence:

> Auf: Whence com'st thou? What wouldst thou? Thy
> name?
> Why speak'st not? Speak, man, what's thy name?
> Cor: (Unmuffling) If, Tullus,
> Not yet thou know'st me, but seeing me, dost not
> Think me for the man I am, necessity
> Commands me name myself.
> Auf: What is thy name?   (*Cor.* IV, v, 53-57)

Coriolanus withholds the name "Coriolanus" partly out of tact before the man whose defeat it celebrates. But he withholds all his names ("Caius," "Martius," and "Coriolanus") for the additional reason that all of them, and "Coriolanus" most of all, declare his dependence upon society. Banished from and banishing the society which had given him his names, he presents himself in Antium as "the man I am." In this he is both like and unlike Satan as he asks "Know ye not mee?" Both exiles have supreme confidence in their native merit, but whereas Caius Martius Coriolanus wishes to be recognized without reference to names added by society, Satan scorns Ithuriel and Zephon with the unspoken name "Lucifer" in the belief that it is manifest in and obvious from his "sudden blaze."

Coming just two lines before the poet's "said Satan," Zephon's "enemie" is a gloss. The good angel does not speak the meaning of Satan's name with an awareness that this is what he is doing, but he identifies Satan even as he asks for his name. Ithuriel and Zephon are not cowed by the rebel Chief, but they draw back from calling him "Satan": "Think not, revolted Spirit, thy shape the same" (IV, 836). John M. Steadman speculates from this that Ithuriel and Zephon are still unaware of Satan's identity even after his scornful taunting of them: "Zephon's words give no clear-cut indication that he recognizes his prisoner as the archfiend himself, and the first explicit awareness of his identity is voiced by Gabriel . . . it is Gabriel who first addresses Satan as 'Satan.'"[17] Gabriel is the first speaker to address Satan as "Satan" in the entire poem, not just this episode. Zephon does recognize the intruder once Satan speaks (he scorns him with his change of "shape"), but his "revolted Spirit" is wisely politic. Only in the confrontation with Gabriel, "best with the best," is Satan called "Satan" to his face.

Gabriel makes a point of doing so. In each of his four speeches to Satan at the close of Book IV he drops his enemy's name into the opening words or lines: "Why hast thou, *Satan*, broke the bounds prescrib'd / To thy transgressions?" (IV, 879–80). This is the first time in the poem that the name has been spoken by a voice other than the poet's. Its position between two caesuras gives it an unusual stress. In Gabriel's next speech it is held in abeyance and then delivered in the third person: "O loss of one in Heav'n to judge of wise, / Since *Satan* fell, whom follie overthrew" (IV, 904–05). The name is dangled before Satan as a taunt, spoken at him rather than to him. In Gabriel's third speech the name comes after Satan has shifted his explanation for intruding:

> To say and strait unsay, pretending first
> Wise to flie pain, professing next the Spie,
> Argues no Leader, but a lyar trac't,
> *Satan*, and could'st thou faithful add? O name,
> O sacred name of faithfulness profan'd!   (IV, 947–51)

Once again the name is held in suspension, having to be "trac't" by the reader through three syntactically tortuous lines. Our suspense is not as to who the unsayer is, but when the familiar name will appear. It turns suddenly on Satan, addressing him directly for the first time in this speech. The "profan'd" name Gabriel refers to in the same line is "faithful," but the repetition of "name" in a context of profanation reminds us that "Satan" is itself the result of a profanation. Gabriel's fourth and final addressing of Satan by name is more potent for its simplicity: "*Satan*, I know thy strength, and thou know'st mine / Neither our own but giv'n" (IV, 1006–97). Here is no taunting of Satan, the name is spoken matter-of-factly as something which, no less than both angels' strength, is "giv'n." But Gabriel's strength is given also in his name, for "Strength of God" is its literal meaning.[18]

Satan's reactions to Gabriel's baiting of him change throughout the scene. After Gabriel's first speech, his reply affects supercilious unconcern: "*Gabriel*, thou hadst in Heav'n th'esteem of wise, / And such I held thee" (IV, 887–88). The immediate concession of Gabriel's name strikes a patronizing tone. This self-control does not last long. When Gabriel accuses him of cowardice, Satan enters the exchange in earnest:

> To which the Fiend thus answerd frowning stern.
> Not that I less endure, or shrink from pain,

> Insulting Angel, well thou know'st I stood
> Thy fiercest.   (IV, 924–27)

"Insulting Angel" is an insult. Satan's withholding of Gabriel's name is unprecedented among angels of high rank. When Uriel had warned Gabriel of Satan's escape he had addressed him in a way which endorsed the meaning of his name as "Strength of God":

> *Gabriel*, to thee thy cours by Lot hath giv'n
> Charge and strict watch that to this happie place
> No evil thing approach or enter in.   (IV, 560–62)

Gabriel had employed the same courtesy, describing Uriel's office so as to corroborate the meaning of his name as "Light of God":

> *Uriel*, no wonder if thy perfet sight,
> Amid the Suns bright circle where thou sitst,
> See farr and wide.   (IV, 577–79)

Satan does not concede "the warrior Angel" his name of strength when a trial of strength seems imminent, but he is powerless to deny that Gabriel is an "Angel," an admission which gives the poet's "Fiend" the force of a distinction between the two.

III

As Sin hails Satan in Book X, her words gesture to the bridge which she and Death have built:

> O Parent, these are thy magnific deeds,
> Thy Trophies, which thou view'st as not thine own,
> Thou art thir Author and prime Architect.   (X, 354–56)

Satan's children praise the work and they also praise the "Architect," but he speaks that name which, until this moment, has been unheard and unadored throughout the Infernal Deep:

> Fair Daughter, and thou Son and Grandchild both,
> High proof ye now have giv'n to be the Race
> Of *Satan* (for I glorie in the name,
> Antagonist of Heav'ns Almightie king).   (X, 384–87)

The fallen angel now accepts his role as Satan Antagonistes, an evil foreshadowing of the title Milton is later to confer upon Samson. Both terms come from the Greek *agōnia*, meaning both "suffering" and "contest." But whereas Samson grows through suffering to a renewed faith in God, Satan is degenerated by his inflicting suffering upon others. Both are also contestants in games, but whereas Samson uses the public spectacle of the Philistines' games to serve God, Satan's name "Antagonist" confesses that any war against one who is named — not just "styl'd" (IX, 137) — "Almightie" can only be a game.[19] When Samson labored in the theatre of Dagon, he did so alone, "None daring to appear Antagonist" (SA, 1628). The daring of "That mighty leading Angel, who of late / Made head against Heav'ns King" (II, 991–92), is without limit, but his role as "Antagonist" places him on the opposite side of a barrier from Samson: Samson is to "quit himself / Like Samson . . . on his Enemies / Fully reveng'd" (SA, 1709–12), but Lucifer has quit himself like Satan, himself becoming "th' Arch-Enemy."

Sin's "which thou view'st as not thine own" (X, 355), though applied to Satan's "deeds" and "Trophies," recalls her last meeting with her father when he had viewed herself and Death as not his own: "I know thee not, nor ever saw till now / Sight more detestable than him and thee" (II, 744–45). Satan's failure to recognize his daughter has often been put down to forgetfulness. Thus Fowler writes: "it is part of the change in Satan that he should have forgotten and should not even recognize his sin for what it is."[20] I feel that the change from "Sin" to "his sin" and from "she" to "it" is a change for the worse. Sin and Death have allegorical significance, but they are not allegorical beings. Satan does not identify the "double-formd" Sin with his lover and daughter until she identifies herself, but there is evidence to suggest that he does recognize her in another way. The key words for this reading occur in Sin's recounting of their incestuous affair:

> I pleas'd, and with attractive graces won
> The most averse, thee chiefly, who full oft
> Thy self in me thy perfect image viewing
> Becam'st enamour'd.   (II, 762–65)

Satan's infatuation with his own reflection may (as Douglas Bush has argued for Eve's) allude to the Christian tradition that "some of the newly created angels looked up to God, others fell in love with themselves."[21] But Sin's "perfect" similitude to her father has more than just an allegorical significance. Her resemblance to him, "in shape and count'nance bright" (II, 756), is a reflection of his "count'nance as the Morning Starr" (V, 705). The creature Satan fails to recognize in Book II is a half serpent who bears the face of Lucifer.

He has not necessarily forgotten the birth of Sin when he sees her transformed shape, but he does not think this is she. Why should he? That previous appearance of a stranger bearing his face is evidence that such marvelous encounters happen to him, and it is consistent with his pride that he should not attribute this new development to a lost concubine. He shuns the recognition of this mirror self, not because he has forgotten the being who sprang from his head like Athene from the head of Zeus, but because he remembers her. She had been held a "Sign / Portentous" (II, 761–62), commanding fear by her sudden appearance, but displaying to all eyes the splendor Lucifer knew to be his. Now Satan is confronted for a second time by his perfect likeness, but this is different: here is no "Goddess armd" but "a Serpent armd / With mortal sting" (II, 653–54). In Sin, Satan sees no daughter or lover from Heaven, but he sees a "Sign Portentous" of a different kind: Satan the Serpent.

When she has called him "Father," there is both bewilderment and insistence in his reply:

> So strange thy outcry, and thy words so strange
> Thou interposest, that my sudden hand
> Prevented spares to tell thee yet by deeds
> What it intends; till first I know of thee
> What thing thou art.　　　　　　　　　　(II, 737–41)

Only Sin's "outcry" and her "words," not her features, are said to be "strange," but in the chiasmic repetition of "strange" we hear Satan's determination to keep the serpent-self a stranger. Bentley yielded to Satan's urging of the newness of the encounter by altering the second "strange" to "new," but, in thus breaking the chiasmus and the sense of general strangeness that it brings, he emphasized the fact that Sin's newness is limited to her "words." Though Sin's appearance is "strange" to him, Satan can say to her, as Chaos is soon to say to him: "I know thee, stranger, who thou art" (II, 990). Steadman, who interprets this recognition in Aristotelian terms, argues that it is only after Sin's "detailed explanation" about herself and Death that Satan experiences a "change from ignorance to knowledge": "This fuller revelation of their nature and identity completes the process of discovery."[22] Sin's explanation does bring a change from ignorance to knowledge, but it also brings a change from knowledge to ignorance: her placing of herself in a particular, recognizable place in Satan's personal history allows him to place the serpent only with her, not, as he had first feared, with himself.

His words "I know thee not" are as much a command as a statement of what he takes to be fact. I am reminded of the newly crowned Henry V's use of these words in *Henry IV, Part II;*

> I know thee not, old man. Fall to thy prayers.
> How ill white hairs become a fool and jester!

> I have long dreamt of such a kind of man,
> So surfeit-swell'd, so old, and so profane;
> But being awak'd I do despise my dreame.   (V, v, 47–51)

Whereas Henry's words are spoken by one who is self-knowing, Satan's are spoken by one who wishes to be, but cannot quite become, ignorant of his darker self. There is no disgust in Henry's scrutiny of Falstaff; instead, he is dismissed as a waking man dismisses a dream. Sin, however, steadfastly refuses to fade into a dream image. Satan's "what thing thou art" is revealingly similar to, but different from, Henry's "Presume not that I am the thing I was" (V, v, 56). "I was" acknowledges that the repudiated thing can make some claim upon him, though only to his past. As in Prospero's acknowledgment of Caliban as "this thing of darkness mine," the otherness insisted upon by "thing" is allowed to pass because the speaker is humble enough to accept that the thing of darkness cannot be completely sloughed. This humility Satan does not have. He uses "thing" only with the second person, denying any knowledge of the serpent self which confronts him.

As Satan meets Sin and Death for a second time, he acknowledges them without protest. In Book II he had failed to recognize Sin as his daughter, but now she recognizes him "though in disguise" as "an Angel bright." As Sin and Death greet Satan, the word "dear," which he had used to them in Hell, returns to cement the relationships he had conceded only for the sake of expediency. Satan had claimed the appellation back as soon as it was given: "Dear Daughter, since thou claimst me for thy Sire" (II, 817). But this time it is the poet who calls Sin and Death his "Children dear" (X, 330) and "his Offspring dear" (X, 349).

Satan claims the name "Satan" as a name of glory, but in doing so he relinquishes his hold on "Lucifer." This is made clear thirty lines later when "Lucifer" appears for the third and last time in the poem. Satan finds his followers huddled

> about the walls
> Of *Pandaemonium*, Citie and proud seate
> Of *Lucifer*, so by allusion calld.
> Of that bright Starr to *Satan* paragond.   (X, 423–26)

To a modern reader, the words "by allusion calld" and "paragond" suggest resemblance between Satan's identities as "Lucifer" and "Satan," but when read aright, they do just the opposite. In Milton's lifetime "allusion" was most often used as we use "illusion." The *OED* cites the one word "illusion" as its first definition of "allusion" and quotes an example from 1618: "Resolved in the error of his allusion, he strongly conjectured that . . ." But for the presence of "allusion," "paragond" might mean "To set forth as a paragon or perfect model" (*OED*, 4). This action of the word is not just absent from the text (its presence enables us to feel how the devils hold their chief in reverence), but it is excluded from the poet's sanction. The presence of "allusion" gives greater prominence to the meaning "To place side by side; to parallel, compare" (*OED*, 1). The *OED* does not quote the following example from *Anthony and Cleopatra*, but it can help us to feel the tension between "Lucifer" and "Satan" in Milton's lines:

> Cleo: . . . Did I Charmian,
> Ever Love Caesar so?
> Char: Oh that brave Caesar!
> Cleo: Be chok'd with such another emphasis,
> Say "the brave Antony."
> Char: The valiant Caesar!
> Cleo: By Isis, I will give thee bloody teeth,
> If thou with Caesar paragon again
> My man of men.   (I, v, 66–72)

It is dangerous to paragon unlike persons or things distinguished by a sovereign. Milton's lines, with their three italicized proper names in as many lines, present the most complete withholding of "Lucifer" from Satan in the poem. The two previous applications of "Lucifer," to a building in Book V and a star in Book VII, here come together to welcome the rebel chief by name: he is "Satan (not Lucifer)." The old name doesn't even sit squarely upon the palace (as it had done in Heaven) for the presence of "Pandaemonium" gives this structure's true name: "Seat of all devils."

Satan's recounting of the judgment on himself reflects in small the pattern I have tried to trace in the poem:

> True is, mee also he hath judg'd, or rather
> Mee not, but the brute Serpent in whose shape
> Man I deceav'd: that which to mee belongs,
> Is enmity, which he will put between
> Mee and Mankinde; I am to bruise his heel;
> His Seed, when is not set, shall bruise my head.   (X, 494–99)

The key word here is "mee." This small but decisive word is first yielded to the curse, then at once claimed back in "or rather / Mee not." This is Satan recoiling from his serpent image, locating it with another. Then comes the concession: "that which to mee belongs / Is enmity." This is the nearest Satan ever comes to speaking his name to his followers. Like the poet invoking his muse, Satan calls upon "The meaning, not the Name" (VII, 5). The poet had been cautious in his use of the name "Urania" lest he throw away his prayers upon an "empty dreame" inherited from mythology, but Satan eschews that name which confesses the particular applicability of God's curse to him. His newly accepted name already proclaims him a serpent.

Trinity College, Cambridge

NOTES

1. *The Works of John Milton*, ed. Frank Allen Patterson et al. (New York, 1931), vol. II. All of Milton's poetry cited in this essay is from this edition, hereafter cited in the text.

2. Richard Bentley, *Milton's "Paradise Lost"* (London, 1732), p. 19.

3. Zachary Pearce, *A Review of the Text of the Twelve Books of Milton's "Paradise Lost."* (London, 1733), pp. 31–32.

4. Alastair Fowler, *John Milton: Paradise Lost* (London, 1971), p. 71.

5. Fowler, *John Milton*, pp. 66–78, cites the various sources and draws attention to the appropriateness of the names' meanings to their contexts.

6. The Lucifer of Isaiah is first identified as Satan by Origen and Tertullian. See Stella P. Revard, *The War in Heaven* (Ithaca, 1980), pp. 33–34.

7. P. H. (Patrick Hume) *Annotations on "Paradise Lost"* (London, 1695), p. 100.

8. Samuel Beckett, *The Unnamable* (London, 1975), p. 42.

9. Christopher Ricks, *Milton's Grand Style* (Oxford, 1963), p. 92.

10. The point was first made by Hume, *Annotations* p. 100.

11. Revard, *The War in Heaven*, pp. 33–34.

12. William Empson, *Some Versions of Pastoral* (London, 1935), p. 185.

13. Fowler, *John Milton*, p. 302.

14. Jonathan Richardson, *Explanatory Notes upon "Paradise Lost"* (London, 1734), p. 770.

15. Thomas Newton, *Paradise Lost . . . With Notes of Various Authors* (London, 1749), p. 414.

16. This article is drawn from a book I am writing on the Adamic language of nature in *Paradise Lost*.

17. John M. Steadman, *Epic and Tragic Structure in "Paradise Lost"* (Chicago, 1976), pp. 63–65.

18. Fowler, *John Milton*, p. 227.

19. See James G. Mengert, "Styling the Strife of Glory: The War in Heaven," in *Milton Studies*, XIV, ed. James D. Simmonds (Pittsburgh, 1980), pp. 95–115.

20. Fowler, *John Milton*, p. 126.

21. Douglas Bush, *Milton: "Paradise Lost"* (London, 1966), p. 286.

22. Steadman, *Epic and Tragic Structure*, p. 63.

ADAM IN HOUYHNHNMLAND:
THE PRESENCE OF *PARADISE LOST*

James V. Falzarano

T HE ANTAGONISM between Swift's vocation as a Christian minister and the apparently anti-Christian pessimism expressed in part
4 of *Gulliver's Travels* has persistently generated critical controversy. On
one side of the debate, Roland M. Frye stresses Swift's priestly participation in the Christian tradition of sermons that lament man's fallen condition; he considers this participation as evidence that in *Gulliver's Travels* Swift attempted to reassert the doctrine of original sin to an age which
had exaggerated the goodness inherent in man. Other critics, beginning
with Thackeray, have refused to read Gulliver's final voyage as the product of a Christian motivation; they regard Swift's satire as embodying
a darker attitude toward human nature than even the idea of the Fall
would allow. In a recent instance of this position, Patrick Reilly sees in
Swift "an epistemological pessimism which, though often supporting
religious belief, occasionally threatens it; suspicion of human reason
sometimes deepens to a level inhospitable to any creed."[1] The division
between those who perceive Swift as a Christian sermonizer and those
who think of him as a despairing Christian cannot be resolved by re-
sorting to biographical and historical — to extratextual — evidence, as both
critical camps have attempted to do. I argue that it is a textual element
of *Gulliver's Travels*, the repeated and varied presence of Milton's *Paradise Lost*, which fuses a Christian tone with a satiric purpose, thereby
undermining the critical dichotomy.[2] Swift's allusions to the crucial episodes of Milton's epic enable his readers to compare Gulliver's actions
and attitudes with those of Satan in his rebellion and fall, as well as to
contrast Gulliver's travails among the Houyhnhnms with the central
Christian paradigm of Adam's sin, fall, repentance, and redemption.[3]
When judged against the normative context provided by *Paradise Lost*,
it is Gulliver's misanthropy, and not Swift's, that encounters an orthodox rebuke. The comprehensive presence of Adam, as the implicit *vir
bonus* of Gulliver's Fourth Voyage, demonstrates Swift's knowledge of
and belief in the Christian ideal.

Allusions to *Paradise Lost* help to play a constitutive role in investing

Augustan poetic satire with the moral weight of tradition. As Reuben Brower describes it, the poetry of Dryden and Pope reveals references to Milton as evidence of "the active pressure of older literary traditions." The satiric energy of this poetry often grows out of a reader's awareness that the allusive presence of Milton stands at odds with the explicit meaning of the verse; such "allusive irony" confronts the butts of Augustan satire with the moral force of a literary tradition which reflects the shared interests of Dryden and Pope. Similarly, Barbara Lewalski refers to Pope's use of allusion in "evoking Miltonic contexts for brilliant ironic or satiric effect." Christopher Ricks also shows the Augustan reliance on Miltonic allusion in the service of satire; he reads the Augustan idea of allusion as that of an inheritance, a store of traditional value which has been built up by poetic predecessors. Ricks sees the concern of Dryden and Pope with Miltonic allusion not as a Bloomian sense of anxiety over belatedness, but rather as the wish to invest their inheritance wisely in the interests of satiric truth.[4] The work of all three of these scholars testifies to the great subtlety with which the Augustan poets invoke Miltonic elements in order to lend traditional authority to their satires.

If Dryden and Pope allude to Milton in an effort to strengthen satire, then one might ask whether Swift, as fellow Augustan and satirist, does the same. In current discussion of Swift's poetry, the subject of allusion is undergoing a reassessment. While only several years ago it was believed that "Swift was rarely subtle about including allusions; usually, he footnoted them or even mentioned them within the poem itself,"[5] the latest view holds that "the verbal texture of Swift's poetry is more dense and richly fraught than was once supposed" and that Swift's verse contains "intricately allusive subtexts." Pat Rogers's notes to the new Yale edition of *The Complete Poems* shows that these subtexts owe much to Swift's "traditional devotion to a core of classical and modern authors."[6] Rogers cites *Paradise Lost* as a key text; in the case of several poems, Rogers's annotations reveal Milton's account of the Fall as a structural support for Swift's satiric strategies.[7] The reconsideration of the technique of allusion in Swift's poems, when combined with the discovery of the greater presence of Milton as a source, should indicate at once both the complexity of method and the strong sense of a tradition operating in Swiftian allusion. The case posed by Swift's poetry, together with a knowledge of Augustan satiric practice, should make one suspect that Swift alludes to Milton to add satiric irony to his prose. In so doing, Swift would be asserting a "community of mind," a tradition shared with his Augustan peers.[8]

The analysis of a Miltonic reference in part 2 of *Gulliver's Travels* illustrates both the great subtlety and the traditional character of allusion in Swift's prose. Swift refers to *Paradise Lost* in the seventh chapter of Gulliver's voyage to Brobdingnag. Seeking to ingratiate himself with the king, Gulliver tells him about gunpowder and its use in European warfare to destroy enemies and annex their territories. Gulliver proposes artillery to the king as an efficient way to expand his domain. After listening to Gulliver's account of the death and destruction attendant upon man's rapacious use of guns, the king reacts with horror; he shuns "those destructive machines, whereof he said, some evil genius, enemy to mankind, must have been the first contriver."[9] This passage alludes to Satan's discovery of gunpowder and his invention of the cannon, as described in *Paradise Lost* (VI, 469–523); Satan creates the weapon in an effort to vanquish God, against whom he has rebelled. Although the idea of Satan creating the cannon does not originate with Milton, the context in which Swift places the reference establishes the allusion as Miltonic. Swift compares Gulliver to Satan: Gulliver attempts to seduce the king much as Satan seduces his victims in *Paradise Lost*. Satan extends promises of power and godhead to his fellow angels, and later, to Eve; his motives are evil, and in both cases the results of his seduction are disastrous. The allusion contains much irony: unlike Satan, Gulliver is ignorant of the potentially harmful effects of his proposal. Further, he is obtusely unaware that the king is correct to shun his offer; with hurt pride, Gulliver privately rebukes the king for being so narrowminded as to reject his suggestion. Though haughty like Satan, Gulliver lacks his mental acuity. He also fails in his attempt to seduce.

Not only does Gulliver represent Satan in the allusion, but the king's prelapsarian innocence and instinctive rejection of sin suggest the very figures in *Paradise Lost* who rebuff Satan's temptation: Abdiel, in the case of the rebellion in Heaven (V, 809–95), as well as Eve, whose better judgment resists Satan briefly in Book IX (615–54). The king manifests man's intuitive goodness; he contrasts with that in man which has been corrupted and is capable of further corruption. The allusion connects Swift's text with both the moral and immoral exemplars of Milton's epic.

When allusion links two texts, as in the preceding instance, the meaning and structure of the old text enrich the meaning and structure of the new. At such times the act of allusion therefore assumes "an established literary tradition as a source of value" as well as a knowledgeable audience who can share the tradition and its values with the author who invokes them.[10] Implicit in Swift's allusion to Milton is not only a confluence of Swiftian satire and Miltonic epic, but also a union of Swift and his reader, both of whom become joined by the tradition which they reenact.

In the act of reading a passage like the one from part 2 of *Gulliver's Travels*, the knowledgeable reader begins to notice the presence of allusion through a cue: "some evil genius, enemy to mankind . . . the first contriver."[11] The cue, often by seeming out of place in its present context, urges the reader to consider other contexts in which it might be more appropriate. When the reader discovers the proper context of the cue — the text to which the cue refers — the reader can then summon an entire episode or episodes from that source text in order to compare these episodes meaningfully to corresponding ones in the new text. The fruitfulness of the reader's comparisons in turn validates the cue and confirms the presence of allusion. The reader must complete the process of allusion, which the author can only begin.[12] It is improbable that the reader would consider larger parallels between two texts without the author's cue; it is also unlikely that the cue would possess any significance if it did not urge the reader to consider larger contexts. The reader's realization of the cue, his identification of its source, his consideration of larger contexts, and his comprehensive comparison of contexts from both texts enumerate the significant stages of Swiftian allusion.

The reader who misses the cue might still sense that the Brobdingnagian king is superior to Gulliver for being, as the latter arrogantly calls him, the victim of "the miserable effects of a confined education" (p. 108) and an example of the "strange effect of narrow principles and short views" (p. 109). Even without the cue, the reader might also realize that, though Gulliver does not know it, he is at fault for proposing what he does; the fact of Gulliver's ignorance strengthens Swift's satire, which makes Gulliver a representative of modern man's vices. But the reader who perceives the cue and understands the extent of the allusion apprehends more forcefully Gulliver's depravity and the king's innocence by forging a connection between Swift's satire and the moral perspective of *Paradise Lost*. Modern man, Swift implies, is vicious precisely because of the legacy of the Fall. Satan's sin of pride leads ultimately to wholesale death and destruction in human history; the allusion labels Gulliver's pride as the true "enemy to mankind."

Aside from uniting text with text, the allusion joins reader with writer. The discerning reader perceives that Swift himself inscribes the Christian element in his text; the author has self-consciously evoked the tradition that *Paradise Lost* represents. Of course, the king is as unaware of the English literary tradition as he is of the English military one. And Gulliver, in his role as satiric butt, is himself as totally ignorant of the allusion as he is of the satanic implications of his actions. Precisely because Swift cannot speak in his own voice but must allow his judgments to filter through Gulliver's limited perspective, it is the task of allusion to reinforce Swift's satiric intention.[13] It is Swift who initiates the connection between Gulliver and Satan, between the king and prelapsarian innocence. In so doing, Swift both reminds the reader of the Christian tradition and demonstrates his own knowledge of that tradition. As a result, the understanding reader judges Gulliver as Swift wants him to judge and as Swift himself judges. This sense of shared judgment, based upon a shared tradition and shared values, is the most significant implication of Swift's allusion to *Paradise Lost*, as it allows the reader to know that he is collaborating in the union of Milton's work with Swift's. Swift's deliberate uniting of text with text implies to the reader a joining of minds, through which the reader transcends the narrow focus of Swift's narrator in order to discover authentic authorial motives.

Since the process of allusion relies fundamentally upon the creation of a proper context as well as a community of mind between reader and author, and since the skillful use of Miltonic allusion by Swift's Augustan peers suggests that these men possessed those two requisites, it is very probable that the Augustans had an ability to recognize a Miltonic presence that is greater than our own. What to the modern reader, deprived of the necessary context and community, seems merely a casual reference could have appeared fraught with allusive meaning to a Pope; in like manner, what to a modern seems no reference at all might at one time have echoed a Miltonic presence.[14] To restore the kind of context that Swift's original audience enjoyed would aid greatly in attuning the modern ear to the types of reverberations that the Augustans may have heard. Restoration of the relevant context can change a commonplace or random reference into a meaningful allusion, or silence to an audible echo.[15] One should be aware of a sliding scale of Miltonic reference in Swift; the degree of presence one hears depends upon the quality of context one enjoys. Certain passages in *Gulliver's Travels* allude to *Paradise Lost;* other passages only echo Milton's epic. The phenomenon of echo, as its name suggests, is not as voiceful or as forceful as allusion: one cannot say with certainty that the author intends echo as he intends allusion. Also, echo by itself cannot support the presence of another text in the same way that allusion can; but if the reader is reasonably sure that allusion exists between two texts, and has urged him to consider larger contexts, then he should expect echoes to arise as a natural part of those contexts.[16] The process of allusion generates the contexts in which echoes may be heard.

An example from *Gulliver's Travels* part 4, will show how the ear that is sensitized by proper context can detect even the faintest of echoes. Gulliver appears to the Houyhnhnms in part 4 in much the same satanic way that he confronts the Brobdingnagian king in part 2. In fact, *Gulliver's Travels*, part 4, contains a conversation between Gulliver and the Master Houyhnhnm that suggests the dialogue between Gulliver and the king: both verbal exchanges intimate that warfare is the result of the Fall. Gulliver is amazed that the Master knows so little about the procedures and the effects of battle:

I could not forbear shaking my head and smiling a little at his ignorance. And being no stranger to the art of war, I gave him a description of *cannons*, culverins, muskets, carabines, pistols, bullets, powder . . . my master commanded me silence. He said, whoever understood the nature of yahoos might easily believe it possible for so vile an animal to be capable of every action I had named, if their strength and cunning equalled their malice. But as my discourse had increased his abhorrence of the whole species, so he found it gave him a disturbance in his mind, to which he was wholly a stranger before. He thought his ears being used to such abominable words, might by degrees admit them with less detestation. (Pp. 199–200; emphasis added)

The presence of "cannon" in the catalogue's privileged initial position recalls the cannon allusion from *Gulliver's Travels*, part 2. Once the reader summons forth this context, then the Master's remark seems to echo Eve's reaction to the seductive dream provoked by Satan, who sat "Squat like a Toad, close at the ear of *Eve*" (IV, 800).[17] The next morning, Eve tells Adam that she dreamed "of offense and trouble, which my mind / Knew never till this irksome night" (V, 34–35). Both her mental irritation and its cause resound in the words of the Master Houyhnhnm. The echo brands Gulliver once again as a satanic tempter, while the auditor of his speeches represents man's original innocence.[18] The Houyhnhnm does not fall as a result of hearing Gulliver's discourse; even after Satan's provocation, Eve is without sin, since as Adam explains, "Evil into the mind of God or Man / May come and go, so unapprov'd, and leave / No spot or blame behind" (V, 117–19). As in the case with the Brobdingnagian king, Gulliver's fallen knowledge meets with just rebuke. The reader perceiving only Swift's satire might still apprehend the moral perspective that Swift intends: Gulliver is wrong to promote deadly violence. One armed with the sense of echo can be more certain: Gulliver is morally culpable because he is satanic. The reader who notes the echo working within the satire will see how the one reinforces the power of the other to convey a stronger sense of Swift's moral judgment.

If Gulliver becomes utterly fallen, like Satan, while the Houyhnhnms possess a primordial innocence, then what should prevent the reader from concluding that the Houyhnhnms provide Swift's idea of what man can be? Similarly, if Gulliver is so clearly evil, what should deter one from thinking that Gulliver is an illustration of Swift's idea of man as he is? Another body of references to *Paradise Lost* suggests that modern man, like Gulliver, cannot aspire to Houyhnhnm status just as Adam cannot recover the lost Eden: original sin hinders both wishes. On the other hand, although man may become totally fallen like Gulliver, there is another possibility for man, which Gulliver does not consider because he is blinded by satanic pride. If Gulliver at certain points appears satanic, at other times the presence of Milton's poem reveals his missed opportunity for Adamic repentance and redemption. Many of the conversations between Gulliver and the Houyhnhnms suggest similar dialogues in *Paradise Lost*. The implicit presence of Milton's dramatis personae helps to determine the meaning and define the narrative substructure of Swift's satire. In Gulliver's final voyage, Swift carefully places a pattern of structural allusion, which in turn fosters a host of verbal and thematic echoes.[19] Both forms of Miltonic presence evoke the pivotal dialogues of the latter part of *Paradise Lost:* the confession of Adam and subsequent judgment of God the Son in Book X; the notice of eviction given to Adam and Eve by Michael in Book X; and Michael's glimpse of the future of mankind, given to Adam on the Mount of Speculation in Books XI and XII. Each of these episodes touches upon corresponding elements in *Gulliver's Travels*, part 4, to reflect Swift's idea of man.

The complex nature of Gulliver's sin and fall emerges when the Master Houyhnhnm confronts a naked Gulliver in chapter 3 of part 4. The relevant context for this episode comes from Books IX and X of *Paradise Lost*. After Adam and Eve commit the original sin, they become ashamed and decide to cover themselves. Adam advises that they "cover round / Those middle parts, that this new comer, Shame, / There sit not, and reproach us as unclean" (IX, 1096–98). The desire to hide the genitals is a sign of Adam and Eve's guilt for their sin; Adam is "naked left / To guilty shame: hee cover'd, but his Robe / Uncover'd more" (IX, 1057–59). When God the Son visits the Garden, Adam hides from him. God commands Adam to appear and asks Adam why he hides himself. Adam responds that he fears God's voice because he is naked, that is, ashamed. God then asks, "without revile," "that thou art naked, who / Hath told thee?" (X, 118; 121–22). God already knows what Adam has done and why he is ashamed; his question is meant to elicit Adam's willing confession of his sin. After this necessary confession, Adam may receive God's grace, and the machinery of divine justice, tempered with mercy, may be set slowly in motion.

In chapter 3 of his final voyage, Gulliver is shocked to learn how similar in appearance he is to the detested Yahoo. His nightly nakedness exacerbates this similarity; only his clothing, Gulliver thinks, separates him from being a Yahoo. After a groom discovers the secret of his clothing one morning and reports it to the Master, the latter is struck with curiosity and visits Gulliver. Ashamed at his nakedness before the Houyhnhnm Master, Gulliver relates his behavior: "I let my shirt down to my waist, and drew up the bottom, fastening it like a girdle about my middle to hide my nakedness" (p. 191). The Master does not at all comprehend why Gulliver should feel shame at his physical appearance: "he could not understand why nature should teach us to conceal what nature had given. That neither himself nor family were ashamed of any parts of their bodies; but however I might do as I pleased" (p. 191). Through this highly allusive passage, Swift juxtaposes the situation of Adam before God with that of Gulliver before the Houyhnhnm. Whereas Eve sins by assenting to satanic pride, Adam errs by joining Eve in her disobedience of God's command. Adam knows that he has wronged a God who deserves better from him. Gulliver, however, mistakenly perceives his sin to be his physical likeness to the Yahoos; yet his real sin, his pride, causes him both to deify and later to emulate the Houyhnhnm Master. In denying the Yahoo and embracing the Houyhnhnm, Gulliver rejects the human nature which he thinks would only impede the attainment of his equine goal. In striving to be godlike, both our first parents and Gulliver wrongly deny their essential human natures. Gulliver may be more to blame in this, however, since his god is hardly as worthy of emulation as is the Christian deity. Whereas Adam and Eve sin through pride and disobedience, Gulliver sins through pride and obsequiousness. He enslaves himself by worshipping a less-than-perfect being. In glorifying the Houyhnhnm Master, Gulliver adopts an inadequate analogue to the Christian God. This glorification adversely affects all of Gulliver's future attitudes and actions.

Just as Swift's allusion implicitly compares the sins of Adam and Gulliver, it also examines the standards of judgment with which God and the Houyhnhnm treat their respective supplicants. While judging Adam, the Son of God treats man with knowledge and sympathy; he understands well the notion of original sin and knows his own future role in overcoming man's sin. The Son can feel for Adam because he, as Christ, will become man; his love for man is based in part upon his sympathy for man. In marked contrast to the Son, the Master Houyhnhnm has neither knowledge of original sin nor compassion for the human post-lapsarian problem; he is in fact astonished at Gulliver's behavior. His perception reflects not that of the omniscient Christian God but rather that of the prelapsarian Adam. Gulliver's behavior absurdly asks a pre-lapsarian being to grasp a postlapsarian problem. All that the innocently ignorant Houyhnhnm can do in response is wonder at Gulliver's attitude and agree to keep the secret of his nakedness. While the Son covers the penitent Adam with "the Skins / of Beasts" and his "Robe of righteous-ness" (an act which prefigures the greater sacrifice that Christ will make on man's behalf), the Houyhnhnm can only afford Gulliver puzzlement and the skins of dead Yahoos (X, 220–21; 222). Further, without the in-cisive questions of an all-knowing God, Gulliver cannot realize, let alone admit or repent, his real sins of presumption. With such a misguided idea of his sin, and with such an unfortunate choice of deity, Gulliver can neither see the need for true redemption nor achieve it. Gulliver's skewed sense of the Christian paradigm requires the reader to judge him harshly. This harsh judgment of Gulliver depends upon Swift's evoca-tion of the Christian myth, which in turn is derived from the allusion to *Paradise Lost*.

Gulliver's aspirations toward the Houyhnhnm ideal lead him to a rejection of mankind, whom he comes to see as merely Yahoo. Later, however, when Gulliver cannot escape the conclusion that he too is a Yahoo, his earlier rejection of man leads him into a full-blown despair. He cannot be Houyhnhnm and dare not think himself human, which is for him Yahoo. For a time in *Paradise Lost* Adam also lapses into de-spair. Yet Swift's contrast of Gulliver's despair with Adam's — the causes and consequences of each — reveals the significant differences between the two men: their antithetical attitudes toward wife and children, to-ward their treatment by their superiors, and toward the future which will culminate in death. These differences show the superiority of Adam's ways as well as the problems inherent in Gulliver's.

Not only does Swift allude to the Miltonic presentation of sin and judgment, but in his account of the ejection of Gulliver from Houyhn-hnmland he exploits a major dramatic moment from *Paradise Lost*: the expulsion from Eden. Despondent over the ramifications of his sin — his emotional estrangement from Eve, his fear that his children (the race of man) will curse him in perpetuity for his transgression, his inability to perceive the justice of God's plan as a whole, and his fear that death may not come to end the stings of conscience — Adam has yet to learn that he must leave Eden. God the Father realizes that the news of his expulsion might be the last blow that Adam could bear. He therefore instructs Michael carefully:

> drive out the sinful Pair,
> From hallow'd ground th' unholy, and denounce
> To them and to thir Progeny from thence
> Perpetual banishment. Yet lest they faint
> At the sad Sentence rigorously urg'd,
> For I behold them soft'nd and with tears
> Bewailing thir excess, all terror hide.   (XI, 105–11)

Since man is truly sorry for his sin, Michael will use the same nonthreatening tone that the Son employed while judging Adam. The Father continues his instructions:

> If patiently thy bidding they obey,
> Dismiss them not disconsolate; reveal
> To *Adam* what shall come in future days,
> As I shall thee enlighten, intermix
> My Cov'nant in the woman's seed renew'd.   (XI, 112–16)

God shows mercy toward Adam and Eve because they are repentant and no longer proud or disobedient. The greater expression of God's mercy consists in his telling Michael to reveal the providential plan to Adam. If Adam understands his own role in that plan and the reason behind his present suffering, he will be better able to bear his pain and will escape the despair that would otherwise cripple God's scheme for man's salvation.

Swift alludes to the banishment of Adam and Eve in chapter 10 of *Gulliver's Travels*, part 4. Just as God orders the sinful pair to be purged from his good garden, the council of Houyhnhnms decides to expel Gulliver lest he might foster a rebellion among the Yahoos. The council entrusts the Master Houyhnhnm with the task of delivering its sentence to Gulliver. The Master does this with little sympathy or understanding:

In the midst of all this happiness, when I looked upon myself to be fully settled for life, my master sent for me one morning a little earlier than his usual hour. I observed by his countenance that he was in some perplexity, and at a loss how to begin what he had to speak. After a short silence, he told me, he did not know how I would take what he was going to say. (P. 225)

As in the incident with Gulliver's clothes, the Master cannot comprehend Gulliver's human motivation. The Houyhnhnm's innocence knows no passion and is therefore singularly unsuited to consoling Gulliver. Unlike Michael, who knows what great value Adam and Eve place on their residing in Eden, the Master does not realize the importance which Gulliver has come to place on his existence in Houyhnhnmland. The uncertainty with which the Houyhnhnm performs his duty stands in great contrast to the care and understanding with which Michael accomplishes his.

When Michael tells Adam and Eve that they must leave Eden, the pair are at first shocked and deeply distressed: "*Adam* at the news / Heart-strook with chilling gripe of sorrow stood, / That all his senses bound" (XI, 263–65). But Adam soon recovers and thanks Michael for not being as severe as he might have been: "gently hast thou told / Thy message, which might else in telling wound, / And in performing end us" (XI, 298–300). Adam seems to sense God's concern and is grateful for it. Because of God's thoughtful anticipation of Adam's state of mind, Adam and Eve can bear the news of their exile. On the contrary, when Gulliver hears of his expulsion, he plunges into the very despair which Adam largely avoids:

I was struck with the utmost grief and despair at my master's discourse, and being unable to support the agonies I was under, I fell into a swoon at his feet; when I came to myself he told me that he concluded I had been dead. (For these people are subject to no such imbecilities of nature.) (P. 226)

Gulliver's faint represents an even stronger reaction than that of Adam and Eve; the absurdity of Gulliver's despair emerges when one compares Houyhnhnmland, where happiness for Gulliver depends upon self-deception and misanthropy, to Eden, a true paradise. Adam and Eve have greater reason to lament their loss, since it is a more grievous one. Yet because of the nature of their God and their willing submission to divine justice, they do not faint or despair.

After Gulliver learns that he must leave Houyhnhnmland, he succumbs to many of the same causes of despair that temporarily afflict Adam. Whereas Adam eventually avoids despair through the goodness of his God and the aid of his Eve, Gulliver falls victim to despair because of his misanthropic pride and the insensitivity of his deity. When Gulliver recovers from his swoon, he laments his banishment by telling the Master, who had assumed him to be dead, that in his present condition, "death would have been too great an happiness" (p. 226). Gulliver adds that "the certain prospect of an unnatural death was the least of my evils: for, supposing I should escape with life by some strange adventure, how could I think with temper of passing my days among yahoos, and relapsing into my old corruptions, for want of examples to lead and keep me within the paths of virtue?" (p. 226). For Gulliver, even a violent death seems preferable to the prospect of returning to England and living among his fellow men. In fact, while later embarked upon his "desperate voyage" (p. 228), he tries to commit suicide by jumping ship; a concerned captain, Don Pedro de Mendez, wishes to know Gulliver's reason "for so desperate an attempt" (p. 231). Despair has produced desperation.

Gulliver's desperate wish for death is ridiculous for two reasons: first, it stands in direct opposition to the Houyhnhnm attitude toward death, an attitude that he should be obliged to adopt; second, his death wish echoes Adam's initial desire for, and later rejection of, a quick death as an end to present pain. When Adam first learns God's judgment in Book X, he wonders why God does not take his life at once:

> why do I overlive,
> Why am I mockt with death, and length'n'd out
> To deathless pain? How gladly would I meet
> Mortality my sentence, and be Earth
> Insensible, how glad would lay me down
> As in my Mother's lap!
> . . . .
> Yet one doubt
> Pursues me still, lest all I cannot die.   (X, 773–78; 782–83)

Later, Michael instructs Adam that death will come peacefully to those who live a life of moderation. He tells Adam: "So may'st thou live, till like ripe Fruit thou drop / Into thy Mother's lap" (XI, 535–36). Adam then agrees to wait for death calmly. Adam's mature view of death recalls that of the Houyhnhnms whom Gulliver is supposedly mimicking. This view becomes clear when Gulliver tells the story of the female Houyhnhnm who apologized for being late for dinner, as she had been busy burying the body of her newly deceased husband. Gulliver further explains that the word for "death" in the Houyhnhnm tongue means "'to retire to his first mother'" (p. 221). Without the proper guidance of a Michael, and burdened with an immoderate pride which causes him to loathe the idea of a future among men, Gulliver is unwilling to accept the natural death that Adam does: a concept of death that Gulliver's adulation of the Houyhnhnms should require. A look at Adam's first improper and then proper responses to death underscores this view.

Adam learns his lesson about death, as well as many other important lessons, when he ascends the Mount of Speculation with Michael in *Paradise Lost*, Books XI and XII. Before he can see the visions of God, however, Adam must have his eyes cleansed: "to nobler sights / *Michael* from *Adam's* eyes the Film remov'd / Which that false Fruit that promis'd clearer sight / Had bred" (XI, 411–14). Even though Adam is able to see the sights that Michael shows him, he often misinterprets them because of his fallen reason. Michael reveals to Adam many scenes of death and destruction from human history; he reminds Adam at every turn that it is Adam's fault that these scenes will be possible. When Adam views a more peaceful scene, he understandably errs in thinking that the sight is a good one: "True opener of mine eyes, prime Angel blest / Much better seems this Vision" (XI, 598–99). The vision turns out to be a depiction of the seduction of the sons of Seth by the daughters of Cain. Michael warns Adam: "Judge not what is best / By pleasure, though to Nature seeming meet" (XI, 603–04). Michael is always present to correct Adam's error and to lead him toward greater knowledge of himself and his role in God's plan. The angel tempers harsh criticism with ameliorating instruction.

Both by his personal example and his harsh words, the Master Houyhnhnm reminds his listener of his human failings. Just as Michael constantly draws the connection between future human corruption and Adam's original sin, the Master (after Gulliver has given him the necessary information about European man) seems never to tire of exposing the faults of all Yahoos (both domestic and European) as well as the faults of Gulliver, a representative English Yahoo. The Master's persistent reminders of human weakness are a great part of the reason why Gulliver despairs of man in general. Gulliver openly admits his abandonment of the human race:

But I must freely confess, that the many virtues of those excellent quadrupeds, placed in opposite view to human corruptions, had so far opened my eyes and enlarged my understanding, that I began to view the actions and passions of man in a very different light, and to think the honour of my own kind not worth managing; which, besides, it was impossible for me to do before a person of so acute a judgment as my master, who daily convinced me of a thousand faults in myself, whereof I had not the least perception before. (p. 208)

The Master opens Gulliver's eyes only to the dark side of man; Gulliver wrongly concludes from the Houyhnhnm's diatribe that man is utterly devoid of worth and should be discarded. Gulliver, like Adam, incorrectly thinks that he now can see clearly. Unfortunately for Gulliver, the Houyhnhnm cannot correct his mistakes as Michael can rectify Adam's; unlike Michael, the Master is ignorant of an aspect of man which inspires hope.

In a brief episode which is a *reductio ad absurdum* of Michael's education of Adam on the Mount of Speculation, Swift illustrates both the inadequacy of the Houyhnhnms as judges of human nature and the blindness of Houyhnhnms toward human concerns. After telling Gulliver that he must leave Houyhnhnmland, the Master directs his servant, the sorrel nag, to help Gulliver with his preparation for departure. Gulliver is thankful for the aid of the nag: "I told my master, that his [the sorrel nag's] help would be sufficient, and I knew he had a tenderness for me" (p. 227). Accompanied by the nag, Gulliver ascends a hill in order to decide upon his future course:

I got upon a height, and looking on every side into the sea, fancied I saw a small island, towards the northeast: I took out my pocket-glass, and could then clearly distinguish it about five leagues off, as I computed; but it appeared to the sorrel nag to be only a blue cloud: for as he had no conception of any country beside his own, so he could not be as expert in distinguishing remote objects at sea as we who so much converse in that element. (p. 227)

In this version of the Mount of Speculation, it is ironically Gulliver, and not his guide, who has the better vision. The Houyhnhnm, by contrast, cannot perceive what Gulliver does because of the narrowness of his range of experience. The utter insufficiency of the Houyhnhnms as a help to Gulliver is underscored by the fact that the sorrel nag is the only one of his tribe who has any real sympathy for Gulliver; yet even his concern pales before the care of God for Adam as expressed through Michael.

Michael's harping upon Adam's fault and its detrimental effects might have led Adam into despair had Michael not seasoned his criticism with other, more positive lessons. Chief among these is the concept of Christ's redemption of man, his paying for Adam's original sin. Milton uses the strategy of typology to join Adam, through a line of exemplary men, to the eventual redeemer of mankind. In Books XI and XII, Michael's theme of the "one just man" provides a continuum of virtue from Adam, through history, to Christ, that will show Adam just how important his own perseverance will be. Michael explains to Adam that as long as one good man exists in any age, God will not destroy man because of his general corruption, but will allow the race to continue. The first "one just man" is Noah; after being shown Noah's ark and its preservation of mankind, Adam is visibly refreshed: "O thou who future things canst represent / As present, Heav'nly instructor, I revive / At this last sight, assur'd that Man shall live" (XI, 870–72).

Deprived of the knowledge of exemplars such as Noah, as well as of their possible relation to himself, Gulliver cannot conceive of any human being but himself as being worthwhile; certainly, he thinks, there could be no man who would resurrect his faith in humanity as a whole. Because he wishes to be like the Houyhnhnms and because he shares their pessimistic view of human nature, Gulliver cannot see that Don Pedro de Mendez is just the sort of man that he should regard as evidence that the human race is not wholly depraved. If God the Father should be satisfied with one just man, then why shouldn't Gulliver? Don Pedro's exemplary treatment of Gulliver as well as his general human excellence mark him as a strong contrast to the many negative human images that are exhibited in the final voyage.[20] As such, Don Pedro occupies the same relationship to these negative portraits as the one just man holds to the larger picture of future human corruption in *Paradise Lost* Books XI and XII.

After taking extremely good care of Gulliver during the journey back to England, Don Pedro bids a warm farewell: "He took kind leave of me, and embraced me at parting, which I bore as well as I could" (p. 233). Gulliver's barely concealed disgust at the embrace stems from his pride: he cannot bear to think that he has any affinity with human beings. Although banished from his beloved Houyhnhnms, he persists in trying to be like them and in shunning the hated Yahoos among whom he now must live. The words with which Adam rebukes Nimrod, whom Milton sets against the example of Noah, provide a useful comment upon Gulliver's attitude: "O execrable Son so to aspire / Above his Brethren" (XII, 64–65). In his rebelliousness and pride, Nimrod is linked typologically to Satan; in spurning a man like Don Pedro and maintaining his proud distance, Gulliver reasserts his satanic nature.

Gulliver's callous treatment of Don Pedro extends to that of his own wife. A significant difference between Gulliver and Adam is that only the latter becomes reconciled to his Eve, both because he realizes the great love she bears him and also because he has understood her great part in the future of man. Immediately after the two commit their sin, Adam blames Eve for his own lapse: "Out of my sight, thou Serpent" (X, 867). The emotional reunion of Adam and Eve begins in Book X, where Eve, "with Tears that ceas'd not flowing, / And tresses all disorder'd, at his feet / Fell humble, and imbracing them, besought / His peace" (X, 910–13). Gulliver's final lack of an Eve can be attributed to his great pride which causes him to reject the embrace of his wife (to whose touch he responds much as he does to the assault of the female Yahoo) just as he repulses the embrace of Don Pedro: "As soon as I entered the house, my wife took me in her arms, and kissed me, at which, having not been used to the touch of that odious animal for so many years,

I fell in a swoon for almost an hour" (p. 234). Gulliver's view of his wife echoes Adam's view of Eve just after the Fall; but Gulliver's attitude regresses while Adam's progresses. Gulliver suffers from the absence of the understanding which leads Adam to renew his faith in and love for Eve; the change from "wife" to "that odious animal" effectively charts the extent of Gulliver's fall.

Adam's reconciliation with Eve means that he no longer fears the prospect of fathering the human race. Once he thought that men would blame him forever for burdening them with original sin: "All that I eat or drink, or shall beget, / Is propagated curse" (X, 728–29). Now he knows that his union with Eve will beget the line that will ultimately bear Christ. For Adam, propagation need no longer be accursed. Gulliver, however, reacts with disgust at the realization that he has helped to bring children into the world: "And when I began to consider, that by copulating with one of the yahoo species I had become a parent of more, it struck me with the utmost shame, confusion, and horror" (p. 234). While Adam's initial despair at the thought of siring mankind comes from his sense of having failed those yet unborn, Gulliver's shame stems from the conviction that he is far superior to mere humans. Adam at first fears that he has corrupted the human race; Gulliver fears that he has polluted himself.

Gulliver's choice of god and his persistent pride deprive him of the many consolations granted to Adam; thus, in the end, he lapses into abject despair. Ironically, he remains arrogant to the last; he warns "those who have any tincture of this absurd vice [pride], that they will not presume to appear in my sight" (p. 239). Gulliver's problem is that he cannot recognize himself as the prime offender. Like Satan, Gulliver can never escape from the despair to which extreme pride leads. Unlike Satan, however, Gulliver cannot detect the connection between pride and despair; Satan at least admits his fault: "myself am Hell" (IV, 75). Gulliver's despair will continue to haunt him because his pride prevents him from seeing the true cause of despair, just as it prohibits him from obtaining the relief from despair afforded to Adam.

A consideration of the complex presence of *Paradise Lost* in *Gulliver's Travels* substantiates the view that Gulliver does not express a Swiftian despair any more than the Houyhnhnms portray a Swiftian ideal. Gulliver's Fourth Voyage may seem overly pessimistic to some because the situation of Gulliver castigates man's weakness while it overtly lacks Christian consolation; yet the Miltonic presence not only shows that such castigation is well within the Christian tradition but also suggests hope by referring to the case of Adam. The reader who is aware of allu-

sions and echoes will regard Gulliver as a failed Adam; Gulliver falls
short of Swift's ideal of man insofar as he lacks Adam's humility and hope.
In joining Gulliver ultimately with Satan, and contrasting him with
Adam, Swift gives his readers a doubly negative exemplum. By linking
his own satiric perspective with the moral force of Milton's Christian epic,
Swift also resolves the problems posed by the narrative necessity of speaking through Gulliver's morally indeterminate voice; Swift's installation
of Adam as the *vir bonus* of his satire provides the sure moral authority
which is the essential requisite of that genre. If Swift's reading of Milton
appears unduly conservative (when compared to a Romantic reading,
for example), it should be noted that a revisionist reading would have
undercut the authority of tradition that Swift sought to provide for his
satire: Swift's mode of intertextuality underscores the fact that to revise
authority is to compromise authority. To Swift, Milton is not a precursor
to be overcome, but rather a respository of Christian belief. Rather than
deprecate Swift's orthodox interpretation of *Paradise Lost*, one should admire the skill with which Swift employs allusion in the search for truth.

Marquette University

NOTES

1. Roland M. Frye, "Swift's Yahoo and the Christian Symbols for Sin," *JHI* XV,
no. 2 (1954), 201–17. Cf. Louis A. Landa, "Jonathan Swift," *English Institute Essays, 1946*
(New York, 1947), pp. 20–40; Kathleen M. Williams, "Gulliver's Voyage to the Houyhnhnms," *ELH* XVIII, no. 4 (1951), 275–86; Patrick Reilly, *Jonathan Swift: The Brave De-
sponder* (Carbondale, 1982), p. 214. See also John J. McManmon, "The Problem of a
Religious Interpretation of Gulliver's Fourth Voyage," *JHI* XXVII, no. 1 (1966), 59–72.

2. I use the word "presence" in my title and elsewhere to reflect the tenor of *Milton Studies XI: The Presence of Milton*, ed. B. Rajan (Pittsburgh, 1978). See Rajan's introductory essay, "The Varieties of Presence," p. xiii: "The essays in this volume [show]
how the poetry of allusive reference to Milton involves the commentary of one poem on
another as part of the advancement of a heritage." In *Gulliver's Travels*, the presence of
Milton and the advancement of an essentially Christian tradition are profoundly joined.

3. Earl Miner, "Allusion," in *Princeton Encyclopedia of Poetry and Poetics*, ed.
Alex Preminger (Princeton, 1974), p. 18, says that structural allusion "gives form to a new
work by suggesting the structure of an older work." See my discussion of allusion and
larger contexts.

4. Reuben Brower, *Alexander Pope: The Poetry of Allusion* (Oxford, 1959), pp. 5,
8; Barbara K. Lewalski, "On Looking Into Pope's Milton," in *Milton Studies*, XI, 1978,
35; Christopher Ricks, "Allusion: The Poet as Heir," in *Studies in the Eighteenth Century*, III (Toronto, 1976), 231. Lewalski makes the same point about Pope: "There is no

evidence here of the dark Oedipal anxieties and desperate Satanic resolutions which Harold Bloom has recently offered as a paradigm for the relations of poetic fathers and sons — a paradigm which, one suspects, pertains only to Romantic or post-Romantic poets, and only to a few of those" (45).

5. Peter J. Schakel, *The Poetry of Jonathan Swift: Allusion and the Development of a Poetic Style* (Madison, 1978), p. 4; cf. Nora Crow Jaffe, *The Poet Swift* (Hanover, N. H., 1977), p. 1.

6. Jonathan Swift, *The Complete Poems*, ed. Pat Rogers (New Haven, 1983), p. 24; Richard Wendorf, "The Canonical Dean," *Times Literary Supplement*, 22 July 1983, p. 787.

7. For example, see Rogers's notes to Swift's "On Cutting Down the Old Thorn at Market Hill," in *The Complete Poems*, pp. 782–83; also, see the discussion of Miltonic allusion in Swift's "Ode to Temple" in A. C. Elias, Jr., *Swift at Moor Park: Problems in Biography and Criticism* (Philadelphia, 1982), pp. 85–86.

8. Robert Folkenflik, "'Homo Alludens' in the Eighteenth Century," *Criticism* XXIV, no. 3 (1982), 218. Folkenflik borrows the phrase from Boswell's Johnson. Brower, *Alexander Pope*, p. 9, also considers Augustan allusion as expressing "a community in attitudes and standards of art."

9. Jonathan Swift, *Gulliver's Travels*, ed. Louis A. Landa (Boston, 1960), p. 109. All subsequent references will be to this edition.

10. Miner, "Allusion," p. 18. Miner also mentions "metaphorical allusion," which is "found chiefly in periods setting value on tradition." This form of allusion "uses the echoed element as a vehicle for the poetic tenor that it acquires in the new context."

11. I use the word "cue" to suggest the call to action which allusion gives the reader. Compare this term with the word "marker" in Ziva Ben-Porat, "The Poetics of Literary Allusion," *PTL: A Journal for Descriptive Poetics and Theory of Literature* I (1976), 105–28. Ben-Porat notes that the marker need not be identical to its form in the evoked text (110).

12. Ben-Porat, ibid., 108, acknowledges the importance of the reader's role in allusion; the reader is free to effect the "formation of intertextual patterns whose nature cannot be predetermined." The goal of allusion, as Ben-Porat sees it, is the forming of "Maximum Intertextual Patterns" (111).

13. Cf. Folkenflik, "'Homo Alludens,'" p. 231: "It has frequently been objected to religious interpretations of the Fourth Voyage that there are no explicit references to religion of the sort we might expect to find if Swift's intention were to inculcate Christian doctrine. Yet Gulliver's lack of religious concerns means that Swift cannot have his speaker explicitly deal with religion and that he must make his own views known through irony . . . and other forms of implicit meaning, including allusion."

14. See John Guillory, *Poetic Authority: Spenser, Milton, and Literary History* (New York, 1983), pp. 74–75: "Verbal echoes are often meaningless to us because we have no context within which to understand what appears to be an arbitrary recollection." My use of the term "echo" reflects the discussion of that concept by John Hollander in *The Figure of Echo: A Mode of Allusion in Milton and After* (Berkeley, 1981), p. 65. Hollander notes that we lose the ability to perceive echo because we become absorbed in our own particular "community of reading."

15. Hollander, ibid., pp. 65–66: "A scholarly recovery of the context would restore the allusion, by revealing the intent as well as by showing means."

16. Hollander, ibid., p. 66: "Even in patently allusive contexts, echoes of a more covert sort can lurk." I would change Hollander's "Even" to "Especially" or "Principally," since I feel that echo depends upon the presence of allusion, at least in the present case.

17. John Milton, *Paradise Lost*, ed. Merritt Y. Hughes (Indianapolis, 1962). All subsequent references will be to this edition. It is important to note that the same allusion (Satan at Eve's ear) is cited by Jaffe, *The Poet Swift*, p. 12, as occurring in Swift's poem, "The Author upon Himself." Also, Pope employs the same Miltonic allusion in the *Epistle to Dr. Arbuthnot*, lines 319–33; this give further evidence of the community of mind among the Augustans that I have mentioned. In each case, the author condemns the whisperer by comparing him to Satan.

18. Both Steward Lacasce, "The Fall of Gulliver's Master," *essays in Criticism*, XX, no. 3 (1970), 327–33 and Ann Cline Kelly, "After Eden: Gulliver's (Linguistic) Travels," *ELH* XLV, no. 1 (1978), 33–54, regard the Master Houyhnhnm as innocent until he is corrupted by Gulliver. The debate over whether or not the Houyhnhnm falls, as well as the exact moment when he falls, if he does, is strikingly similar to the debate in Milton criticism over the timing of Eve's fall — another indication of the affinity between *Gulliver's Travels* and *Paradise Lost*.

19. Hollander, *The Figure of Echo*, p. 95, observes that the phenomenon of echo may involve verbal, thematic, or structural similarity; not only "a single word or phrase," but also "schemes and patterns" can echo. The echoes operating in *Gulliver's Travels* are "metaphorical" rather than "metaleptic," since they do not revise Milton's meaning, but rather assert that meaning in an ironic context.

20. Kathleen Williams, "Gulliver's Voyage to the Houyhnhnms," p. 284, links Don Pedro to the Christian sermonic tradition, while I connect him to the Christian poetic one: "The sermon *Upon the Excellency of Christianity* [by Swift] shows, in its account of the ideal Christian, a creature who is meek and lowly, 'affable and courteous, gentle and kind, without any morose leaven of pride or vanity, which entered into the composition of most Heathen schemes.' The description applies far more nearly to Don Pedro and the early Gulliver than to the Houyhnhnms, or to Gulliver the misanthrope, into whose composition pride certainly enters."

HAVING DONE ALL TO STAND:
BIBLICAL AND CLASSICAL ALLUSION
IN *PARADISE REGAINED*

Neil Forsyth

A CHARACTERISTIC IMAGE in Milton's poetry is the contrast of frenetic activity with patience, firmness, and quiet resolution. Perhaps the best-known version is the end of *Sonnet XVI*, where "Thousands at his bidding speed / And post o'er land and ocean without rest" is set against the final simplicity of "They also serve who only stand and wait."[1] Similar images of firmness occur not only at endings but in moments of high tension. The Lady in *Comus*, "set in an enchanted chair," proclaims that "Thou canst not touch the freedom of my mind / With all thy charms" (663–64), an early variant of the idea, and several subsequent instances confirm its power in Milton's imagination. There is, for example, Abdiel, "alone / Encompassed round with foes," who proves to be

> Among the faithless, faithful only he;
> Among innumerable false, unmoved,
> Unshaken, unseduced, unterrified,   (*PL* V, 897–99)

and who at Satan's "bold discourse without control . . . Stood up, and in a flame of zeal severe / The current of his fury thus opposed" (*PL* V, 803–08). Here uncontrolled fury is ineffectual against one who simply stands up. The praise of Abdiel is typically negative and passive in grammar (unmoved, unshaken), but the parallel with Milton's situation after the Restoration, "In darkness, and with dangers compassed round, / And solitude" (*PL* VII, 27–28), makes it anything but negative in effect.

Milton even intrudes the idea, in generalized form, into a context where it is not immediately relevant. The denunciation of traditional epic in the invocation to Book IX of *Paradise Lost* contrasts "the long and tedious havoc" of "fabled knights / In battles feigned" with "the better fortitude / Of patience and heroic martyrdom / Unsung" (*PL* IX, 30–33). Neither virtue has much to do with the major themes of the poem, still less with what is about to happen in the garden, although in his next works Milton went on to sing of both. Perhaps the most active instance of firm standing is, indeed, the final image of Samson in *Samson Agonistes*. Near the beginning of the play, when the chorus first see him, he is lying down "at random, carelessly diffused, / With languished head unpropped" (*SA* 118–19), but at the end he manages to find a place to stand, and a purpose to stand there "with both his arms on those two massy pillars" (*SA* 1633). And if Samson's is the heroic martyrdom still unsung in epic, then the patience is surely that of Christ in *Paradise Regained*.

The uninspiring hero of this poem has been a frequent topic of discussion in Milton criticism.[2] Readers have, it seems, often been led to echo Satan's frustrated cry, "What dost thou in this world?" (IV, 372). Yet the image on which the poem culminates is the typical figure of one who stands firm, and a review of the contexts Milton supplies for this episode may help to dispel some of the difficulties. Milton prepares for the final confrontation on the pinnacle of the Jerusalem temple with a series of parallel images, and he characteristically adds layers of allusion, direct and indirect, which increase the reach and resonance of his climax. In particular, the fourth book of the poem, although it begins in the middle of the longest temptation, is given its own structural unity by the images of firm resolution.[3]

Milton followed Luke's ordering of the three temptations rather than Matthew's, and the effect is to make the pinnacle test the climax of the poem. In Luke, however, as in Matthew, the meaning of the scene is different, and tolerably clear. Satan urges Christ to cast himself down, quoting Psalm xci to the effect that angels will uplift him if he chance to dash his foot against a stone, that is, to trip and fall. Christ replies in the accepted manner for Jewish disputants by himself quoting Scripture, the laconic words from Deuteronomy, "Thou shalt not tempt the Lord thy God" (Luke iv, 12; Deut. vi, 16). Traditionally, Christ's reply was taken as a direct response to Satan's temptation: we must not, says Christ in effect, put God's providence to the test by inventing false trials.[4] Satan tempts Christ to presumption, and he resists.

Milton includes all of this, but he brackets the biblical dialogue with his own additions, which complicate and shift the focus of his model. He invents here not a third moral temptation but a test of Christ's identity. Satan has so far seen Christ resist "to the utmost of mere man . . . Not more" (IV, 535–36), so he carries him up to the pinnacle to find out "what more thou art than man" (538). He expects him to fall off, we are told (571), and when he doesn't, Satan falls himself, "smitten with amazement" (562). He returns to Hell defeated, and the concluding hymn assures him that this has been a foretaste of his doom: "hereafter learn with awe / To dread the Son of God" (625–26). Satan is now sure that Christ is the enemy who shall defeat him finally. None of this is in the biblical source.

By converting the biblical temptation into an identity test, Milton raised for his readers all the questions that exercised the tradition about the nature of Christ. Man or God? If both, how? The poem does not resolve these issues, however closely or ingeniously we read the lines. Milton's own views on the matter he set out at length in the *De Doctrina Christiana*, but his poem allows one to read here either a miracle, or a supreme act of nerve, or both.[5] It does not say, for example, whether a man could in fact have balanced on the pinnacle, a point at issue in both biblical and Milton commentaries, nor does it say whether God intervened. The reticence is characteristic of both the hero and the poem.[6] It is Satan who wants Christ to show he is "In some respect far higher" (521), and who says on the pinnacle, "highest is best," but all that this Christ will do is quote Scripture and stand there.

All of Milton's additions to the biblical scene are encapsulated in the enigmatic phrase, "and stood." The word is the climax of the scene. It is prepared by Satan's scornful, sarcastic speech, also added to the source, in which he urges him to try his skill:

> There stand, if thou wilt stand; to stand upright
> Will ask thee skill; I to thy Father's house
> Have brought thee, and highest placed, highest is best,
> Now show thy progeny.   (551–54)

In Satan's "if thou wilt stand" we hear his sardonic version of what Christ has been doing throughout the poem, withstanding him. As usual, he converts the language of moral metaphor to a literalness that damns him. The new focus of the Miltonic scene, Christ standing, is then reinforced by the denouement in which Satan falls, also not mentioned in Luke or Matthew.[7] And in one of the similes to which this fall is compared, the language echoes that of Satan's temptation, ironically: the Sphinx "Cast herself headlong from the Ismenian steep" (IV, 575) as Satan urged Christ to "Cast thyself down" (555), with the linking word "Cast" at the beginning of the line in each case. It is Christ's ability to stand, rather than his verbal reply, on which the fall of Satan immediately follows: ". . . he said and stood. / But Satan smitten with amazement fell" (561–62), where "stood" and "fell" complement each other at the end of the lines. And when the first of the two similes, the allusion to the Hercules-Antaeus battle, is explained, the emphasis again is on the dramatic opposition of standing and falling:

> So after many a foil the tempter proud,
> Renewing fresh assaults, amidst his pride
> Fell whence he stood to see his victor fall.   (569–71)

The explication extends the reference of the simile from the fall of Satan to all his efforts throughout the poem, but the last of these three lines, so compressed one has to pause to unravel its various referents, places the word "stood" at the center between the two parts of the verb "fall," like Samson between his two massy pillars. Everything throughout the scene grows from the central word "stood."

Since neither of the two gospel accounts warrants this new Miltonic focus, we should ask, first, whether there may be any other biblical justification. Part of the answer was supplied by the typological approach of Northrop Frye. He was the first to notice that the context of Satan's quotation from Psalm xci makes an ironic reference to the fundamental Christian myth of combat.[8] Verses 11 and 12, to which Satan alludes, read: "For he shall give his angels charge over thee, to keep thee in all thy ways. They shall bear thee up in their hands, lest thou dash thy foot against a stone." But the next verse is one of several biblical passages about trampling the enemy under foot: "Thou shalt tread upon the lion and the adder: the young lion and the dragon shalt thou trample under feet." Naturally, Satan quotes only the part about the angels' support, but the concluding hymn of the poem echoes this next verse, together with all the parallel passages in the Christian reading of Scripture,[9] and draws the lesson:

> But thou, infernal serpent, shalt not long
> Rule in the clouds; like an autumnal star
> Or lightning thou shalt fall from heaven trod down
> Under his feet: for proof, ere this thou feel'st
> Thy wound.   (618–22)

The temptation sequence is a part of the larger combat and the end is now known to all.

It is odd that neither Frye nor most other commentators take account of the main scriptural passage upon which the Miltonic scene is based.[10] The whole idea of victory over Satan by standing derives from Ephesians vi, 10–14, the famous injunction to "put on the whole armour of God, that ye may be able to stand against the wiles of the devil." The passage, probably pseudo-Pauline, continues with an elaborate military metaphor for Christian struggle:

For we wrestle not against flesh and blood, but against principalities, against powers, against the rulers of the darkness of this world, against spiritual wickedness in high places. Wherefore take unto you the whole armour of God, that ye may be able to withstand in the evil day, and having done all, to stand. Stand therefore having your loins girt about with truth, and having on the breastplate of righteousness.

Milton may conceal the allusion slightly by substituting classical wrestlers ("fiercer grapple joined") in his simile, and a literal high place, the peak of the temple, for the scriptural metaphor. But the phrase "spiritual wickedness" fits well enough as a description of Satan's activity in the poem, and in fact the expression, "ta pneumatika tēs ponērias," was often taken as a reference to the fallen angels who lived "en tois epouraniois," in the heavenlies, the phrase which the King James version translates as "high places."[11] Milton himself took the "principalities and powers" to be devils, both in *Paradise Lost* and in the explicit citation of this passage in the *De Doctrina* (I, ix; *YP*, VI, 349). "And having done all, to stand" is precisely what Milton makes Christ do at this moment. The Pauline metaphor has become the climax of a literal confrontation, and, again, it is Satan's idea to take the metaphor literally.

As well as fusing several biblical sources, Milton typically expands and transforms his scene with allusions to classical victories. Satan begins his fall at line 562, continues falling through the Antaeus and Sphinx similes, and arrives back "to his crew" in line 577. The conclusion of the passage is delayed, however, till line 581 ("So Satan fell"), and the length and complex activity of these twenty classical lines contrast with the brief simplicity of Christ's victorious standing. The *Vergleichungspunkt* of each simile is the fall of the victim, with Satan as first a giant and then a monster, but each simile also recapitulates Satan's repeated assaults throughout the poem: Antaeus "oft foiled still rose," and even the briefer Sphinx simile has the "Theban monster" devouring her various victims before the riddle is solved.[12] The first is a simile of physical combat, but the second picks up both the intellectual and moral aspects of the confrontation and fall: Antaeus was "Throttled at length in the air," while the defeated riddler committed suicide "for grief and spite." In the same way, Satan begins his fall "smitten with amazement," a suitable reaction to a feat of physical skill, but at the end, after the second simile, he is "struck with dread and anguish," and he brings to Hell "Ruin, and desperation, and dismay."

Although the focus of each simile is the loser, each implies, of course, a victor, to compare with Christ. Hercules is named, but only in a prepositional phrase: Antaeus "strove / With Jove's Alcides," which makes Hercules also a "Son of God." Otherwise, he is present, if at all, only as the unexpressed agent behind the passive participle "Throttled," just as Oedipus is implied only by the passive participles attached to the riddle, "once found out and solved." Hercules was a traditional type of Christ, but Oedipus, even with his tragic self-knowledge, could hardly be compared to Christ directly except in the most distant and allegorically generalized way.[13] Images of Christ, then, appear in each simile, but only indirectly and indistinctly. Indeed, he appears in the second, perhaps, more as the riddle itself or its equally riddling answer, "man," than as its solver.[14]

The Sphinx simile, however, contains another, if equally distant, point of comparison to Christ, and one which picks up and completes a pattern of imagery present throughout the fourth book. Epic similes like these, rarer in this poem than in *Paradise Lost*, are more frequent in this book than earlier (Carey, p. 428), and in fact the "Ismenian steep" from which the monster throws herself echoes a cliff at the beginning of Book IV; the cliff too comes at the end of a simile cluster. Indeed, these two groups of similes frame the book, and are linked by other echoes of classical epic in the intervening scenes, most obviously in the denunciations of Rome and Athens, but also in the storm scene.

Satan is again the main point of comparison in the group of three similes with which the book opens. He is first compared to Odysseus, though rather to the debased character of the fifth century than to Homer's hero:[15]

> But as a man who had been matchless held
> In cunning, over-reached where least he thought,
> To salve his credit, and for very spite
> Still will be tempting him who foils him still.   (*PR* IV, 10–13)

Satan's spite is later echoed by the Sphinx's at her death. Then he is, in his repeated assaults, like

> a swarm of flies in vintage-time,
> About the wine-press where sweet must is poured,
> Beat off, returns as oft with humming sound.   (*PR* IV, 15–17)

The Homeric model here compares the Greek warriors milling around the body of Sarpedon to flies buzzing around pails of milk (*Iliad* XVI, 641–43). The substitution of wine for milk, and of vintage-time for Homer's spring, makes the simile apply also to Christ in his sacrificial or sacerdotal role.[16] Sarpedon, we might add, is a son of Zeus, much lamented, whom the god is constrained to yield up for a greater good.

The third simile is the one which contains the cliff, and it follows immediately on the other two:

> Or surging waves against a solid rock,
> Though all to shivers dashed, the assault renew,
> Vain battery, and in froth or bubbles end;
> So Satan, whom repulse upon repulse
> Met ever.   (*PR* IV, 18–22)

The simile has Homeric and Virgilian precedents, and it establishes the solid rock as an important image in the book. But in both Homer and Virgil, the *Vergleichungspunkt* is not the force which attacks, as in Milton (Satan as waves), but those who resist. Homer's Danaans "withstood the Trojans steadfastly, and did not yield,"

> like a cliff ("petre")
> Towering, huge, hard by the grey salt-sea,
> That withstands the screaming winds and their sudden shifts,
> And the waves that swell and burst against it.   (*Iliad* XV, 618–21)[17]

Virgil uses the same image twice, once for Latinus holding off the Allecto-crazed mob at his gates, "like a sea-cliff that . . . stands in its massive bulk unmoved ("immota") amid the howling waves; around it, the reefs and foaming rocks rage" (*Aeneid* VII, 586–90); and once for Mezentius, the savage and embittered Tuscan who beats off the exultant Trojans, "like a cliff, that juts into the wide ocean, exposed to the fury of the winds and the waters, and withstands all the violence, the threats of sky and sea, standing immovable there" ("ipsa immota manens") (*Aeneid* X, 693–96).

To these models Milton adds two details — that the waves are "all to shivers dashed" and that they "in froth or bubbles end," an apt metaphor for Satan's verbal assaults. The additions reinforce the shift of focus to the wasted but desperate efforts of the attacker, but the solid rock remains as an image of firm resistance to frantic pressure. Christ is immediately taken up to a high mountain "Washed by the southern sea" for a view of the Roman *imperium*. Its center is the Capitol on the Tarpeian rock, which Satan (falsely, we know) labels "her citadel / Impregnable" (*PR* IV, 49–50). The image chain passes, we shall see, through other symbolic rocks and stones before it ends in the Ismenian steep from which the Theban monster, like Satan from the Christ-held pinnacle, casts herself down.

The similes which frame the book are linked in various ways. They have parallel images and points of reference. There are verbal repetitions, particularly of the word "foil" — "Still will be tempting him who foils him still," (*PR* IV, 13); "and oft foiled still rose," (565); "So after many a foil the tempter proud, / Renewing fresh assaults," (569–70) — where the language could apply equally to the first three similes as to the last two, and which echoes "the assault renew" of line 19. And all five are attached to Satan. It is appropriate in a book in which Christ rejects both the kingdom of Rome and Athenian wisdom that most of the rhetorical devices and the overt classical similes should be attached to Satan. Yet an image of Christ appears in each of the similes, though indirectly, and there are other places in the book where the language of classical epic, even of epic similes, is used for Christ. The allusions are more muted and distant, but the idea of combat, of victory by standing still, is the key image, however transformed. In the storm scene, in fact, the images from the similes become the language of the narrative itself.

Homer frequently compares his armies to fire, winds, and rushing water, or his fighting soldiers to trees. Among the more relevant of this group of similes, Crethon and Orsilochos fall "like towering pines" (*Iliad* V, 560); Asios and Sarpedon are like oaks or pines cut down (XIII, 389 and XVI, 482); Euphorbos is an uprooted tree (XVII, 53); Ajax is like a torrent that sweeps down trees (XI, 492); Agamemnon, Hector, and Achilles are all compared to forest fires (XI, 155; XV, 605; XX, 490), while Hector, in the most impressive of these comparisons, is like a great oak tree struck by lightning (XIV, 414).

Satan prepares Christ for the third and final test by a terrible night storm and, in the language of this passage, we hear, first, a kind of summary of the Homeric combat similes. Satan watches at Christ's head, and disturbs his sleep, like Eve's, with "ugly dreams" (*PR* IV, 408). He then provokes thunder and

> Fierce rain with lightning mixed, water with fire
> In ruin reconciled: nor slept the winds
> Within their stony caves, but rushed abroad
> From the four hinges of the world, and fell
> On the vexed wilderness, whose tallest pines,
> Though rooted deep as high, and sturdiest oaks
> Bowed their stiff necks, loaden with stormy blasts,
> Or torn up sheer.   (*PR* IV, 412–19)

In the words which describe Christ's resistance to the storm, the tree image continues: "ill wast thou shrouded then, / O patient Son of God, yet only stood'st / Unshaken." Of course, this is not simile: both trees and Christ are there in the wilderness, yet the language is that of the Homeric battle similes. Most of these Homeric warriors fall, and that is the traditional *Vergleichungspunkt* of the falling tree simile, but in one — and only one — the attacked warriors manage to stand firm. Two brothers, Lapiths, resist the furious charge of the Trojans:

> They stood there like two oaks that raise their crests in the mountains
> And through day upon day withstand the wind and the rain,
> Gripped by their great roots reaching far in the ground.
>
> (*Iliad* XII, 132–34)

Milton thus has a Homeric precedent for the isolated instance of resistance to the forces which attack trees.

Here, however, it is as much the Virgilian adaptations as the Homeric models that Milton has in mind. The night winds, for example, are introduced with the obvious allusion to Aeolus, whose winds figure in the journeys of both Odysseus and Aeneas toward the reestablishment of their kingdoms. In Homer he lives on a floating island, where he gives Odysseus a bag of winds, soon untied by his foolish companions, but in Virgil, as in Milton, he keeps his winds in a cave. Juno goes there to bribe him by setting women in his eye, and he lets loose his winds on Aeneas and his fleet, provoking the storm which is the first episode of the poem (*Aeneid* I, 34–156), and which is echoed later by various other storms like the one in the cliff similes quoted above. The "morning fair" which follows the Miltonic tempest is adapted from the figure of Neptune who rises in a splendid Virgilian image to quell the storm. The "radiant finger" of morning is Homeric, but her action is like that of Virgil's Neptune: he commands the winds back to their cave, "collectasque fugat nubes" (*Aeneid* I, 143), as Milton's dawn "chased the clouds and laid the winds" (*PR* IV, 429). But in Milton the Neptune figure becomes a grey-hooded religious, moving "with pilgrim steps in amice grey." The image reinforces the idea of spiritual calm in the face of these wild, ungoverned powers.

Virgil's tree similes are also radically different from Homer's. In Homer, individual warriors in their glory or death evoke the tree comparison, but only the comedy of the boxing match in *Aeneid*, Book V provides a parallel. The echo of the Homeric heroes adds to the absurdity of the foolish giant, Entellus, who swings a wild punch, misses, and falls flat on his face "as a hollow pine will fall on Erymanthus or great Ida, torn up by the roots" (*Aeneid* V, 448–49). Virgil also imitates the Lapith simile, but this time with even more irony, since his two defenders, Pandarus and Bitias, open the gates they are supposed to defend, and are soon killed (*Aeneid* IX, 672–83). However, Virgil also has two much more important tree similes, both concerned with our central theme, and worth exploring a little for the revealing contrast with Milton.

In the *Iliupersis* of Book II, Virgil presents a kind of amalgamation of all of Homer's falling trees: it is not now a single warrior but the city of Troy itself which falls. At the climactic moment, Aeneas is granted a vision of the gods themselves participating in the destruction of the city, and he compares it (he is telling the story to Dido) to a great rowan tree, hacked repeatedly by farmers, which slowly falls, torn up ("avulsa") and tumbling to ruin (*Aeneid* II, 626–31). But the simile represents not so much the objective event as the observer's state of mind. It signals the discovery of his intention to quit the defense of Troy and begin his new career.[18] The simile is immediately followed by the words "ducente deo."

This simile anticipates another magnificent tree image, and one which also caps a visionary experience. In Book IV, Aeneas is eventually reminded by divine messenger that he has another mission than to help rebuild Carthage and console Dido. Her sister, Anna, comes to make a last appeal for him to stay: he listens, but is unpersuaded. Virgil compares this mental act of resistance to one of those strong Homeric trees:

> As when, in the Alps, north winds strain against
> Each other, vying to root out with their blasts
> A stout oak tree, old in its strength; the noise
> Attacks, the trunk is shaken, and the high leaves
> Cover the ground; but the tree grips the rocks;
> Its crown thrusts upward to the heavens as far
> As the roots stretch down to Tartarus.
> So the hero battered on this side and that
> By insistent words, feels care in his mighty chest,
> But his mind stands unmoved, and the tears fall
> Useless.   (*Aeneid* IV, 441–47)

The last line, "mens immota manet, lacrimae volvuntur inanes" iterates a common theme of the poem, and anticipates the Mezentius cliff simile quoted above. The point of comparison shifts from the attacking winds to the strong tree, from the pleas of Anna to Aeneas. As a whole, the simile both echoes and contrasts with the earlier tree: the fall of Troy is to be compensated and transcended in the Roman future. The Stoic firmness with which Aeneas faces the task becomes the chief point of the simile.

Although the simile also echoes the one for the Homeric Lapiths, Aeneas is compared here to no ordinary Homeric tree, however strong. The roots of Virgil's oak, in words transferred from the *Georgics* (II, 291–92) to this more appropriate context, reach as far toward Tartarus as the branches rise to heaven. At this crucial point in his story, Aeneas' mental resolve makes him the very *axis mundi*, the cosmic tree of European and Asian myth, whose roots, according to Mircea Eliade, "plunged down into Hell, and whose branches reached to Heaven." Attaining this spiritual center, says the mythologist, is "fraught with perils, because it is, in fact, a rite of passage from the profane to the sacred. . . . Whatever is founded has its foundations at the center of the world."[19] Troy has fallen, but Rome will stand firm: that, in spite of the uneasiness with which Roman ways are presented in the poem (the empty tears which fall so often), is the obvious implication of these Virgilian trees.

The echo of this great tree in Milton is very faint. Apart from the words, "Though rooted deep as high," the trees of the Miltonic wilderness have become again the ordinary trees of Homer's similes. They bend, and may fall: "*Or* torn up sheer." That "or" is characteristic of this poem, as John Carey points out (p. 426), and its effect is to make things other than Christ's duel indistinct. It hardly matters what happens to these trees, for what counts is the central figure of the tree-like Christ, "who "only stood'st / Unshaken."[20] Homeric warriors, Virgilian Rome, are all fallen, rejected here by the ruler of a new, and different, kingdom.

There is certainly a hint of the miraculous if we apply "Unshaken" to the tree image: even Virgil's great *Weltaxle* shook and scattered its leaves. Both Virgil and Milton are thinking primarily of moral rather than physical strength, and of its source in some extrahuman power. Virgil is explicit: "fata obstant, placidesque viri deus obstruit auris" (*Aeneid* II, 440), but, as usual in the temptation scenes, Milton is reticent about the role of divine grace. The angelic rescue is held back until after the victory is achieved by standing still.

One more echo of epic combat in these lines confirms the series of Miltonic allusions. The dying Euryalus is compared by Virgil to a flower, but in language which echoes that of the tree similes. He dies "like poppies, with weary necks, that bow their heads, weighed down by rain" ("lassove papavera collo / demisere caput pluvia cum forte gravantur"), (*Aeneid* IX, 436–37).[21] Milton has noticed the parallel in Virgil's similes. So, while the Virgilian poppy becomes a Miltonic tree, the language of Milton's line follows Virgil's closely: "Bowed their stiff necks, loaden with stormy blasts." The combined allusions remember all the warriors who die like trees or flowers, as well as the single figures who stand firm. But the epic trials by combat or storm are all subsumed here, as mere foils, while Christ himself *immota manet.*

Given the presence, however faded, of these epic trees, we may wonder why Milton does not offer a more extended or explicit allusion. Why not, for example, a tree simile for Satan's fall, instead of the Antaeus and

Sphinx comparisons? Once we reflect on the question at all, the answer becomes clear and revealing. The storm-temple sequence prefigures, but only by subtle hints (like the earlier wine), the main event in the Christian drama which constitutes, however mysteriously, victory over the enemy. Christ is "shrouded," the pinnacle and the cross were often related in the tradition, and Satan's taunting speech may be read as a foreshadowing of the scornful questioning at the crucifixion.[22] To these we may add, of course, the delicate link between Christ and the trees in the storm scene. But a strong and obvious parallel, such as a simile provides, would suggest the holy rood directly, or even the fatal tree from *Paradise Lost*, and so would distort and disturb the focus.

Indeed Milton makes very little of the common biblical and Christian symbolism which links the tree of knowledge and the cross. He quotes a key text on one occasion in the *De Doctrina* — "1 Pet. ii, 24, *who bore our sins in his own body on that tree*" (I, xv; *YP*, VI, 433) — but his point is the sin, not the tree. Irenaeus' theory of *recapitulatio* had long been popular in typological speculations; Milton applied both the Adam-Christ and the Eve-Mary parallels to his poems; but he never seems to have explored the cross-as-tree idea. The tree was not, for him, a sacrament,[23] and his interest in *recapitulatio* was always confined to the human act, as the opening of *Paradise Regained* shows (e.g., I, 154–55, 161–62; II, 132–43). Indeed, only the Adam-Christ parallel has a biblical warrant (Rom. v, 9), although Genesis, chapter iii, verse 15, the *protevangelium*, lent some support to the Eve-Mary equation.[24]

Besides, other trees, equally symbolic, have reduced the robust trees of classical epic to a mere narrative foil for Christ. Virgil's world tree was, from the Miltonic point of view, only a shadow, a "false resemblance" (*PR* IV, 320), of the Christian tree of life, and it is from this tree, immediately after the triumph, that the angels fetch ambrosial fruit for Christ (583–84). In rejecting what Virgil's tree represented, imperial might, Christ explains that it would be replaced, eventually, by another kingdom:

> Know therefore when my season comes to sit
> On David's throne, it shall be like a tree
> Spreading and overshadowing all the earth,
> Or as a stone that shall to pieces dash
> All monarchies besides throughout the world,
> And of my kingdom there shall be no end.   (*PR* IV, 146–51)

The speech echoes two visions of Daniel (ii, 35–44; iv, 10–12), as commentators note, but it also adapts the visionary language to the form of a classical simile. Christ too is master of the manner, as he shows in his eloquent rejection of classical culture (Carey, pp. 427–28). He prefers, as he explains, the "majestic unaffected style" (*PR* IV, 359) of the biblical prophets, but he too can manage a pair of linked similes.[25]

Christ's prophetic similes also anticipate the climactic scene of the poem. Christ stands like a tree, unshaken, and then Satan tells him, before he carries him up to the pinnacle, that he has so far found him "Proof against all temptation as a rock / Of adamant, and a centre, firm" (533–34). Firm as a rock and, in the context, as a world tree — Satan thus links in his own brief pair of similes the two images of the Virgilian similes for firmness and the two similes of Christ's prophecy.

Satan further echoes the prophecy when, in that final scene, he suggests that Christ cast himself down, for angels "shall uplift thee, lest at any time / Thou chance to dash thy foot against a stone" (558–59). We have seen that he here quotes Psalm xci, and "dash" is the word used in the English version. Milton simply repeats it. But he gives it added force by adapting the earlier images to prepare for it: the waves, we recall, were "all to shivers dashed," and in the prophecy it is Milton's Christ, not the Authorized Version or the Geneva Bible, that makes Daniel's stone "to pieces dash / All monarchies." In this one final effort to get Christ to act, Satan inverts, merely by quotation, the relation of stone to "dash," of calm center to frenetic activity, just as he tries to invert the values Christ represents. But Christ remains still on the pinnacle, the stone and the tree to which all the others point. Satan has feared it, and now he sees it is true.

Biblical allusions, then, are adapted to classical forms throughout the book — distant or muted for Christ, emphatic and explicit for Satan. The contrast of standing and falling, of firmness and desperate action, fuses classical and biblical into this particularly Miltonic version of the single combat recommended by the letter to the Ephesians. The manner of the contrast is also characteristic. Christ's victory takes a line and a half, while Satan's mocking challenge lasts eight lines, and he then falls for fifteen (or twenty) more before returning to his crew. The loud, long fall echoes the first fall of Satan (*PR* IV, 580, for example, recalls *PL* I, 51) and anticipates the last ("like an autumnal star / Or lightning thou shalt fall from heaven," *PR* IV, 619–20). So Satan's fall becomes the final image of frenetic but fruitless activity in Milton's poetry, while the muted and laconic language for the standing victor allows the image of Christ, as in the surrounding similes, to emerge quietly within.

University of Geneva

NOTES

1. Milton's poems are cited from the two-volume Longman edition, *John Milton: Complete Shorter Poems* (London, 1971), ed. John Carey, and *John Milton: "Paradise Lost"* (London, 1974), ed. Alastair Fowler, and are referred to by the editor's name hereafter. Line references are incorporated in the text.

2. E.g., W. W. Robson, "The Better Fortitude," and F. W. Bateson, "*Paradise Regained*: A Dissentient Appendix," in *The Living Milton*, ed. Frank Kermode (London, 1960), pp. 124–37, 138–40. The main issues are summarized in Carey, *Complete Shorter Poems*, pp. 418–23. New arguments have been offered by Irene Samuel, "The Regaining of Paradise," in *The Prison and the Pinnacle*, ed. Balachandra Rajan (Toronto, 1973), pp. 111–34; Stanley Fish, "Inaction and Silence: The Reader in *Paradise Regained*," in *Calm of Mind*, ed. Joseph Wittreich (Cleveland, 1971), pp. 25–48; Alan Fisher, "Why is *Paradise Regained* so Cold?," in *Milton Studies*, XIV, ed. James D. Simmonds (Pittsburgh, 1980), pp. 195–217; and Georgia Christopher, *Milton and the Science of the Saints* (Princeton, 1982), pp. 202–19.

3. My use of terms such as *climax* and *structural unity* is purely formal, and is not intended to contradict the argument of Stanley Fish, "Things and Actions Indifferent: The Temptation of Plot in *Paradise Regained*," in *Milton Studies*, XVII, ed. James D. Simmonds (Pittsburgh, 1983), pp. 163–85, in spite of the strictures offered by Mary Nyquist, "The Father's Word / Satan's Wrath," *PMLA*, C (1985), 187–202.

4. Elizabeth M. Pope, "*Paradise Regained*": The Tradition and the Poem* (Baltimore: 1947), pp. 34–79; Barbara Lewalski, *Milton's Brief Epic* (London, 1966), pp. 177–78, 305–07; Carey, *Complete Shorter Poems*, p. 517.

5. For the Latin of chapters 5, 14, and 15 of Book I, see the Columbia edition, *The Works of John Milton*, 18 vols., ed. Frank Allen Patterson et al. (New York, 1931–38) vols. XIV, XV; for the English translation, see the Yale edition, *The Complete Prose Works of John Milton*, 8 vols., ed. Don M. Wolfe et al. (New Haven, 1953–82), vol. VI, cited hereafter as *YP*. See also Lewalski, *Milton's Brief Epic*, pp. 133–63 for a useful exposition.

6. On the ambiguity, see Lewalski, *Milton's Brief Epic*, pp. 316–17; on the reticence, see Fish, "Inaction and Silence," pp. 46–48. For a range of views, compare Arnold Stein, *Heroic Knowledge* (Minneapolis, 1957), pp. 124–30, with Edward W. Tayler, *Milton's Poetry: Its Development in Time* (Pittsburgh, 1979), pp. 169–72.

7. Pope, "*Paradise Regained*": The Tradition and the Poem*, p. 11, remarks that no other writer has Satan fall at this point, but cf. Merritt Y. Hughes, "The Christ of *Paradise Regained* and the Renaissance Heroic Tradition," *SP*, XXXV (1938), 254–77, on the fall of Malory's fiend, and Carey, *Complete Shorter Poems*, p. 518, on the iconographic tradition.

8. Northrop Frye, "The Typology of *Paradise Regained*," in *Milton: Modern Essays in Criticism*, ed. Arthur E. Barker (Oxford, 1965), pp. 429–46. On Christian combat generally, see Gustav Aulén, *Christus Victor* (1931; rpt. New York, 1969), and Neil Forsyth, *The Old Enemy: Satan and the Combat Myth* (Princeton, forthcoming).

9. Most of these passages derive from New Testament quotations of Psalm cx, 1: see D. M. Hay, *Glory At the Right Hand: Psalm 110 in Early Christianity* (Nashville, 1973). But there are many other parallels: see in particular Luke x, 18–19, "And he said unto them, I beheld Satan as lightning fall from heaven. Behold, I give you power to tread on serpents and scorpions, and over all the power of the enemy," and Romans xvi, 20, "And the God of peace shall bruise Satan under your feet shortly."

10. But see Emory Elliott, "Milton's Biblical Style in *Paradise Regained*," in *Milton Studies*, VI, ed. James D. Simmonds (Pittsburgh, 1974), pp. 227–41; cf. Lt. Col. James L.

Jackson and Walter E. Meese, "'Who Only Stand and Wait': Milton's Sonnet on his Blindness," *MLN*, LXXII (1957), pp. 91–93; and Boyd M. Berry, *Process of Speech* (Baltimore, 1976), p. 185.

11. The most recent discussion of this passage in Ephesians is Wesley Carr, *Angels and Principalities* (Cambridge, 1981), who insists that it must be a second-century gnosticizing interpolation.

12. The famous *Vergleichungspunkt* controversy over whether Homeric similes can be said to have one or more points of contact with the narrative began with Georg Finsler's *Homer* (Berlin, 1908); this was attacked by Hermann Fränkel, *Die homerischen Gleichnisse* (Göttingen, 1921), who in turn was attacked by Gunther Jachmann, *Der homerische Schiffskatalog und die Ilias* (Köln, 1958).

13. On the Hercules typology, see Lewalski, *Milton's Brief Epic*, pp. 227–41, and on Oedipus, p. 319, citing Conti and another mythographer. Northrop Frye, *The Great Code: The Bible and Literature* (New York, 1982), pp. 155–56, suggests that the Oedipus legend is "a domestic form" of the Christian story, since, in the one case, the son kills the father, while in the other the Son dies to appease the Father's wrath.

14. See, however, J. B. Broadbent, "The Private Mythology of *Paradise Regained*," whose argument rather belies the title of the volume in which it appears, *Calm of Mind*, ed. Joseph Wittreich (Cleveland, 1971), pp. 77–92. This and the attached simile are analyzed at length in Edward Tayler, *Milton's Poetry*, pp. 172–83, as the language of "brotherly dissimilitude."

15. W. B. Stanford, *The Ulysses Theme* (Ann Arbor, 1968), pp. 90–108, discussing in particular Pindar, Sophocles, and Euripides. He notes that Odysseus had become a way to whip contemporary politicians, something that Milton is probably doing here.

16. Arnold Stein, "The Kingdoms of the World: *Paradise Regained*," *ELH*, XXIII (1956), 123. In his note on this passage, Merritt Y. Hughes, *John Milton: Complete Poems and Major Prose* (New York, 1957), p. 515, points out that Ariosto's version of the simile has flies attacking ripe grapes (*Orlando Furioso*, XIV, 109).

17. For the *Iliad*, I have used the Oxford Classical Text, 3rd edition, 2 vols., ed. D. B. Munro and T. W. Allen (Oxford, 1920), and for Virgil, *The Aeneid of Virgil*, 2 vols., ed. R. D. Williams (London, 1972–73). References are incorporated in the text, and translations are my own. For another point of view on Milton's linked similes, see Burton J. Weber, *Wedges and Wings: The Patterning of "Paradise Regained"* (Carbondale, 1975), pp. 1–4.

18. On this and the subsequent simile, see the excellent commentary by R. D. Williams, *The Aeneid of Virgil*, vol. I, pp. 256–57, 373.

19. Mircea Eliade, *Images and Symbols* (New York, 1969), p. 44, and *The Myth of the Eternal Return* (New York, 1959), p. 18.

20. Patrick Cullen, *The Infernal Triad: The Flesh, the World, and the Devil in Spenser and Milton* (Princeton, 1974), p. 166, also notes that the words "stoodst / Unshaken" point forward to the pinnacle temptation. The sparer style of this poem is well illustrated by comparison with the Abdiel passage, cited above: he was "unmoved, / Unshaken, unseduced, unterrified" (*PL* V, 898–99). For complementary remarks on the storm scene, see John M. Steadman, "'Like Turbulencies': The Tempest of *Paradise Regained* as Adversity Symbol," *MP*, LIX (1961), 81–88; and on relations to classical epic, see John E. Seaman, "The Chivalric Cast of Milton's Epic Hero," *English Studies*, XLIX (1968), 97–107.

21. For the Homeric, Sapphic, and Catullan echoes in these lines, see W. R. Johnson, *Darkness Visible* (Berkeley, 1976), pp. 59–60. The simile echoes both the Gorgythion flower of *Iliad* VIII, 306, and the Euphorbos tree of XVII, 53. For the implications of such shifts

in both Virgil and Milton, see John M. Coolidge, "Great Things and Small: The Virgilian Progression," *Comparative Literature*, XVII (1965), 1–23.

22. Howard Shultz, "Christ and Antichrist in *Paradise Regained*," *PMLA*, LXVII (1952), 806–07; Lewalski, *Milton's Brief Epic*, pp. 309–14; Cullen, *The Infernal Triad*, pp. 168–70.

23. John M. Steadman, "The Tree of Life Symbolism in *Paradise Regained*," *RES*, XI (1960), 384–91.

24. For Mary as second Eve, see *PL* V, 387; X, 183; Carey, *Complete Shorter Poems*, p. 422; for the *protevangelium*, see C. A. Patrides, "The 'Protevangelium' in Renaissance Theology and *Paradise Lost*," *SEL*, III (1963), 19–30; Georgia Christopher, "The Verbal Gate to Paradise: Adam's 'Literary Experience' in Book X of *Paradise Lost*," *PMLA* XC (1975), 69–77; Neil Forsyth, "If They Will Hear: Regeneration and the End of *Paradise Lost*," in *Anglistentag 1982, Zürich*, ed. Udo Fries and Jörg Hasler (Giessen, 1984), pp. 221–34.

25. Replacing Virgil's world tree with the one from Nebuchadnezzar's dream in Daniel iv, 10–12, has a further warrant in the parable of the mustard seed which becomes a great tree "so that the birds of the air come and rest in the branches thereof" (Matt. xiii, 31–32), words which also allude to Daniel, iv, 12.

IMAGING IN *PARADISE REGAINED*

Albert Cook

M ILTON CHANGED the set of his poetic language so much in
going from *Paradise Lost* to *Paradise Regained* that we are often
forced to assert the continuity of the "brief epic" with the longer one.
And this is in spite of the clear continuity that Milton himself asserts in
the invocation to *Paradise Regained*, an invocation compact, simple,
and "brief":

> I who erewhile the happy Garden sung,
> By one man's disobedience lost, now sing
> Recover'd Paradise to all mankind,
> By one man's firm obedience fully tried
> Through all temptation, and the Tempter foil'd
> In all his wiles, defeated and repuls't,
> And *Eden* rais'd in the waste Wilderness. (*PR* I, 1–7)[1]

While asserting its link to *Paradise Lost*, the invocation to *Paradise Regained* begins, at the same time, by immediately offering a different focus
and register. If we try to assess the difference between the two poems,
it can be found profoundly, and perhaps even most profoundly, in the
imaging they perform.

By imaging I mean the act of bringing images to bear on a topic,
and also the choice of the topic itself, insofar as that involves a visual
situation. "Image" is a term more neutral, and also broader, than terms
like *symbolism* and *metaphor*. *The image*, too, for all its complexity,
is less slippery than a term like *metonymy*, that current jack-of-all-work
which is also a jack-in-the-box of tautology, since references named in
a sequent language must perforce be *contiguous* to each other, and almost any kind of contiguity can be called metonymy. So, in a large view,
it may be said that *Paradise Lost* tends to amplify its images, as well
as its language, while *Paradise Regained* tends to compact them. *Samson Agonistes* shares the amplitude of the first with the condensation of
the latter. So it may be taken formally as a sequel to both, whether or
not it is actually so in time.

More particularly, *image* can be taken in several senses. First, the
image can be taken to mean an item of *imagery* in the sense of Caroline

Spurgeon — an image joining a number of similar ones in the course of a work to produce a pattern of embedded congruences. Barbara Lewalski finds several of these in *Paradise Regained* — rocks versus air, light versus dark, hunger versus food, and a martial imagery that might be opposed to peace.[2] One could augment this list: vegetation versus desert waste, for one. These images tend to enter into patterns of oppositions, patterns that certainly exist on a larger and more explicit scale in *Paradise Lost*, where, to begin with, the anguished dark and turmoil of Hell stands in large contrast to the light and jubilation of Heaven. The situation is more complicated as well as more ample in *Paradise Lost* because in Paradise itself the two contrasts interpenetrate — the contrast of present to future in the garden, and the contrast of past to present in our vision of the garden. In the main action of *Paradise Lost*, the ensuing structure of paradox tends to twist out of shape, and a protracted analysis of image congruences would certainly show this. So would the paradoxes reveal their distortions under the sort of analysis of image-effect by sequential presentation about which Stanley Fish sensitively teaches us while trying to lead us down the garden path of the reader's infinite regress.

In a second sense of image, an image taken singly and by itself will have its own internal rhetorical and propositional structure. This is, of course, a vast and intricate topic, but without getting deeply into the logic of the questions it generally raises one may notice a difference in the number of single images between the two poems. *Paradise Lost* is obviously the lusher, and it also happens to enlist more frequently that protraction of image known as the epic simile.

The most pronounced and climactic of the similes in *Paradise Regained* is the comparison of the confounded Satan to Antaeus and then to the Sphinx (*PR* IV, 562–76). These similes compare one defeat to another: "But Satan smitten with amazement fell," and the somewhat amplified account of the other two defeats follows. The account is also somewhat abstract. It contains elements that could be called visual, but it does not dwell on, nor amplify, visual detail and visual correspondences, as do the similes in *Paradise Lost*. The same may be said of another comparison of one abstraction to another, earlier in Book IV: a comparison of two kinds of persistent trouble. These similes are consciously Homeric, but they consistently avoid the pronounced visualization and vehicle spillover of the Homeric similes:

> But as a man who had been matchless held
> In cunning, over-reach't where least he thought,
> To salve his credit, and for very spight

> Still will be tempting him who foyls him still,
> And never cease, though to his shame the more;
> Or as a swarm of flies in vintage time
> About the wine-press where sweet moust is powr'd,
> Beat off, returns as oft with humming sound;
> Or surging waves against a solid rock,
> Though all to shivers dash't, the assault renew,
> Vain battry, and in froth or bubbles end:
> So Satan. (*PR* IV, 10–21)

The visual gets no deep hold here. We have "froth or bubbles," alternate items. In *Paradise Lost,* on the other hand, a shift from one visual or sensible state to another is often a spiritual shift as well as a physical, accompanied by many plasticities of poetic attribution.[3] In this passage, too, there are many senses present, but their effect is not of profusion but of a sort of coordination that holds in check, as the Savior has been held in check from indulging in food or yielding to images of power. "Sweet" relates to taste, "swarm" to sight, "humming" to hearing, and it may even be said that "wine-press" implies touch. Smell alone is left, and smell would be strong for one standing near a full wine-press. But smell is unmentioned here. "Dash't" could be either sight or sound, and the alternatives tend, again, to mute each other rather than to allow an amplification of image.[4]

Moving away from figurative language, there is a third sense of "image" as a sort of overall focus at a point in the poem. Christ stands in an actual landscape of which an image is constructed, as do Adam and Eve. He is in a wilderness, they are in a garden. At points in both poems an overall focus is offered to the protagonist within the poem. Satan shows Christ a view of Rome (*PL* IV, 25–42)); Michael shows Adam a view of the whole earth (*PL* XI, 375–422) from a hill explicitly compared to the situation of *Paradise Regained:*

> It was a Hill . . .
> Not higher that Hill nor wider looking round,
> Whereon for different cause the Tempter set
> Our second *Adam* in the Wilderness
> To show him all Earths Kingdoms and thir Glory.
> (*PL* XI, 377–84).

The use of overall focus in general, and its enlistment within a dramatic context, is a special characteristic of Milton's poetry, though it is also a feature of epic style generally.

More common to all poetry is local focus, the naming, without recourse to figurative language, of something in the course of the poem that

has visual properties. This fourth kind of image is a sensitive area for
Milton from the beginning. I have elsewhere noted the originality of the
visual imagery even in his youthful translations from the Psalms, which
amplify their Hebrew original in a visual direction.[5] The poet who says
his Swain "twitch'd his Mantle blew" in the final rhyme of *Lycidas* is placing a strange and powerful emphasis on the color "blue" that cannot be
wholly accounted for by studying the rich iconography of that color in
Renaissance usage.

The term *iconography*, of course, may refer not only to such particular significations but to the staple subject chosen by the poet, a fifth
sense of the term *image*. This is what Roland Frye, who documents it
elaborately, calls "the vocabulary of visual images."[6] Milton, like a
painter, presents us with an image of Adam and Eve being tempted and
expelled from the Garden. These are conventional subjects, shown on
the sculptured portals and pillars of scores of medieval churches, as well
as notably in the works of such painters as Masaccio and Cranach, not
excluding Rubens. The temptation of Christ is much less common: it seems
to resist visual representation, just as Milton keeps in check for *Paradise
Regained* the visual elements that are noteworthy elsewhere in his poetry.
To be sure, the Temptations might be included in a very large repertory
of images for the life of Christ. They appear twice at Chartres, for example: once in a group of thirty-eight scenes on the west portal and once
in a window on the south aisle of the ambulatory that represents separately each of the three temptations. Or Milton could have seen his third
temptation on a panel of the north gate of Ghiberti's Bronze Doors.[7] Still,
Chartres is a sort of iconographic encyclopedia, as are the Bronze Doors.
The temptations are singled out as little there as they are in Richard Crashaw's Latin epigram on them:

> Ergo ille, Angelicis, o sarcina dignior alis,
> Praepete sic Stygio sic volet ille vehi?
> Pessime! nec laetare tamen. tu scilicet inde
> Non minus es Daemon, non minus ille Deus.
>
> So he, o burden more worthy than angels' wings,
> Thus by Stygian bird thus he would fly to be borne?
> Wretch, still do not rejoice. Clearly for that
> You are no less Demon, he no less is God.[8]

In one sense this single quatrain of Crashaw's resumes *Paradise Regained*. Yet it is not only short; it is one among many statements, like
the panels at Chartres. Milton has chosen to make a single statement about
the whole Redemption, and he has chosen to center it on a moderately

infrequent iconographic subject. He has taken his license from the typological identification between an Old Testament figure and Christ (which might be called, incidentally, a sixth sense of image, Auerbach's *figura*).[9] Still, for example, Job does not enter into typological comparison as often as David. The long tradition of classifying Job as a brief epic would still not dictate that for his brief epic Milton chose that point of Christ's life most analogous to Job. Nor is Milton's style much like that of the Book of Job, which as a deep student of the bible, Milton would have known well.

There are many differences between *Paradise Regained* and Job — so many that Milton's "humanist" adduction of the biblical "brief epic" is more honorific than it is illuminating about his own poem. With regard to imagery, Job offers a poetry much stranger and more condensed than anything in *Paradise Regained:*

> Hast thou given the horse strength?
> Hast thou clothed his neck with thunder?
> Canst thou make him afraid as a grasshopper?
> The glory of his snorting *is* terrible.   (Job xxxix, 19–20)

The second of these lines synaesthetically merges a tossing mane with an audible portent over the whole sky. The third line is almost Picasso-like in its disengagement of rapid visual effects from two animals whose similarity is, strikingly, the more purely visual for having only this point of contact: the legs of a leaping horse, taken globally, look like the legs of a leaping grasshopper. The fourth line links two Hebrew abstractions, *glory* and *terror* (e'mah; the word is a noun), through a single sensual attribute, *snorting*. None of these effects can be paralleled in *Paradise Regained*, or in Milton generally.

Milton's out-of-the-way choice of the temptations to represent the Redemption has an iconographic as well as an intellectual side. On the intellectual, or theological, side, to call Christ a second Job as well as a second Adam has the effect of countering the Fall directly by providing articulations of justification. Iconographically, it corresponds to the action of *Paradise Lost*, though we should not lose sight of the iconographic caveat that there is a more usual typological reversal associated with the overcoming of sin — the type of Mary as a second Eve. Again, in the long medieval and Renaissance traditions of iconography which preceded Milton, in the visual arts as well as in poetry, Eve and the temptation of Eve are common subjects. Mary is not tempted at all, but if we allow the Annunciation, *Ave Eva*, to focus Mary's typological reversal of Eve, then one of the most common iconographic subjects has been displaced by Milton when Mary is displaced from the center of *Paradise Regained*, as the first Eve had not been displaced from *Paradise Lost*.

The longest account of the Annunciation is in Luke, the Gospel which Milton generally follows for *Paradise Regained*.[10] Luke gives Milton the order of the temptations, which appear in a different order in Matthew. Mark recounts them so briefly that he gives them no order at all, a fact which could have given Milton license to present them in any order at all. As they are given in the poem, they have a climactic order, proceeding at first from simple to complex within each main temptation, and then from direct and personal to subtle and powerful as we move from food to power to suspension of the laws of nature. At the same time, each main temptation is somewhat disjunct from the one that precedes it, and there is a lack, even within the phases of a single temptation, of the sort of logic that governs the actions of *Paradise Lost*. The temptations, seen as the images which unfailingly accompany them, "stand out" in a framed isolation. They stand out against the backdrop of a wilderness which is little described. The wilderness is a sort of black cloth against which the temptations are played out, largely an anti-image, though there is some change from the tundralike background of the first food temptation to the valley where Christ is confronted with the banquet. For the second and third main temptations the wilderness has been left behind. Christ becomes "private"; the wilderness, away from which he has won himself, is especially bleak. All this bareness contrasts against the physical situation in which Christ had stood immediately beforehand: the baptism with John the Baptist at his side, the crowds around him, the water beneath him and pouring over his head, and the dove of the Holy Spirit descending upon him (*PR* I, 20–31). Northrop Frye emphasizes the typological contrasts between the more usual iconographic subject of the baptism and the temptations that immediately follow in *Paradise Regained* and in Luke.[11] Against this chaotic or nondescript backdrop, the temptations, as well as being typologically contrasted, are heightened at once in their dramatic effectiveness and in their special imagistic character.

After protracted councils in both Hell and Heaven, Christ is gradually drawn by the Spirit through his thoughts, a kind of distant echo and perhaps a silent recapitulation of these heavenly thoughts that culminate in laudatory song. He is drawn by his thoughts gradually to change his location, to center himself on the terrain that will serve neutrally to minimize distraction, as we may infer from the very failure of the poetry to provide imagistic substance:

So they in Heav'n their Odes and Vigils tun'd:
Mean while the Son of God, who yet some days
Lodg'd in *Bethabara* where *John* baptiz'd,
Musing and much revolving in his brest,
How best the mighty work he might begin
Of Saviour to mankind, and which way first
Publish his God-like office now mature,
One day forth walk'd alone, the Spirit leading;
And his deep thoughts, the better to converse
With solitude, till far from track of men,
Thought following thought, and step by step led on,
He entred now the bordering Desert wild,
And with dark shades and rocks environ'd round,
His holy Meditations thus persu'd.   (*PR* I, 181–95)

In *Paradise Lost* the physical enviroment and the bodies of angels and devils all undergo perceptible change through spiritual operation, "by likening spiritual to corporal forms" (*PL* V, 573). The whole world itself suffers a slow transmutation after the Fall. *Paradise Regained* offers a different slant, through its images, on the postlapsarian world. That world has, so to speak, hardened into place and the physical no longer yields to the spiritual. Instead, it serves as a staple and appropriate resource for the spiritual. The devil here does not involuntarily change location and shape. He shows only his voluntary changes of shape while staying in one location, his first being that of a humble old man seeking a sheep or scavenging for sticks.

The role of images in society generally is not a stable one. In many societies, and at many periods, there occurs an oscillation between fascination with images and the purging of images, between the tendency toward idolatry and that toward iconoclasm.[12] Milton found himself in the midst of such an oscillation, religious and political; images were at the contested center of both Rebellion and Restoration. Having capped the "idolatrous" tradition of the masque,[13] he not long afterward attacked the image of king and bishop, along with the visible trappings of worship favored by Archbishop Laud and his group. He was *Eikonoclastes*. Christ's withdrawal in *Paradise Regained* to the low visibility, both active and passive, of the desert thus takes its emphasis from a long tradition of image purging. At an earlier point, Saint Bernard shielded his eyes as he crossed the Alps; much later T. E. Lawrence attributed to the desert environment the birth of theological speculation.[14] To choose the desert as an iconographic locus amounts to a sort of protoiconoclasm.

Samson's blindness builds in such a contemplative state (though, of course, Samson is tempted by voices). Samson, like the blind Milton, has a memory for the visual, and he registers, while rejecting it, the word-picture of Dalila sailing toward him. Temptation by a beautiful woman is a motif in a more common iconographic tradition associated with the desert, the temptations of St. Anthony.[15] We cannot know that Milton saw such paintings, however, and Satan rejects Belial's suggestion that beautiful women be sent to tempt Christ (PR II, 152–71). But Milton does associate Christ with the tradition of the desert saints when he calls him, in the first attribution of the entire poem, a "glorious Eremite" (PR I, 8).

While Satan's arguments expand and contract around the images that accompany them, the images themselves are steadily progressive in incidence and complexity from the first temptation to the second, and within the first temptation itself. In the first, Satan begins with a bare mention of hunger. Then he specifies the possibility of turning stones into bread, trailing off at the refusal into a large debate. It is not until Book II that images of food are produced before Satan's return, and then they occur in Christ's dream of spare and proper desert food, the miraculous feeding of Elijah and Daniel (PR II, 262–83). Next, a better dressed Satan, instead of speaking, produces the actual image of "a table richly spred," complete with comely waiters of both sexes, incorporating Belial's suggestion, as it were, and adapting it.[16] Once this lavish spread is rejected and the ensuing debate has been exhausted, Satan switches to the second temptation immediately — power. There, more elaborately, he produces a show for Christ; very soon the whole array of Asia Minor culminates in the battle array of the Parthian king at Ctesiphon. Argument then follows upon the presentation of image. In the next attempt, Satan takes Christ around to the western side of the same mountain and displays the image to him — the perspectival vision — of the City of Rome: "So well I have dispos'd," Satan says, "My Aerie Microscope" (PR IV, 55–56).

The third temptation is abruptly climactic in its series, but anti-climactic in its employment of image. As Christ is told to save himself in midair, Jerusalem is shown from aloft, but its topographical features are not enumerated or described. Instead, its temple is imaged in a comparison reminiscent of, and partially drawn from, Revelation:

> The holy City lifted high her Towers,
> And higher yet the glorious Temple rear'd
> Her pile, far off appearing like a Mount
> Of Alabaster, top't with golden Spires.   (PR IV, 546–49)[17]

This is in contrast to the more expansive and literal description of Rome, though the two descriptions occur within the same imagistic set, which must correctly be felt to be the figural as well as the tonal consistency of *Paradise Regained*. The distinction between allegory and mimesis is too crude to serve here—if it can serve anywhere—since, to begin with, the visual images of Rome and Jerusalem have both allegorical and mimetic properties. Rome and Jerusalem stand for something—they are allegorical—and they are at the same time real places; their depiction is variously mimetic. And the actual presentation has many subtleties throughout, for which we have, so far, just tried to lay out the defining conditions. The effects remain to be explained. Take the description of Rome, or part of it:

> He brought our Saviour to the western side
> Of that high mountain, whence he might behold
> Another plain, long but in bredth not wide;
> Wash'd by the Southern Sea, and on the North
> To equal length back'd with a ridge of hills,
> That screen'd the fruits of the earth and seats of men
> From cold *Septentrion* blasts, thence in the midst
> Divided by a river, of whose banks
> On each side an Imperial City stood,
> With Towers and Temples proudly elevate
> On seven small Hills, with Palaces adorn'd,
> Porches and Theatres, Baths, Aqueducts,
> Statues and Trophees and Triumphal Arcs,
> Gardens and Groves presented to his eyes,
> Above the highth of Mountains interpos'd.
> By what strange Parallax or Optic skill
> Of vision multiplyed through air, or glass
> Of Telescope, were curious to enquire. (*PR* IV, 25–42)

Satan's further description adds hyperbole to this one, as well as qualification. He speaks of a microscope, the narrating poet of a telescope. The laws of "parallax," employed and named but not explicitly identified, introduce perspectival techniques of the science of the day. These laws resemble those of a common aid to perception that Renaissance painters used in constructing proportionate imagery, the *camera obscura*. Some painters active in England during Milton's time used it, as did Vermeer, who was also Milton's contemporary.

The bare naming of "porches and theatres" in this account accords with the figurative curtness of *Paradise Regained*, and it is not entirely foreign to the proportionate literalness in Vermeer's nearly contempora-

neous *View of Delft*. The names offer minimal images, the type images
of the architectural staples they designate, strung together in only a metri-
cal order to label the shapes of the buildings of Rome as they might be
seen. The scale is reminiscent of such paintings as the topographic view
of Rome in the *Sala del Mappemundo* of the Palazzo Publico in Siena,
which Milton might have seen, or the similar panoramas of Italy in a
corridor of the Vatican. In this passage, the image has been reduced to
topographical inventory. Correspondingly, there is little use of the hyperbaton found elsewhere in the poem, a hyperbaton whose capacities
for distorting images Stanley Fish has so actively described.

There is also present in this matter-of-fact and nearly paratactic
passage an undercurrent of pride, of *superbia*, in the Rome which Christ
will reject, and toward which his own elevated position of vantage from
the mountaintop is a kind of physical temptation, a potential counterpart. This Rome is described as protected from northern blasts much as
Paradise had been before it was lost. In that sense, in a physical sense
only, Rome is a simulacrum of that Paradise. Confining the image presentation to the physical may be taken to suggest the flat deceptiveness
of such a possible inference.

But the words connoting *superbia* do run through the passage like a
thread of warning—"high," "Imperial," "proudly," "elevate," "adorned,"
"Triumphal," "highth." Still, half these words denote a description in
physical space. If the physical space is to have significance read into it,
then this Rome has the significant situation of being "long in bredth not
wide," again a description preponderantly physical. At no point, though,
does the description, except in the mouth of the Tempter, take on the
full allure of imagistic figuration. It is checked at the physical, and its
figurative properties are confined to such intermittent if persistent hints.

The images, or the lexically implied protoimages, of this passage
are quite far over on the "general" side of the general-to-specific scale
that Wayne Shumaker has devised for Milton's imagery.[18] Yet they do
not just happen to be general, any more than the brief description of
Jerusalem happens to be figural. Milton's theology, taken all around, is
fairly conventional: his originality appears in the poem through the instinct that deploys images for local effect and for overall focus. If he goes
from general to specific, there is a kind of instinctual appropriateness in
the change. *Paradise Lost* is imagistically lusher than *Paradise Regained*
because we are being induced to sorrow over the loss. *Paradise Regained*,
though, does not recount the simple recovery of Paradise, or it should
be properly joyous rather than sorrowful, and still lusher. Instead, *Paradise Regained* is bracing for the reader or for the poet. Milton is not Christ

any more than he is Adam. The effect of compacting the poem away from lushness is to induce him to "put on the whole armour of God" and imitate Christ by resisting temptation, rather than letting go in a great paschal celebration of the Redemption. It is from that vantage that Milton is induced to abjure great sources of imagery in the classical poets, again following his Christ's expressed rejection of them. In that perspective only does the great admirer and imitator of the classics, which Milton does not cease to be, abjure Vergil and Homer.

In fact, Milton abjures even the more extravagant imagistic effects of Job and Isaiah. A biblical model may have inspired his brief epic, but Milton is not inspired in the biblical sense. He is not a writer of scripture, and he keeps an austere distance from the full outpouring of the biblical poets by keeping his own considerable imaging faculty under fairly tight rein.

Spenser, too, holds his images on a tight rein, but his is a tight rein of figuration. Spenser's presentation is even, whereas Milton's is variable, even within the limits he sets himself. Spenser is uniformly figurative, Milton only incidentally so in presenting his images, general or specific. The images in Milton tend to separate, and yet the underlying vision coordinates them to what he would have us register. In *Paradise Regained*, Milton cannot be assimilated to the method of "mosaic," the laying of separate image next to image, the *intarsie* that Galileo finds in Tasso.[19]

Milton does not exactly think in images, as Marvell, Emily Dickinson, and Blake, among others, may be said to do. Rather, the antistyle of *Paradise Regained*, by varying and, at the same time, restricting its deployment of images, undercuts the traditional distinction of styles. In *Paradise Regained*, Milton is grand, medium, and low all at once. On his theological ground, as in his handling of images, he manages to get past the Renaissance criteria of stylistic decorum for these three styles as expounded by Bembo, Tasso, and others.[20] These criteria justify the use of *durezza* in Tasso, and they sanction, as F. T. Prince has shown us, the abruptness of Milton's sonnets — and indeed their virtual absence of imagery. So their models, the sonnets of Della Casa, have little recourse to imagery. But again, in *Paradise Regained*, Milton has managed to modify this abruptness while retaining it, and he has done so by virtue of modulating his presentation of images.

In this particular sense, removal from the three classical styles, Milton in *Paradise Regained* may be said to capture something of the style of Isaiah and Job. Or, in visual analogy, he may be said to offer at once the space-filling solidity of Poussin, and the effects of mysterious light and dark of Rembrandt. Wylie Sypher's suggestive alignment of Milton with Baroque and late Baroque procedures in architecture and painting, even if we accept it, can be said to succeed only in naming organizational constituents of the poem. In the case of Milton, the particular mix offered by the poem — its particular structure of vision — is distinct not only for the given poet but, as Wylie Sypher asserts concerning Milton, from poem to poem within the work itself.[21]

In this "brief epic," a principle of brevity operates not only in the overall span of the poem but in the restrained economy of sentences that seem to be making a point of not adopting the diapason of *Paradise Lost*. And there is a persistent brevity in the treatment of images, but also a principle of expansion. A commentary has expansiveness built into its conception to begin with, and *Paradise Regained*, like *Paradise Lost*, exists modally as a commentary on a very specific segment of scripture. To locate a tension between brevity and expansiveness in the special register of this brief epic is to raise still further questions about the kind of image perception that can lend itself to such treatment. That tension, indeed, fortifies the images. We are left with the effect of the poem to which the images, rudimentary as they are, remain mysteriously intrinsic while at the same time residually intractable to the critical approaches we may bring to bear upon them.

Brown University

NOTES

1. The text is cited according to *The Student's Milton*, ed. F. A. Patterson (New York, 1933).

2. Caroline Spurgeon, *Shakespeare's Imagery and What It Tells Us* (Cambridge, 1936). Barbara Lewalski, *Milton's Brief Epic* (Providence, 1966), pp. 386–88.

3. Albert Cook, *The Classic Line* (Bloomington, 1966), pp. 288–92.

4. Roland M. Frye, *Milton's Imagery and the Visual Arts* (Princeton, 1978), p. 321, relates the scene around the wine-press, and other points of the poem, to the tradition of genre painting. He also adduces pastoral elsewhere. In general iconographic choice we might so classify such images of Milton, but his specific handling lacks the preoccupied attention to abundant detail that characterizes such paintings.

5. Cook, *The Classic Line*, p. 282.

6. Roland Frye, *Milton's Imagery and the Visual Arts*, p. 4.

7. Roland Frye, ibid., reproduces this, along with a plate showing the debate between Christ and Satan in the Holkham Bible, the Sistine Chapel fresco of the temptation by Botticelli, and a more focused view of the same subject by Tintoretto in the Scuola di San Rocco. However, Frye cites Gertrud Schiller, *Ikonographie in der Christlichen Kunst*

(Gütersloh, 1966–71) as documenting the fact that the Temptation is not an especially prominent iconographic motif in painting, any more than it is in poetry.

8. Richard Crashaw, *Poems*, ed. A. R. Waller (Cambridge, 1904), p. 311.

9. Erich Auerbach, "Figura," in *Scenes from the Drama of Western Literature* (New York, 1959), pp. 11–78.

10. Matthew's "the devil taketh him unto an exceeding high mountain and sheweth him all the kingdoms of the world and the glory of them" (Matt. iv, 8) is more suggestive for the account in *Paradise Lost* than is the corresponding passage in Luke, "And he led him up, and shewed him all the kingdoms of the world in a moment of time" (*en stigme chronou*, Luke iv, 5).

11. Northrop Frye, "The Typology of *Paradise Regained*," *MP*, LIII (1956), 227–38, as reprinted in *Milton: Modern Essays in Criticism*, ed. Arthur Barker (New York, 1965), pp. 429–46.

12. My discussion here has been informed by works in progress on the idolatric-iconoclastic ambivalence by John Erwin and Irving Massey.

13. Angus Fletcher, *The Transcendental Masque: An Essay on Milton's "Comus"* (Ithaca, 1971); Stephen Orgel, *Jonsonian Masque* (Cambridge, 1965), and *The Illusion of Power: Political Theater in the English Renaissance* (Berkeley, University of California Press, 1975). The elaborate explanations of Fletcher and Orgel spell out how the traditions of hyperbole and display in the masque traditions were at the service of extravagant eulogy of the royal person and the self-celebration of the court for which they were written.

14. T. E. Lawrence, *Seven Pillars of Wisdom* (Garden City, 1935), pp. 39–42.

15. Heironymus Bosch painted many versions of *The Temptation of St. Anthony* at the turn of the sixteenth century, and the subject remained an iconographic staple thereafter.

16. This connection is touched on by Arnold Stein in *Heroic Knowledge* (Minneapolis, 1957), pp. 56–57. Roland Frye, *Milton's Imagery and the Visual Arts*, p. 338, relates this scene to the *vanitas* motif in still life painting of the time.

17. The details of spire and pinnacle, Roland Frye demonstrates, (Ibid., pp. 320–29), are drawn not from any text, but from contemporary and prior visual representation.

18. Wayne Shumaker, *Unpremeditated Verse: Feeling and Perception in "Paradise Lost"* (Princeton, 1965), 104–32.

19. F. T. Prince, *The Italian Element in Milton's Verse* (Oxford, 1954).

20. Prince, ibid., points out Tasso's use of the three ancient divisions of style in his *Discorsi*.

21. Wylie Sypher, *Four Stages of Renaissance Style* (New York, 1955), pp. 203–11; 217–34.